FUSSBUSTERS
at home

AROUND-THE-CLOCK
STRATEGIES AND GAMES

FOR SMOOTHING THE ROUGH SPOTS IN

YOUR PRESCHOOLER'S DAY

CAROL BAICKER-McKEE, Ph.D.

Ω
PEACHTREE
ATLANTA

Dedicated to my mother,
Teddy McKee, who, thanks to me,
the formerly crabby daughter,
is as expert as they come
in handling children who fuss.

—C B-M

Published by
PEACHTREE PUBLISHERS, LTD.
1700 Chattahoochee Avenue
Atlanta, Georgia 30318-2112

www.peachtree-online.com

Text © 2002 by Carol Baicker-McKee, Ph.D.

Photographs © 2002 by Corbis Images: Asian girl, girl smiling, girl covering ears, pouting baby, angry boy, boy crying, girl showing teeth, boy rubbing eye; EyeWire/GettyImages Creative: serious girl.

Book and cover design by Loraine M. Joyner
Composition by Robin Sherman

Manufactured in the United States of America
10 9 8 7 6 5 4 3 2 1
First Edition

Library of Congress Cataloging-in-Publication Data

Baicker-McKee, Carol, 1958-
  Fussbusters at home : Around-the-Clock strategies and games for smoothing the rough spots in your preschooler's day / by Carol Baicker-McKee.-- 1st ed.
     p. cm.
   ISBN 1-56145-262-9
  1. Preschool children. 2. Parenting. 3. Parent and child. 4.
Creative activities and seat work. I. Title.
   HQ774.5 .B35 2002
   649'.5--dc21
                        2001007565
                        Rev.

Table of Contents

CHAPTER FOUR
Rest for the Leery 84

CHAPTER FIVE
Putting the "Great" in the Outdoors 108

CHAPTER SIX
Arsenic Hour Antidotes   144

CHAPTER SEVEN

Don't Throw In the Dish Towel Yet:
Winning Food Fights

167

CHAPTER EIGHT

Sleep-Ease: From Twilight to Nightlight

191

CHAPTER NINE
The Mush Pot
229

Acknowledgments

No one ever writes a book alone. Oh, you may wish you could write it alone, but there is bound to be someone hanging over your shoulder whining that you *promised* we could go to the pool after just one more page. At least that's what happens if you have kids and you don't quite meet your deadline and get the thing done before school gets out.

That wasn't what I meant, of course. This is where I get to thank all the people who have made this book possible. I am enormously grateful to all of them. I thank my parents, who were super parents and role models and who have also offered suggestions on format and ideas to include. To my enormously patient and helpful husband, the kind who brings me ice cream and rubs my shoulders when I feel like I just can't type another word, I say, "Thank you, thank you, thank you, and more chocolate chip cookie dough, please." Steve, I appreciate all the reading and photocopying and computer-problem troubleshooting you've done, too. And most of all, thanks for being my partner in this parenting adventure. You are the Best Dad in the World, as it says right there on the Father's Day card the kids started making but I forgot to make them finish.

I thank my three kids, Kyle, Eric, and Sara, who let me practice my parenting skills on them and cheerfully helped me test things I'd forgotten how to do. Thanks, too, for laughing at my jokes even when they didn't include boogers, and for being understanding about the pool and my forgetting to practice spelling words. Again. Spelling is overrated anyway, now that there is Spell Checker.

I also need to express my appreciation to my writer friends who have given me excellent advice and unfailing support in the creation of this manuscript—and unselfishly shared their favorite parenting ideas. A very special thanks to my sister-in-law, Karen Baicker, who helped me reshape my early versions of the book and offered invaluable advice and encouragement at every stage, and who is a truly outstanding and fun mother herself. Special thanks, too, to Judy Press and Andrea Perry, two super writers, great mothers, and wonderful people to boot. I also owe gratitude to Pat Easton and my buddies in her Monday evening writers workshop.

The Mt. Lebanon, Pennsylvania, Public Library has been an invaluable resource for me, and I thank the stellar staff of librarians in the Children's Library, headed by Judy Sutton.

I thank Sarah Smith for believing in me and FussBusters and for continuing to offer help even when things were tough in her life. And Kathy Landwehr for picking up editorial duties so seamlessly (and being very patient and encouraging), and all the other staff at Peachtree Publishers.

And last but not least, thanks to the many parents, preschool teachers, and babysitters who shared ideas, field-tested activities, or offered suggestions about what to include. Also thanks to all the kids who helped. (I hope I'm not forgetting any-one—please forgive me if I am!) Thanks to my sisters and their husbands, Anna and Doug Grossman-McKee and Cory and John Polena, practically perfect parents all. I thank my brother, Evan McKee, who is a super father to Matt and a fun uncle. Thanks to my parents-in-law, Macky and Joe Baicker, who are outstanding role models as parents and grandparents and endlessly supportive. My appreciation also to Keith and Mary Elizabeth Baicker, Karen Baicker (again) and Paul Schmitz, and Kate Baicker and Alan Durell, who are wonderful aunts and uncles and the kind of people who always have neat ideas to try. Thanks to all my nephews and nieces—John Michael, Mark, Scott, and Erin; Morgan, Alex, Brent, Geoffrey, and little Evan; Jake and Lucy, Michael and Andrew, and Matt. You're great guinea pigs as well as kids. I am grateful to Mary Lou Vanzin, the most organized mother I know (and a source of many great ideas) and the rest of the McMonagle family. Thanks to the Morycz fami-ly, including Peggy the amazing preschool teacher, the Edson family, Eileen (I wouldn't have survived my kids' preschool years without you), the Seidel/Blaushild family, the Owens family, Dr. Nancy and family, the Stormer family, the Barinas family, Nancy Mac (another terrific child and family therapist) and the rest of the Mac/Carnon family, and Tracy Plassio. I thank the teachers at Begindergarten Preschool, including Mrs. Walker, Mrs. O'Connell, Mrs. Nave, Mrs. Fox, and Mrs. Frye; and the kindergarten teacher at Lincoln Elementary, Ms. Mimi Frey, who let me try out many of these activities on groups of her kids. Thanks to Dianey, Abby, and my Polena nephews, all of whom were the best babysitters in the world.

May you all bust the fusses that blow your way.

—*C B-M*

Introduction

About the Author
OR, HOW I CAME TO WRITE A BOOK THAT MENTIONS THE WORD "POOP" AT LEAST A DOZEN TIMES

I entered parenthood with my eyes open—and my nostrils pinched shut, since I already knew something about stinky pants.

I grew up in a family with four children, the youngest of whom was born when I was ten, in suburban neighborhoods teeming with children. By the time I entered college, having logged zillions of babysitting hours, I'd seen most baby and kid stuff firsthand, much of it repeatedly. I could change poopy *cloth* diapers with one hand (the other, naturally, was holding my nose), wrestle four rambunctious, fighting brothers into pajamas and their beds at something reasonably close to their ordained bedtime without using a single four-letter word, and laugh hysterically at fart jokes when the situation demanded. And, as a former "challenging" child myself, I had some insider knowledge about how to handle the toughest of the tough.

I picked up more knowledge about kids over the next ten years or so. I majored in psychology at Yale University and earned a Ph.D. in clinical child psychology at the University of Virginia. In and around my schooling I garnered additional practical experience. I volunteered at a daycare center in college, taught in the toddler room at Harvard Yard Child Care Center after graduation, and spent a couple of summers during graduate school teaching in the U.Va. laboratory preschool. Later I worked as a child and family therapist in various inpatient and outpatient settings. In the process, I helped tame kids who manipulated their parents into buying toys by threatening to speed dial the number for Child and Youth Services, and hyperactive four-year-olds whose desperate parents had been forced to install iron bars on all the windows and settle for furnishings constructed entirely from foam rubber. As a teacher, I even dressed a dozen toddlers in snowsuits, boots, hats, *and* mittens in under an hour—with only two other adults helping! What more could there possibly be to learn?

So, when parents coming for therapy challenged my credentials by asking whether I had children of my own, I smiled serenely and reassured them that although I didn't have kids, I'd had *plenty* of experience with young children and knew *exactly* what they were going through.

To those parents I say, "Sorry!"

Because of course I didn't have a clue. There is not a class, book, or experience that can prepare you for the reality of parenthood.

Two things make parenthood more difficult than other childcare jobs. The first is the 24-7-52-eternity-every-single-little-detail nature of it. Whether you stay home with the little tykes or go off to work in an office for ten hours a day, once you become a parent you are never really "off duty." The responsibility travels with you wherever you go. The worries, hopes, and memories weigh down your shoulders and clog your brain cells. And fill your pockets with sticky black things you'd rather not examine closely.

The second is love.

Parent love is the kind that keeps you up all night watching the breathing of a baby with the sniffles. The kind of love that chokes your throat with an impossibly big lump when you even watch *commercials* with toddlers prancing about in tutus. The kind of love that makes you willing to discuss your child's boogers with perfect strangers in line at the grocery store while he's wiping same on the sleeve of your new winter coat.

You'd think that kind of love would give you some kind of advantage in the childcare game. That it would endow you with endless patience, wisdom, and compassion. But it doesn't. Partly because no amount of love can surmount the fatigue and general grinding down of your personal reserves that comes with parenting young children. But mostly because it's almost impossible to remain calm, objective, and rational when you *care* so much. And it makes it hard to believe that *your* child would turn out to be the kind who throws temper tantrums that register on the Richter scale because you won't let him wear the ripped Captain America suit he found at a garage sale to Aunt Karen's wedding, who teases his sister unmercifully by making funny noises with his armpits, who whines that there's nothing to *doooo-oo* right after you've spent $300 on new toys, and who sneaks off to visit the neighbors at six o'clock in the morning absolutely buck naked when he is nearly four and surely old enough to know better, for good-ness' sake!

But probably he will. At least mine did. All three of them. And that's why I wrote *FussBusters*. Kids and fusses go together like barf and diarrhea (we can thank my middle son for providing that last analogy—see what I'm up against?). And, although I never learned the secret for raising perfect little angels, from the many talented teachers, therapists, parents, and grandparents I've encountered in my schooling, work, and around the neighborhood, I *have* acquired strategies and ideas that often can nip everyday fusses in the bud. And sometimes prevent them outright. And, best of all, that can actually make life with young kids the enjoyable adventure it should be. Boogers and all.

About This Book

FussBusters at Home features quick and easy activities and tips for the everyday difficult moments that are all too common with young children. You know, like waking up, getting dressed, eating breakfast,...and so on throughout the day. With *FussBusters*, you can transform boring or aggravating at-home events into experiences that your child—*and you*—may actually find pleasurable and stimulating. And you can enjoy these activities and ideas without a magic wand (though that helps—pretend is fine), a degree in early childhood education, or even a stockpile of egg cartons and Styrofoam trays!

FussBusters at Home is arranged to make it easy to find the right activity or tip you need *when* you need it. The chapters loosely track the events of a day at home with young children from the moment when their little fingers peel your eyelids open to the final moments spent shooing monsters out from under the bed. Within chapters, I have grouped activities into subcategories to fit specific situations or needs. For example, in chapter 5, "Putting the 'Great' in the Outdoors," I've included ideas for setting up a low-fuss play area, solving common play problems, and coming up with fun activities in yucky weather.

Each chapter opens with an introduction that highlights common problems, relevant developmental issues, and general suggestions. The individual activities are described with brief, easy-to-follow instructions. Occasionally, I have included safety tips, real-life anecdotes, or references to enriching resources, such as books, music albums, and websites.

Preschooler Principles

The following are some characteristics of young children that have guided the development and selection of the activities in *FussBusters*. Understanding these principles may help you interpret your child's responses and guide you in choosing activities to suit your child's needs. Plus, this section gives me a chance to use that expensive education I spent years pursuing.

- ***Preschoolers like consistency, rituals, predictability.*** Life is full of surprises for young children. Anything that makes the world more predictable, that lets them know what to expect, makes them feel safer and braver. Repetition helps them master new skills, ideas, and language. Finally, routines help them develop responsibility—they learn what they should do when. "Do it again" is the credo of the young child. That's why they want to have peanut butter and banana sandwiches on white bread with the crusts removed and cut into perfect triangles for lunch. Every day. For the next four years.

- *As inconsistent as it seems, preschoolers like novelty and variety.* They like novelty and variety—within a framework of predictability. Serve that perfect peanut butter and banana sandwich on a doll's plate inside a cardboard box, and you'll be a hero! On other occasions, your support and encouragement will help your child to welcome the new and accept changes.

  Young children also have short attention spans and may need more frequent shifts of activities, with a balance of quiet and active things to do. That's why they alternate between teasing their little sister in whispers and tackling her with Tarzan yells.

- *Preschoolers need to move their bodies.* Young children are developing their muscles and the neurological connections that control them. They need space and permission to be active and use their large muscles. They'll use them in the dining room on the chandelier if you don't send them outside. And don't forget opportunities to use the small muscles in their hands and eyes as they do art projects, manipulate small toys, look at books, and disassemble the VCR.

- *Preschoolers use all their senses.* They learn with their whole selves. Sensory activities will capture their attention, and many, such as water play, have a wonderfully calming effect.

  Preschoolers' drive to use their senses can still cause trouble, though. Even though their emerging self-control helps them to refrain from touching things they shouldn't or putting everything in their mouths, temptation may override their better judgment, leading them to try out your best makeup on the dog. Supervise and continue to childproof their play areas. Pay attention to the safety notes included with some *FussBusters* activities.

- *Preschoolers' temperaments continue to shape their actions and reactions.* Individual differences can be quite striking—and perfectly normal. Be flexible and respect your child's special needs, interests, tastes. Even if they run more strongly in favor of slugs and superheroes than yours do.

- *Gender rules.* Gender identification is quite strong during this period. Young girls may reject seemingly neutral activities as "just for boys," and boys may refuse to do anything they see as "girl stuff." If you have a little girl, odds are good that she will spend hours enveloped in tulle waiting for Prince Charming; and if you have a boy, expect to spend a great deal of time discussing the relative merits of various dinosaurs and arguing about whether he is allowed to pretend the hose nozzle is a ray gun that can annihilate his sister. These sexist attitudes will make you want to gag, but don't get too worked up. By first grade, most will have faded dramatically, even if you skip the equal rights lectures.

Preschooler Management 101

Ever wonder why your child is more cooperative with his teacher or grandparents? The main reason is security—he feels comfortable enough with you to risk making mistakes or even misbehaving. You can't (and wouldn't want to) change that. But another reason may be that teachers and grandparents have acquired skills from long and repeated experience with young children. Adopting these attitudes and strategies can make your life with your child easier—and more fun.

Anticipate

Remember both senses of this word:

- *Be prepared.* Thinking ahead will help you avoid problems and set the stage for success. For example, buy clothes your child can fasten himself or place dishes where he can reach them easily. You can also help prepare your child, whose sense of the future, recall of the past, and awareness of time is just developing, for events on the horizon. As much as possible, tell him what to expect, warn him of upcoming transitions, and remind him of important rules, like "Don't say 'poo-poo butt' to Great Uncle Walter."

- *Look forward to.* It's easy to get bogged down in the drudgery of everyday life with a preschool child. Changing your mindset to expect pleasure, though, can improve both your mood and your child's behavior. Take advantage of the opportunities young children offer you to slow down, to live in the here and now, to notice and marvel at all the small miracles in the world.

Communicate Clearly

Language is still a new skill for small children, so you have to make it easy for them to understand you. What works:
- Make sure you have their attention.
- Exaggerate your facial expressions, tone of voice, body language.
- Give only one or two directions at a time.
- Be specific.
- Don't offer choices unless you mean them.
- Make sure you understand their messages.
- Give them the words they need.
- Use the word "poop" when you really need them to hear you.

Invoke Imagination and Humor

Making believe is an important and emerging skill during the preschool years. *And* it's probably the easiest route to securing your child's cooperation. He might balk at dressing for church, but he'll cheerfully don his Sunday-best space suit! A good dose of silliness helps, too.

Reset Your Clock

Preschoolers have short legs, and most of the time we remember to adjust our strides to match their slower pace. But we also need to remember that *many* tasks take young children longer. Allowing enough time will reduce stress for everyone and boost your child's emerging competence.

Conversely, we sometimes need to speed things up, to adjust for children's shorter attention spans and smaller energy reserves. Two hours at the art museum is probably an hour and a half too long for most young children. Accept that, for a few years, you'll need to be flexible and accommodating.

Refocus and Reframe

Distraction, so effective with toddlers, is also a useful tool with preschoolers. Finding an element of challenge may be the best way to keep a child this age from noticing how much he dislikes something. For example, "I'll bet I can scrub my hands longer than you can!" can produce some impressively clean hands for both of you.

Just as reframing an old picture can bring out its beauty, so can describing an event differently change its impact. If your child was scared by a thunderstorm, you may be able to influence her perception of the experience by helping her notice how well she coped by closing her eyes and covering her ears.

Put Yourself in Your Child's Shoes

Stooping down to your child's size, sometimes literally, will help you make sense of his behavior and remind you of ways to structure his environment so he can succeed. It's good to remind yourself that he may not be able to see what's on the countertop, reach the rack to re-hang his towel, or carry that heavy plate.

Take Care

- *Of Your Child* Your child may loudly assert her competence and independence, but the next minute she may beg for you to help take off her socks. You should expect her to need you especially when she is tired, ill, or stressed by new experiences or problems with her friends or at home. And, no matter how capable she seems, she will need frequent encouragement and reassurance, as well as regular physical contact and demonstrations of your love and affection.

- *Of Yourself* On airlines, flight attendants instruct you to fit your own oxygen mask before you help your child—if you pass out, you'll be no use to your child, and she may not be able to help you. The same principle holds true in everyday life. So don't feel guilty about using activities just to give yourself a half-hour to read a magazine. And feel free to skip suggestions that you find unappealing.

A Word on the Worst Parent in the World

It isn't you. Even if, like me, you suddenly feel like the *worst* parent when you flip through a book crammed with fun activities to do with your child and tips on managing her behavior. I always start thinking, "Geez Louise! I could never do all that with my kids!" I even started thinking that when I read through the final draft of this book. Especially since while I was doing that, I was *completely* ignoring my kids.

Actually, lots of the activities and strategies in this book *are* things I did with my kids—at least at some point in the *eight* years that I had preschoolers. If you have eight years of preschoolers ahead of you, you might get in lots of them, too. Usually, we would go on sort of activity jags. For example, for a while we would really be into sensory wake-ups. A few weeks later, everyone would be waking up fine, and we'd be into playing bubbles while mommy typed on the computer. Or eating dinner under the table to encourage my notoriously picky eaters to consume at least a handful of calories.

Most of the ideas in here worked for us, but in all honesty some of them didn't. The same will probably be true for you. If I included them in here anyway, it's because I know parents who did find them helpful.

Families and kids are like snowflakes—no two alike. Other activities are ones that I wish I'd done—things I've learned about when it was too late for me.

This book isn't a textbook. You need not read it cover to cover—I promise, no pop quizzes. Pick and choose a few activities or strategies that suit you and your child, adding to your repertoire over time. Before long, you too may be a professional (or at least a highly skilled amateur) FUSSBUSTER!

I welcome your comments and suggestions for future editions of this book. You can reach me care of Peachtree Publishers or at baickermckee@adelphia.net

CHAPTER ONE

Eyeopeners!
Energizing Ways
to Start the Day

I am not a morning person. Neither are two of my three children. The third is a cheery ray of sunshine. We hate her. Just kidding. We've actually managed to reprogram her, and now on school mornings she's nearly as grumpy as the rest of us.

That's why I feel a little hypocritical giving some of this advice like, "Get up before your children do." During my years of preschoolers, I could never manage it. I was too exhausted. There was always someone nursing, having nightmares or growing pains, wetting the bed, being awakened by a queasy stomach or raging ear pain, or simply feeling a bit lonely and in need of a cuddle. Or I was pregnant and getting up every two hours to pee. Whatever the reason, I think something like seven years passed before I got a full night's sleep. So my strategy was to stay in bed until there were simply too many people tugging on my eyelids and jumping on my stomach. (Oddly, these days I do get up early and reasonably cheerfully.) I'm leaving the advice in, though, because my morning-people friends swear by it, and because nowadays I enjoy the peace of a first cup of coffee all by myself.

The one piece of advice I mostly did try to follow, despite strong temptations to ignore it, was: *Don't get hooked on TV.* If you need a half-hour's breathing room to get your shower, go ahead and plop the kiddies in front of something like Mr. Rogers or their 8,942nd viewing of *Winnie the Pooh and the Blustery Day.* But the minute you give in to Cartoon Network or even an extra hour of *Sesame Street,* you're sunk. Oh, all right, take away those bamboo slivers! I confess! I did give in at times, at least to Bert and Ernie (we didn't have cable or it probably would have been *Rugrats*). But I regretted it then, and I regret it now. An hour or two in front of the TV did not make my morning easier; it made it worse, beginning the moment I wrested control of the remote. Pick one show max, and make it early, because you can expect a fight anytime you have to skip "their show" for an early appointment.

Most threes and fours are early risers, so waking them may not be an issue unless you have to leave very early for work or something. Older preschoolers, though, may be starting to shift to staying up later and sleeping in a bit if they can. Also, some kids just come wired more like night owls than larks, and these kids can have a very tough time if your morning routine has to start early. And a bad morning mood can stay with young children (and adults) all day. I have used the gentle "alarm clocks" described in this chapter with my own kids (and myself) and they really do help—they may not completely remove the crabbiness, but they tamp it down to livable levels.

Even those remarkable children who wake up sunny and energetic may struggle with the rest of getting going. Morning involves so many transitions—from asleep to awake, from pajamas to clothes, and, often, from home to school or daycare or even just out to play. And preschoolers *hate* transitions. Mornings also involve routines that are frequent sources of conflict with young kids, like washing, toileting, and eating. You may not be able to avoid some of the triggers, but these general reminders can usually help ease the morning "madness":

- Try to get up before your child—even ten minutes will help.
- Give your child enough time. More than you think.

- Make it easy for your child to take care of herself by choosing supplies she can use herself and storing them within her reach.
- Do as much preparation as possible the night before.
- Don't bother with the unnecessary—your daughter will survive without an elaborate hairstyle, and no one will die of starvation if you don't serve a hot breakfast.
- Unplug the television set. Really.
- Create consistent routines and rituals for reconnecting.

The activities in this chapter address the most common morning hot spots—waking, dressing and grooming, and getting out the door—and should help pave the way for you to create a kinder, gentler morning.

Un-Alarm Clocks:
GENTLE STRATEGIES TO ROUSE YOUR SLUG-A-BED

Do not wake a sleeping child! Unfortunately, sometimes you must ignore this good advice. Try some of these sensory tactics to wake your child gently.

Wake Up, Toes!

Touch your child awake, starting with his toes. Gently squeeze them through the covers while whispering, "Wake up, toes!" Work your way up his body, waking his legs, back, belly button, etc., saving his eyes for last. Gently stroke his eyelids, brushing away the sleepy dust. Finish with a hug. Let your voice increase in volume as you work your way up. Add some humor. For example, wake his toes again and again, as they keep going back to sleep. Many kids will be giggling and snuggly by the time you finish.

Another "touching" way to wake your child: Try stroking his face with various soft objects, such as a piece of silky fabric, your hair, a feather, a makeup brush. Can he guess what you're using?

The Smell-a-roma Wake-a-matic

Don't you love waking to the smell of freshly brewed coffee and home-made muffins? The sense of smell is housed in a primitive part of our brains, and scientists have long recognized the powerful ways that smell is linked to emotions and memories. Use pleasant smells to waken your child in a happy frame of mind. To make a good "smeller," soak a cotton ball with scent (try flavorings like vanilla, hot cocoa, or orange juice) or sprinkle on a pleasant aromatic substance (like a dash of cinnamon or other spice, some pine needles or flower petals, etc.). Put the cotton ball in a plastic squeeze bottle, place the opening near your child's nose, and give the bottle a gentle squeeze. Make this game-like by having your child try to guess the scent. You may want to link the scents to breakfast.

SAFETY ZONE

Some people are sensitive to scents, especially artificial ones like those added to perfumes, soaps, and detergents. Be sure to avoid anything that seems to cause a reaction in your child, and try to stick to "natural" scents in their normal concentrations.

A fun variation on this game is to offer your child a tiny taste of an appealing food or liquid (you can use an eyedropper). Whisper for her to sit up, keeping her eyes closed, and stick out her tongue. You'll start to awaken her senses and her brain; her body will soon follow.

Read 'Em Up

Bedtime reading is a wonderful routine: soothing and intimate. Morning reading can be *invigorating* and intimate. Aim for something short and sweet —poetry is excellent. Or, try a bit of an exciting story, with promises to finish it when your child is up and ready to go. Humor is especially successful.

Music is another wonderful waker. Experiment with something rousing like a march, soothing like New Age music, or complex like Bach. Help your child identify what music she likes best.

Let Tinkerbell Wake Them

A gradual brightening of light will waken most people easily, and sudden bright lights are effective—but jarring. Try this "light" touch on a dreary morning: Grab a flashlight and shine it on the ceiling of your child's darkened room. Move it in swirling patterns around the room. As you notice your child stirring, tell your child to wake up and try to catch Tink. As his eyes open, shine the light nearby and allow him to "capture" the fairy. Give him a turn with the flashlight as he heads to the bathroom.

Another visual waking game: Hold a picture or object near your child. Before she opens her eyes, whisper clues about what she'll see when she does. Can she guess? She'll have to open her eyes to check.

Early Bird Delay Tactics:
ENCOURAGING YOUR CHILD TO SLEEP LATER

Many young children naturally wake early, especially in the spring and summer. These strategies may help your child—and you—squeeze in a few extra winks in the morning.

Prolong the Night

Keep your child's room dark longer by using room-darkening shades or drapes. (A nightlight can help a child tolerate sleeping with a closed door, if light from the hall is a problem.) Mask morning noises like singing birds or traffic with a white noise machine, fan, or tabletop fountain (all located out of your child's reach). Whenever possible, locate your child's room away from the street side of your home. Finally, cool temperatures promote better sleep, so take care not to overdress or over-cover your child. If, however, your child tends to kick off the covers and get cold, dress him in heavy sleepers during the winter and skip the blankets.

Adjust Bedtime

One major cause of early waking is too late a bedtime. Yes, too *late*. Overtired children tend to sleep more fitfully, and this pattern can become chronic. On the other hand, if your child is getting plenty of hours of sleep, you may want to consider gradually shifting to a later bedtime and/or eliminating the afternoon nap.

Deal with Night-Wetting

If your child is still wetting at night (and a high percentage of preschoolers do), take steps to prevent nighttime discomfort. Absorbent pull-ups or continued use of diapers may help your child wait comfortably until morning. An older preschooler may also be able to take care of accidents himself. Lay out an easy change of clothing the night before, and provide a sleeping bag or extra bed to switch to. Many children can even be taught to pull off wet bedding and place it in a plastic hamper in their room. You may be able to get away with dealing with it in the morning and not having your sleep interrupted.

Prevent accidents by limiting fluids before bedtime, taking your child to the potty just before you retire (this works very well for many children), setting your alarm to take the child once during the night, or even providing a potty chair next to the child's bed (many cannot hold off long enough to actually get to the bathroom once they notice they have to go).

Hunger Pangs

Young children can be awakened by hunger. Some can be helped by having a light snack just before going to bed at night. High-protein, high-tryptophan foods like milk, tuna, and turkey may promote falling asleep and stave off hunger longer.

Snooze Buttons:
KEEPING YOUR WIDE-AWAKE CHILD FROM WAKING YOU

The following tips may not prevent your child from waking at the crack of dawn, but they might help her stay in her room or bed long enough to give you a better rest. These tactics can be especially useful on weekends and holidays. Don't forget that you can combine strategies—such as Time Tellers *plus* So Much to Do.

Morning Companions

"Company" may keep your child in his room longer by preventing fear, boredom, or loneliness when your child wakes early. Possible buddies include siblings (many children *like* sharing rooms or at least visiting one another); an audiotape (get a child's tape player ready the night before and have your child practice pressing the "play" button); and stuffed animals or imaginary friends. At bedtime, remind your child what to do when she awakes.

Time Tellers

Most three- and four-year-olds cannot learn to tell time. However, once your child knows numerals, use electrical or duct tape to cover the minute display on a digital clock in your child's room. Post a *large* sign showing the acceptable numerals (whatever is okay with you) for getting out of bed. (You may want a different sign for weekends.) On an analog clock, use paint, glass markers, or cellophane to mark off a pie-shaped wedge from the center of the clock to the appropriate numerals. If the *little* hand is in that area, your child can get up. (Look for a clock where the minute hand is a different color or design from the hour hand—otherwise you can expect many false alarms.) You can also tell them to wait until they hear the shower running

SAFETY ZONE

Make sure your child knows safety rules before you allow him to roam the house by himself. He should know to stay inside, to avoid poisonous or dangerous objects, not to use the phone, and not to engage in risky play like climbing. Five- and six-year-olds can often handle the responsibility; most threes and fours cannot.

or smell the coffee brewing. Or, if you want your child up by a certain time, set an alarm to go off when she *can* get up.

So Much to Do

Make a picture list of things your child must do *before* she wakes you in the morning. Possible activities include going to the bathroom, singing certain songs, drawing a picture, feeding a pet, doing "exercises," listening to a tape, looking at a stack of books, brushing hair, building a block tower, doing five puzzles, and practicing an emerging skill (like writing her name). The specific activities matter less than the time they take, so be flexible and creative. Be sure the skills are not too difficult or unpleasant.

Breakfast-in-Bedroom

Another option for weekends or special occasions. Leave a juice box and a breakfast bar or similar "snack" breakfast out for your child to eat when she gets up. For clean-up ease, serve the meal on a waterproof picnic cloth. Play this up as a special treat for your child (or better yet, children) to increase chances of success. We found this method bought an extra half-hour of sleep on holiday mornings.

Holding Pens

If you want your child to wait in his room, try setting out a container of special toys to play with only in the morning. Rotate these frequently, and be sure they are quiet, high-appeal toys. Or, if your child needs to be near you, create a special place just outside your room where he can wait. A sleeping bag or cushion can be enough to create a welcoming spot. If you have a well-child-proofed room in your house, you can also allow your child to wait there.

The Pot Stop:
TO THE BATHROOM, ROBIN!

The downside of toilet training is that the bathroom traffic jams get worse than ever. And if the bathroom becomes a morning battle zone on top of that, you may find yourself longing for the good old diaper days. So, here are ideas to reduce the problems you face with your child's morning toilette without returning to Huggies.

Toilet Taming

Most preschoolers will need to use the toilet urgently if they are staying dry at night. Encourage sleepy boys to aim accurately by floating a square of toilet paper in the bowl for them to sink. Little girls may need to remove panties or pajama bottoms so that they can spread their knees and lean forward—when they need to go badly, their urine may shoot out of the toilet unless they adjust their posture.

Even if your child is not yet dry at night, you should still take him to the bathroom upon waking to get cleaned up and try to use the toilet. (This also helps discourage children from wetting simply because it's easier.) Encourage a wet child to handle as much of the cleanup himself as possible. Most preschoolers can remove their wet disposable diapers and pull-ups and dispose of them (though they may not want to). I once knew a two-year-old who changed his own diapers. Kids can also put soiled laundry in a hamper or by the washing machine.

Clean Hand Club

Hand washing should be automatic after your child uses the toilet or gets changed. Make it game-like to encourage cooperation. Sing while your child scrubs, wash together, or draw a face on her hand with a washable marker and have your child quickly soap it away. Sing the ABC song to make sure your child scrubs long enough.

Habit Forming

Most of the time, a consistent routine and simple praise will be sufficient to establish good toilet habits. Slow wakers, oppositional children, or those who are simply less regular by temperament may need additional support. Here are some tried and true strategies:

- *Sticker Charts* Keep these simple. A plain piece of paper stuck on the wall is sufficient. Offer a small reward for achieving goals (e.g., for every five stickers earned, your child gets to play an extra game with you or choose dessert that night.)
- *Game Theory* Races, competitions ("I'll bet I can wash longer than you can"), trails to follow from bed-to-toilet-to-sink, songs, and silliness will enlist cooperation.
- *It's the Rule* This is good for children who never "feel" like doing things. "Even if you don't feel like you have to go potty, it's the rule that you try when you wake up." (Run the water when he tries to help get his plumbing flowing, too!)
- *Peer Pressure* Older children can serve as models, as well as offer rewards (such as playing with their toys) that trump anything you have to offer.

To Tell the Tooth:
TOOTHBRUSH TIPS AND TIMERS

Even little kids need to take care of their chompers, because dental problems in baby teeth can lead to even more serious ones in the permanent teeth. Most preschoolers are proud of their teeth, but they may have trouble with the mechanics and habits needed to keep them pearly white. These ideas will help your child put his best smile forward.

Tips

- Brush teeth during the first potty stop rather than waiting until after breakfast. After breakfast, it's too tempting to skip it if you are in a rush.
- Or, keep an extra toothbrush and tube of toothpaste by the kitchen sink for ease.
- Make a clay model of the right amount of toothpaste (the size of a pea or less). Glue it to a piece of cardboard and position the "artwork" at child height for easy comparison.
- Teach an order for brushing teeth—e.g., top outsides, top insides, top flats (and same for the bottoms)—so that your child will get all surfaces. Use the same order when you help your child brush so it becomes a habit.
- Show your child how to bite down a little to brush the back outsides of her teeth and how to open extra wide and angle the brush for doing the middle insides.
- Most preschoolers cannot brush their teeth adequately by themselves. I usually helped at night but let them do it alone at other times to encourage self-sufficiency.
- A child-height mirror, especially a magnifying or fish-eye mirror (get one in the auto supply department), will encourage interest in the activity and help your child find all his teeth.

Timers

Two minutes—really, and yes, it does feel like forever—is recommended by most dentists. Even if you don't always make it that long, using a timer will usually increase brushing time—and with luck reduce time (and money) spent in the dentist chair.

- *Gamepiece Sand Timer* Hunt around for one that is two minutes. A one-minute timer done twice is fine, too. Some of the liquid timers are also good lengths.
- *Music* We used to sing Raffi's toothbrush song ("When you wake up in the morning and it's a quarter to one, and you want to have a little fun, you brush your teeth!"), but any song you can adapt to a two-minute length will do. It's easy to play around with lyrics to well-known songs and make them about brushing (e.g., "There was a tooth who had a friend and Brush was his name-o. B-R-U-S-H" ...and so on to the tune of "Bingo"). You can also make a tape consisting of a series of two-minute segments of songs, stories, noises, etc. Use a child's portable tape player to play a different segment each time.
- *Story Timer* Bring in a book of poetry or jokes. Read to your child for two straight minutes. Time is guaranteed to pass quickly!

Face Scrubbers:
WASH UP WAKE UP

I have to admit that for years my usual method of washing my kids' faces was to ambush them with a wet paper towel when they least expected it. Eventually, though, I learned it was possible to make the process less of an ordeal—and even to transform it into a pleasant-ish experience. Try these ideas to elicit a little cooperation, if not enthusiasm, for the morning scrub-up. (And if these fail, lurk behind the doorway and grab your kid as she walks through.)

Washing Ways

Washcloths are difficult for many preschoolers to handle on their own, and water splashed from the basin is likely to go everywhere (yet still not manage to rinse away all the soap). Let your child try washing instead with cotton balls or pads. She'll enjoy noticing all the dirt that shows up so well against the white background. Use just a small dab of liquid soap or facial cleanser—too much soap is hard to rinse off. Another alternative is to have your child wet her face with a clean paintbrush (try a soft makeup brush). She can also apply soap with a shaving brush.

Most preschoolers do not need moisturizer on their faces, but a little petroleum jelly feels good on chapped lips in the winter.

Wash Your Mandible, Please

Direct your child to wash her face, part by part. Add extra pizzazz (and a cool educational component) by teaching her some fancy words for the facial parts. Introduce the vocabulary gradually, adding a new term every week or two. Pretend she is an artist and have her "paint" (with her washcloth) or "sculpt" the areas you name. You can also narrate the washing process when you do it for her.

- Lower jaw (including chin)—*mandible*
- Upper jaw and lip—*maxilla*
- The little indented place between the upper lip and nose—*filtrum*
- Holes in your nose—*nostrils*, or (really fancy) *nares*
- Nose—*nasal bone*
- Cheeks—*zygomatic bones* or *arch*
- Area around the eyes—*occipital area*
- Forehead—*frontal bones*
- Area beside eyes over to hairline—*temples*
- Eyebrow area—*superciliary arch*
- Back of the neck—*nape*
- Behind the ears—*behind the auricles*

You can also use this opportunity to teach names of facial parts in a second language, if you know one, or you can even make up your own silly names for each section.

Facial Fancies

Groggy children may also enjoy a pretend facial that you give them. Place a slightly warm washcloth over your child's upturned face. After a few seconds, remove it, add soap and gently "exfoliate" each area while talking in a soothing voice and complimenting your child's "complexion." Pat dry and finish with moisturizing smoochies.

Robo-Valet:
DRESSING-SQUABBLE SQUASHERS

Choose clothes for your preschooler that he can manage alone. Elastic waists, pullover tops, colors that mix and match, and inexpensive play clothes that can get tossed in the washing machine are best for children of both genders. Teach one step and one garment at a time. For example, you can pull your child's shirt over his head and then ask him to slip his arms in the sleeves himself. Don't forget to budget extra time in the morning once he starts dressing independently.

Robo-Valet

When you do need to help your child get dressed, boost cooperation by letting a robot take charge. Use a choppy robot voice to direct your child while you dress him. "Time-for-your-shirt. Lift-your-arms. Poke-them-into-your-sleeves," and so on. The robot can tell the child to do certain parts of the process himself as well, or even simply narrate the steps of the process, offering suggestions as needed. Occasionally, the robot can give some silly directions, like "Put-your-sneakers-on-your-ears," to add humor to an often crabby situation.

Other theme approaches to assisting and/or narrating the dressing process include:
- British valet
- Backstage dresser (This is good when you are in a rush.)
- Astronaut (Pretend your child is putting on components of a space suit.)
- Puppet (It is amazing what children will do for a puppet with a silly voice.)
- Drill sergeant (I like this when *I* feel crabby and demanding.)

- Fairy godmother (Perhaps she has a broken wand, so she has to work her magic manually.)
- Sales clerk or dress designer ("You look mah-velous!")
- Pro athlete locker room attendant, helping to suit up for the big game

Feel free to pretend that your child's clothes are something other than what they are. Many preschoolers will be delighted to head off to play-group in an imaginary police officer's uniform, Cinderella's ball gown, or Tarzan's leopard skins.

Into the Phone Booth, Clark Kent

Distractible kids may dawdle less if they are away from their toys, the telly, etc. Try popping them in the closet where they can transform into Superman (incognito in his jeans and T-shirt). Hand them their clothes, saying, "Quick Clark Kent! Into this phone booth! We need Superman immediately! Bad guys are coming!" Another trick is to throw a blanket over your kid. Pretend it's a magician's hanky, say the magic words, and (pause a minute) *poof!* He's dressed! And if that isn't magic, I don't know what is.

Code Blue Days

I wish I had heard of this method when my kids were small. Instead of sorting your child's clothes by type (i.e., socks in one drawer, shirts in another), arrange them by outfit—and bag the outfits in grocery sacks or clip them together with clothespins. No hunting around for socks at the last minute and no cringing when your child shows up wearing the green striped pants with the orange plaid shirt. And *one* dumped-out drawer—*max*—to clean up!

Place each set in color-coded drawers (stick a color dot on the drawer front). Use different colors for different types of outfits (e.g., warm vs. cool weather, play clothes vs. dressy clothes, etc.). Tell your child it's a code blue day, and then let her choose which code blue set to wear!

Capes Go with Everything!
COPING WITH CLOTHING FETISHES

Many parents of preschoolers report that their biggest battles occur when their children insist on wearing inappropriate clothing.

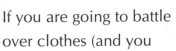

TRY THIS!

If you are going to battle over clothes (and you probably will), at least shift the battles to the evening, so you don't have to be fighting when you're frantically getting ready for work. The rule in our house was that children could choose their own outfits—*if* they did so during the evening. If they waited for morning, they had to wear what we selected. Naturally, we reserved a last-minute veto, in case the weather or plans for the day changed. For best results, select items for every category, from underpants to barrettes.

Unseasonable Duds

This issue crops up most frequently during transitional weather. To avoid conflict, try these approaches:

• *Let the thermometer decide.* Make a picture chart of appropriate clothes for different temperatures. Then simply check the outside thermometer or the forecast.

• *Compromise.* She can wear her bikini in January—but she has to wear pants and a shirt over it.

• *Acclimate gradually .* Some children need to get used to the feel of air on their arms and legs again after a winter of being covered (and vice versa). Push sleeves and pant legs up or down a little each day or opt for mid-length clothes. Or, have your child wear the new clothes for a brief period each day, gradually lengthening the time he wears them.

• *Let natural consequences prevail.* If it isn't a major health risk, allow your child to make a mistake and learn for himself that it's not a good idea to wear his snowsuit to the kiddy pool.

Costumes and Strange Outfits

This was a major issue in my family!

- *Designate costume days.* Or times of day. Perhaps he can be a fireman every evening, but he has to wear other clothes to school and friends' houses.

- *Remove the offending items.* Parents can make things disappear. This technique will undoubtedly cause tears in the short run, but most kids recover quickly.

- *Live with it.* You may feel embarrassed, but most people find it charming when your daughter goes shopping with you in her fairy princess dress. (My oldest was Peter Pan every day for the better part of a year and my daughter wore her Halloween dog costume for longer than I care to admit. She also barked.) Perhaps you can stomach letting your kid wear a portion of the costume most of the time. As my son explained once, "Capes go with *everything!*" (Just beware of potentially dangerous items, like high heels or items that tie around the neck. We fastened capes with small pieces of Velcro for quick release.)

LITERATURE LINKS

There are two great books for kids with strong clothing preferences. For younger children, search out *Red Is Best* by Kathy Stinson. It's a tiny, hard-to-find book but worth the hunt. Older preschoolers will enjoy Lotta's reaction to her sweater, which tickles and scratches, and her preference for her Sunday-best velvet dress in *Lotta on Troublemaker Street* by Astrid Lindgren.

Insistence on Sameness

Some children have to wear the same item or outfit day after day or in inappropriate situations (such as to bed or in the bath).

- *Go along.* These are usually short phases. It really won't harm your child to wear the same shirt every day for a week or those too-short pants. If it looks to be a long phase, try to buy multiples of the desired item and just keep telling the disapproving neighbors that your child actually owns five identical skirts. Or, allow her to carry her favorite tights in a backpack when she's not wearing them.

- *Involve your child in choosing new clothes.* Try to identify the key features of favorite clothes (usually size/tightness, color, texture, or emotional association). Take him shopping and buy what he likes, even if you don't like it. Also, look for hand-me-downs (or as my son called them, "handy downs") or used clothing. Many children prefer these for their softness and/or associations.

Hair Doozies:
UNTANGLING HAIR-DO DON'TS

I, for one, am very grateful whenever buzz cuts are "in" for boys. If only girls would decide they were stylish, too! When you can't go for the Michael Jordan look, try these techniques to minimize tangle terrors.

Distract

Do hair while your child is busy with something else. For a time, we had a no-morning-TV rule—except during hair-dos (not entirely satisfactory, since it then meant that we had to devote half an hour to doing hair). Also try letting your child play with play dough, Legos, water in the sink, or some other absorbing (but stationary) material while you comb and style. Or pretend your child is a champion poodle being groomed or that her head is a dinosaur fossil dig site—who knows what you'll find under all those curls? (This last technique is especially useful when your child comes home from preschool with one of those charming letters informing you that one of her classmates has lice.)

Involve

Help your child enjoy the sensory pleasures of having his hair done. Put on some slow music, seat him on some cushions or a child's chair so that his head is just above your knees. Provide a hand mirror so he can study his reflection. Talk about how wonderfully soft/thick/smooth, curly/straight, etc., his hair is as you comb or brush it with slow, gentle strokes. Periodically look at hairstyles in magazines and experiment with new looks. Try small amounts of hair care products (look for ones formulated for children) or cool new accessories. Let him do the final styling, even if he needs your touch first to get all the tangles out or the part straight.

Simplify and Soothe

Some preschoolers have exceptionally tender scalps. These are often the children who are more sensitive about everything, from food tastes and smells to the seams in their socks. Typically these children cannot be distracted and do not enjoy the hair care process, no matter how hard you try to make it pleasant. For these children, swallow your dreams of long curls, and let them keep their hair as short as possible. Avoid styles requiring hair accessories like barrettes or ponytail holders—they will pull and bother (and your child will remove them at her first opportunity). Restrain growing-out bangs with a little gel or mousse instead of clips. Use a baseball cap to keep hair out of her face during vigorous play.

Get the softest brush that will go through your child's hair (ones designed for babies are often best). Save combs (wide-toothed) for wet hair and quick parts. Brush hair in sections, lifting it so you don't tug on her scalp and slowly work out tangles from the bottom up. Spray detanglers work well for some children, even on dry hair. A quick mist with warm water reduces static and sometimes minimizes tangles, too. Finally, some children are bothered less if they do the de-tangling (but most preschoolers take forever and cannot do a thorough job).

Help desensitize scalps by playing with your child's hair when she is relaxing. Give her gentle scalp massages, making small circles all over her head with your fingertips. Grasp sections of her hair close to her scalp and tug gently. Give her "head scritchies" as you would a pet and encourage her to nuzzle against you.

Skills Seminar:
A DO-IT-MYSELF OUTERWEAR OVERVIEW

You'll be relieved when your child learns how to get all those outer garments on all by himself, won't you? The best thing is your child will be delighted, too! These tips really work—I've seen them in action in school settings with kids of all levels of coordination and motivation.

Putting on a Jacket

All preschool teachers love this trick—and so do all independent-minded preschoolers. Teach your child these do-it-himself steps:
1. Put your jacket on the floor, zipper-side up. Kneel or stand with your toes by the hood (or neck), facing your jacket.
2. Bend over and put your arms part way into the sleeves. It will look like you are going to put on your jacket backwards and upside down.
3. Stand up and flip your coat over your head! Raise your arms and let your hands slide to the ends of your sleeves. You did it!

Most three-year-olds can master this task. The most common error is starting from the bottom. (The jacket will then be on upside down.) To help your kid remember the steps, have him recite the following rhyme:

My hood's by my toes,
My hands in the sleeves.
I stand up and flip!
Right on it goes!

Another option is to have him drape his coat, front open, over a low chair. He sits down, slips his arms into the sleeves, and shrugs it on.

Gloves and Mittens

- Mittens are usually better than gloves because they keep small fingers warmer and are easier to put on. Check to be sure the thumbs are in the thumb place.

- If your child insists on gloves, shop for ones that are easy to manage. To get the fingers sorted out, have your child pretend they are trains, heading into their berths at the roundhouse or little bunnies crawling into their burrows. You can also sing, "Where is Thumbkin?" (but start with "Pointer" and do "Thumbkin" last). Be patient—gloves take concentration.

- For snow play, your child should put on her mittens *before* the jacket, so they will already be tucked into the sleeves.

Snowsuitable

First of all, don't put on a snowsuit if you don't have to. If you are driving and just scooting a short distance from the car to the door, you can even skip boots. But if you're walking or going on a snowy romp, take a deep breath and get to work.

SAFETY ZONE

Remove all cords from hoods or hats (cords pose a strangulation hazard).

- First have your child go potty!

- Show your child how to hold her shirt sleeves in her fist as she slides on her jacket, and tuck pants legs into socks before she puts on her snowpants.

- Set up snowpants firefighter-style. Hold them by the waist, then collapse them so that the waist is centered over the two foot holes. Now your child can simply step in and pull them up.

- Offer an assortment of hats. Have a mirror handy—preschoolers are much more likely to put on a hat when they can watch themselves in the mirror. Develop a silly hat-talk ritual, like repeating the lines from *Go, Dog! Go!* by P.D. Eastman. (Your child asks, "Hello again. Do you like my hat?" You respond "I do! What a hat! I like it! I like that party hat!")

Anticipate Undressing

Walk your child through what she should do with clothes she removes. Also, lay out old towels or rugs from the outside door to the bathroom before going out to play. Five minutes after everyone is dressed, someone is bound to have to go potty, even if you followed the first tip.

Boot Camp

I suspect that calling an ordeal "boot camp" came not from the military, but from someone with experience dressing preschoolers for outdoor play. Try these tips to make the struggle easier:

- To get boots on the correct feet, use an indelible marker to make a design on the inside edges of each boot. If the marks touch, your child knows she has them the right way.
- If you buy boots with liners, your child may find it easier to put the liners on first.
- To help your child get her foot into a tight boot, have her sit on the floor with her back against the wall. On three, she should push her *heel* toward you, as if she were trying to push you over. (You hold the boot firmly in place.) Or have her stand in front of you, with her foot partly inserted in the boot. On three, have her stomp down hard, while you provide resistance. If all else fails, let her be Cinderella. You get to be Prince Charming. How can she prove she is Cinderella? Why, by getting her foot into that glass galosh, of course.
- Keep boots near a radiator or heating vent. Warm boots are much more inviting.
- Make a "boot gnome" from an old-fashioned clothespin to keep mates together.

Howdy Do, Dee:
WELCOMING RITUALS

Helping your child develop a friendly ritual for greeting caregivers will ease separation anxieties. These routines give structure and predictability to the change—and help your child to feel in control of the situation. The following hello games will feel good for everyone:

Great Shakes!

Help your preschooler develop a tricky handshake to do with his caregiver (he can have a different one for each caregiver). An example: Slap five, up high, down low, spin, double clap, wiggle fingers at each other. (Watch the remade version of *The Parent Trap* if you need help visualizing this kind of handshake.) You and your child can probably come up with a great variety of ideas that suit his temperament. For example, stick in some hugging and kissing for kids who need cuddles; whispers and soft tickles for quiet sorts; and jumps, squeezes, and spin-arounds for kids who need an active hello.

We Are Glad to Sing You!

Many preschools begin their days with a welcoming song. Songs work well on an individual basis, too. Here is a good greeting song (or chant), based on one from my Girl Scout days:

Hello, hello, hello, hello!
I am glad to see you!
I am glad to greet you!
Hello, hello, hello, HELLO!

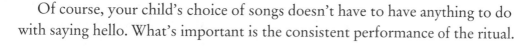

Of course, your child's choice of songs doesn't have to have anything to do with saying hello. What's important is the consistent performance of the ritual.

Butler Duty

Some children like to have a job at greeting time, especially one that will give them some back-and-forth contact before they settle in. Your child may like to take the wraps for arriving caregivers or stand near the door (with an adult) to act as greeter for other arrivals at school or daycare. Other errands and tasks will work, too.

Sign Language

"Hello" is signed in American Sign Language with a salute. Show your child how to hold up the "I love you" sign, too: Palm out, extend the thumb and hold up the pointer and pinky fingers (tall man and ring man fold down). This silent greeting works well with shy kids, who may need a few minutes before they're ready to speak out loud around a newcomer.

Bye and Seek:
TRANSITION INTO A GAME

You will find that your child is more accepting of your departure when he is actively involved in a game as you leave. You'll feel better, too, when your child is happy and busy.

Where's Waldo?

Hide a stuffed animal or other toy before you say good-bye (I recommend using the same one or two each time). Give your child a clue or two about where to find it. Let him start searching with the sitter before you leave. (You might want to tell the caregiver where it is so you don't get a frantic call at work.) Your child can continue to play the game with the caregiver—and he can hide the stuffed animal for you to find upon your return.

Bye and Seek

Let your child hide as the caregiver arrives. Have a ritual for finding her. For example, the sitter might hunt for a minute or two, then wave a magic wand and say, "Abracadabra!" and have your child pop out. Or, you might give the sitter "warmer, colder" clues until she finds her. For safety reasons, just make sure your child is found before you go.

Guess Who?

While you are getting ready to leave, help your child pick a character from a nursery rhyme, book, video, or TV show. Help him think of three clues to give the sitter. For example, for Curious George your child might say, "I'm a monkey. I live with the Man with the Yellow Hat. I'm always getting in trouble. Guess who I am?" Let the sitter engage your child with another "Guess Who?" game or read the appropriate book as you wave good-bye and scoot out the door.

Can You Do It?

Assign your child a task to learn while you are gone, like whistling, snapping his fingers, hopping all the way from the front door to the kitchen, or whatever. Aim for something he is close to being able to do, so he has a good chance of success by the time you get home. Get him started practicing just before you go. Don't forget to have him demonstrate when you return.

More Ideas

Have an activity ready for your child and his caregiver to do. Your child can help you plan if he'd like. Suggestions:

- Puzzles or board games
- An art project
- A cooking project
- A science experiment
- Blocks to build
- A walk to take
- A visit from a friend (if the sitter doesn't mind)
- Swing
- Dance
- Peg board or marble run
- A treasure hunt

End of the Rode:
SHARING A MINI-COMMUTE

When my brother was small, he loved to "go to work" with our dad. Most weekday mornings, he put on his tie and Daddy-jacket (a white shirt that my mom had embroidered his name on so it resembled my father's lab coat), grabbed his briefcase (a yellow scrub bucket), and drove to work with Dad. What this meant was they got in the car together, and my dad drove from the garage to the end of the driveway. He put the car in park, helped my brother hop out, and watched until he walked up to the door of his "office" (our house), and my mom let him in.

This ritual was deeply satisfying for my brother. My dad reports that they had many nice conversations during these short commutes. Undoubtedly, the ritual added as much as ten minutes to his morning departure some days (Evan wasn't always a speedy dresser and sometimes their conversations were lengthy), but for the few years it lasted, it was well worth the investment in their relationship.

TALES FROM THE TRENCHES

My five-year-old daughter was once asked what her father's job was. She thought for a moment, then looked at me, uncertain. I prodded her to answer, saying, "Remember, you've visited daddy at his office. What does he do all day?" "Oh yes!" she said enthusiastically. "He types!" (Her father is a lawyer.)

Look for ways for your child to share a piece of your commute. She may be able to walk to the bus or subway stop with you (and another parent, older sibling, or sitter to walk her home), share a journey down the driveway, or simply stand and watch for your car pool with you. Use the moments to share information about what you do at your job (not that your child will necessarily get it) and to ask about her activities.

A costume and props related to your job can enrich the experience for your child, as they did for my brother. They can also stimulate imaginative play that distracts her as she completes her separation from you.

Blast Off Together!
READY ON THE LAUNCH PAD

When the whole family is heading off in the morning to work, daycare, school, or errands, you'll need to be a little extra organized and prepared. That way you won't have to do lots of last-minute running around looking for missing sneakers or the particular tutu your daughter must have for dance class. Or lecturing and screaming, which is what comes next in my house. The other key to reducing out-the-door fusses is a blast-off attitude, which is easier to adopt once you're organized properly. These ideas may help your family to launch into the day more peacefully.

The Launching Pad

Create a central place to store *everything* family members will need as they go out the door. If at all possible, aim for setting up a "cubby" area, such as those daycare centers and preschools use.

- Be sure that hooks and shelves are at child height, so your child can be independent.
- One easy way to make a cubby is to separate a small bookcase into sections with baskets or boxes. (Closet organizing systems work well, too.) Attach hooks to the side for children's jackets. Use a small basket (or clothespins mounted to the uprights) to hold hats and mittens. Place boots on a tray or an old towel or carpet remnant on the bottom shelf.
- If your child insists on just dumping everything, try a laundry basket or large box (stow footwear on a mat beside it).
- Papers, toys, snacks, supplies, etc., for the next day can be stored right in backpacks and hung on a hook or placed on a shelf. Or you could use a rural-style mailbox, personalized with your child's name; a plastic dishpan; an empty cereal box, covered with contact paper and decorated to your child's taste (tape it to whatever you use for a cubby); or an in/out box from an office supply store.

• Use separate backpacks or totes for each activity and restock them right after use. We were constantly heading off to soccer without clean socks until I realized it was better to buy two pairs and pop the clean one in the soccer bag as soon as we got home from practice or the game. I put clean uniform items in the bag as soon as they're washed, too, so I know where to find them. If there is something that can't go in the bag until the last minute (like perishable food), attach a note or other visual reminder to the outside of the bag.

TRY THIS!

Have special clothes for an activity that need to be washed each time? Have your child get in the habit of sticking them on the washing machine when she removes them. That way, you'll be reminded to do them when you put in a load—and if you don't get to them in time, at least they'll have aired out and you'll be able to find them.

• Use visual checklists and hang them on the door to check each time you leave. Something you always forget? Make a *big* picture of it, and stick it at eye level.

• Mount a dry-erase calendar or large paper calendar near the launching pad. Use markers color-coded for each family member so you can see quickly who has appointments. (Let your child cross off the previous day—that's a chore a preschooler will relish.)

• Place an outdoor thermometer in a window near the launching pad to help moderate outdoor clothing disputes.

• Each night, check to be sure that all items needed for the next day are in the appropriate pack or basket.

Out-the-Door Approaches

Set an alarm or timer to go off when it's time to start last-second preparations, such as gathering packs or putting on coats. (Be sure to allow a few minutes breathing room.) Then try one of these "Let's Go!" approaches:

- **Stepping Out** Divide the task into a series of steps (e.g., Step One is go potty, Step Two is put on your coat and other gear, etc.). Then you can call out each step, drill sergeant style, with a one- or two-word description, like "Potty!" or "Coat!" This terse approach often cuts down on crabby lectures and fussy arguments.
- **Fire Drill** Pretend you're firefighters scrambling to get on the hook and ladder and to the fire. Your kid can imagine that his pack is firefighting equipment, like a hose or ax. From time to time, have your child be the Fire Chief, so you don't always get stuck being the ordering-around guy, and so he learns the routine, too. Other imaginative themes (like space launch, of course) work, too, as long as there is an element of urgency.
- **Last One Out Is a Rotten Egg!** I hate this one, since it leads to bickering among the kids, but I must admit it is remarkably effective in getting everyone together quickly (as long as I do a double check once we're in the car to make sure we have everything). And I don't have to do the yelling, and I like that better.
- **Final Check** Make a list of everything you need to have or do, including buckling up. Then get the list laminated and keep it in the car. If it's a picture list, your child can call out each item. Then do a countdown and blast off to have a great day!

Time Machines and Other Safety Seat Lures:
BUCKLE UP FOR SAFETY STRATEGIES

Getting your kid in his safety seat and buckled up can be one of the most maddening steps of the morning rush. *But never skip this step no matter how big your hurry!* I've seen kids with serious brain injuries from very minor accidents (one was in a parking lot). Teach your child to do as much of the process herself as possible. This will make life easier for you and decrease power struggles. Practice with the straps and buckles when you're not in a rush. Finally, the following imaginary themes can greatly increase your child's cooperation (just vary the theme so it doesn't get dull). And, trust me, it's better than using your knee to force a struggling kid into her seat.

Time Machine Maneuvers

Invite your child to hop in, saying something like, "You like dinosaurs, right? Well, hop in my new time machine, and we'll head back millions of years, so you can see some. What dinosaurs would you most like to see?" Continue to play up the dinosaur theme. Or pick another time destination your child might enjoy. An old remote control or broken cordless phone makes a good prop for this game. Naturally, it would be very dangerous to travel through time unrestrained, so be sure your youngster secures her time-warp webbing before you begin.

Magic Carpet Magic

Your three-year-old may cheerfully bind herself safely to your magic carpet with strands of pearls or gold chains. Be sure to allow her to use the magic words ("Open, sesame!") to make the door to the cave (car) open, as well as the magic words that will start you on your journey: "Abra-cadabra, peanut butter sandwich! Fly, magic carpet! Fly!" During your journey, narrate the wondrous sights you are passing. Encourage your child to join in. Say things like "Look! I see an elephant lumbering along the trail. I wonder if it is carrying the Rajah to the castle over there. Are those rubies or diamonds on the elephant's headpiece?"

Flight Attendant

Invite your child to settle in comfortably aboard the Concorde and run through the in-flight safety instructions, including information on fastening her seatbelt and remaining seated until you are parked at the gate at the other end. Let her know your destination, any interesting sights you'll see, and approximate time of arrival. Magazines and in-flight snacks will naturally be appreciated on longer journeys.

Other imaginary transportation themes that preschoolers love include:
• Police Officer (Use some good siren sound effects.)

- Super Heroes (Fly or ride in a super-powered vehicle.)
- Army Guys (Ever feel like driving a tank to work? Here's your chance.)
- Animal Play (horse loaded in a trailer, puppy in a crate, riding on a wild stallion, etc.)
- Pilot (commercial jet, helicopter, Air Force stealth bomber, hot air balloon, etc.)
- Fantastic Creature Transport (back of a dragon, unicorn, Pegasus, etc.)
- Submarine or Pirate Ship

Static Guard:
HELP FOR THOSE UNSIGHTLY CLING-ONS

Separation anxiety and the resulting clinginess usually peak during the toddler years. Nonetheless, many preschoolers will periodically struggle with separations, and a handful will continue to have consistent difficulty. In extreme cases, you may need to seek professional help, but these strategies have helped ease good-bye grab-ons in many families.

Rule Number One: *Keep Good-byes Short and Sweet and Ritualized.*

If this represents a major change for your family, have a meeting to *tell* your child the new routine. Make a picture diagram of the steps, and keep the steps to four or fewer. An example:

Step One: Mrs. Williams arrives at 7:30.

Step Two: You tell her your new joke.

Step Three: I give you my piggy pin and you give me an action figure.

Step Four: At 7:40, we have our special hug and kiss, and I get in the car.

In my family, we always say last thing, "*Hey!* Let's be careful out there." (Remember *Hill Street Blues*?) When my kids hear that (or say it, if they're leaving me), they know the good-byes are over. Make sure you have a "closer" too.

For the next two weeks, follow the good-bye routine, including the timing, *exactly*. Once your child feels more confident, you can develop Plan B or C patterns for mornings that go differently.

Collateral and Tokens of Affection

Remember those cute heart necklaces that split in two, so you and your best friend could each wear half? Or ID bracelets, fraternity pins, engagement and wedding rings? Giving a loved one a token to remember you by has been a tradition since before the days of knights when ladies gave a scarf to their shining-armored sweethearts. Choose something to exchange with your child. My son and I wore these cute little piggy pins on school days when he was three-and-a-half and suddenly developed an urge to stay with his pregnant mother. The little piggy pins solved the problem to his satisfaction and mine. Another friend of mine used to give her son a "credit card" (which was really an expired video store card, but the kid couldn't read) every day when she went to work. He tucked it in his pocket and rubbed the raised lettering when he missed her. Occasionally he used it to charge goods at the daycare play store, so it came in handy, too.

Humor Helpers

As always, be a little careful with humor in emotionally charged situations. It's a magic bullet for some kids but a dagger in the heart for sensitive ones.

Do something like walk your kid into his classroom. Then pretend to flush a toilet. Your child can get swirled down the drain and shoot through the sewer to land where his friends are playing. Or maybe your child would prefer to flush *you* down the drain. Or, pretend the kid's a baseball, and slug him over the fence. Make believe he's a sack of moldy old potatoes you're unloading, and pick him up and dump him in the block corner with his buddies. Goofy stuff, but it lets your child (or maybe you) express a little of that aggression/frustration safely and the slightly violent separation may be just a bit easier, like ripping off a bandage instead of gently trying to work it off. *Final Warning: Do not sneak out on your child. Ever!*

CHAPTER TWO

Please
Hold!

I am sure you are a wonderful parent who spends Quality Time
teaching your child all the important things he needs to know, like the
alphabet or how to spit for distance. But even the Best Parent in the
World needs a few moments to himself to take care of things like shampooing wads of play dough out of his hair or paying the Toys 'R Us bill.
That's why this chapter is here—it's a compilation of cool stuff your child
can do *all by himself*. Unfortunately, it's also cool stuff your child could
do *with* you. For me, the biggest problem with these activities was that I
sometimes forgot to take advantage of the opportunity to slip away and
shampoo my hair or pay my bills or write my books. Because I still *like*
playing with beans. And with my kids, too, of course.

Although everything here is manageable and intriguing for a four-year-
old by herself, some activities are more effective if you supervise or join in
the first couple of times you set them out. For example, if you invest five
minutes here and there to play bubbles with your kid and show her what
neat stuff she can do, like driving a miniature truck through a bubble
dome, later she will stick with her experiments for a longer period of time.
Maybe even long enough for you to shave your legs and apply mascara
after you get the play dough out of your hair. Or shave your face and apply

deodorant, if you're a dad sort and that's more your thing. Either way, your spouse will like that, and you will, too.

Other activities like Nice Ice! require you to do some simple advance preparation. You have to have some ice on hand, after all, to play with it; and the best ice, the "big" kind, won't be produced by the automatic ice-maker, even if you're lucky enough to have one. So plan ahead and keep at least one water-filled milk or ice cream carton in the freezer at all times. (You can always use it in the picnic cooler if you don't need it for fun.) And some activities require materials that are totally standard supplies in my house, like lots of food coloring, something friends of mine claim they don't always have in their cupboard. Some people don't normally have dried beans! Hard to imagine, but they swear it's true. Stock up if you need to.

Even with these caveats, there are plenty of ideas here that you can do with stuff you are bound to have on hand no matter what—surely you're never completely out of water or pennies or bouncy balls, right? Most are simple activities that don't require you to be especially nimble to set them up from scratch once you're already on the phone. (You might want to post a list of your kid's favorites next to the phone, though, so you don't have to comb the house for this book when you need something desperately.)

In case you haven't mastered the Bug-Me-and-You'll-Deeply-Regret-It-Glare-of-Doom, this chapter starts with a couple of kinder, gentler techniques for keeping kids from interrupting you. Then, once you have the pestering problem under control, you can have fun with these. I mean, let your kid have fun with these. You can have a turn later, after you get the bills in the mail.

Red Light, Green Light:
TRAFFIC CONTROL FOR BUSY TIMES

Even if you dress in neon pink and hold a glowing orange phone to your ear, your child will not "see" that you are talking on the phone when she comes running into the room. She will see only a ready and willing listener for her story about how Georgie next door can put a straw in his nose and blow bubbles in his milk. This "blindness" is why you need a nonverbal method or two like these to help your child tell when you're available—or not.

Red Light, Green Light

Use a traffic-light analogy to let your children know when you should not be disturbed and when you can give them attention. Even three-year-olds generally "get" the traffic-light concept.

- *Red Light* means "Do not interrupt me, except for emergencies (usually involving major bodily fluids, like blood, poop, vomit)."
- *Yellow Light* means "I'm busy, but you can ask a quick question or get me to lend a hand for a moment."
- *Green Light* means "Go ahead and demand my attention. I'm more than ready to have an excuse to stop talking with Mrs. Snoggis about her cat's arthritis."

Most of the time, you can just use finger signals to indicate different lights—one finger is a red light, two is a yellow, and three is green. Add unmistakable facial expressions and head nods or shakes to emphasize your communication. If you work at home, though, you might want to make and post a

TRY THIS

You can buy realistic traffic lights at places like Spencer's Gifts and if you work at home, it might be a worthwhile investment. Okay, a fun investment. Plus, the kids will be so busy playing with it and arguing about who gets to push the buttons that they might leave you alone a little longer.

traffic signal for your office door (with an arrow to indicate the color) to help your kids understand when they can have access to you.

Don't forget that you can use the traffic-light system to protect time with your child or family, too. For example, your evening Crazy Eights tournament can be a "red light time" when telemarketers, chatty neighbors, your boss, and even pesky siblings have to wait while your child has your attention all to herself. Kids will buy in better if the tactic benefits them, too.

LITERATURE LINKS

Read *Five Minutes' Peace* by Jill Murphy. It probably won't solve the problem, but it will make you and the kids laugh, and that's worth five minutes' peace in itself.

The Timer Treatment

Timers can help kids wait a little more patiently—and successfully. When they have a concrete image of the time you'll be busy (and of how much time remains), they are more likely to let you be. Kitchen timers are the classic method, but sand or drip timers are great for short, busy periods. You can also use tapes of stories or music, music boxes, or even activities (like building a castle with every block in the bin) to mark off a chunk of uninterrupted time.

Interruption Interrupters

Have a discussion with your child about how you will stop her when she interrupts you, especially during a red-light time. The technique you choose will vary with your child's temperament and yours. Aim for something silent and quick, so you don't inadvertently reinforce your child's interruption habit.

Nice Ice!
HELP YOUR CHILD "CHILL OUT" WHILE YOU ARE BUSY

This activity is especially inviting on a sultry day, but my kids love it even in the winter. They can wear gloves to keep their hands warm. It generally lasts as long as the ice does.

Dump some ice cubes into one or more containers. Offer your young scientist a variety of ways to melt a cube. Some fun techniques:

- Spray it with a mister of warm water. (Put the mister on spray and try to blast a hole through the middle of a cube!) Be prepared for them to mist themselves, too.
- Sprinkle it with table salt and feel the interesting surface.
- Float it in a bowl. What happens to the water temperature? Will it melt in milk or another liquid? Can you make the ice sink?
- Rub it with a metal spoon. Try using both the bowl of the spoon and the edge. Try a Popsicle stick, too. Which works best? Why?
- Use an eyedropper or straw to drip water onto the cubes. Make a valley!
- Many kids will get a kick out of just playing around with the ice. Provide some small figures or plastic animals, and many children will create a playscape with the ice. (Show them how to make cubes stick together: melt a cube slightly with warm water, then place another on top. As the water is cooled by the ice, it will re-freeze, gluing the cubes together.)

Big Ice

Get in the habit of keeping *giant* ice cubes in the freezer for extra-big fun. Make these in any large *disposable* containers: old ice cream cartons, waxed milk cartons, plastic food trays, heavy-duty latex balloons, or old rubber gloves (these last two make *very cool* ice). Just remember that water expands as it freezes (it may destroy the container) and either the opening must be as large as the "ice cube" or the container can be pulled apart and off (like a balloon).

Rainbow Ice

Add food coloring for an interesting variation. The ice will typically have variations in color density—beautiful and intriguing. Freeze different colors in successive layers for a festive look!

TRY THIS!

These make for some very different and memorable party favor "bags." Freeze a giant ice cube for each child, adding things like plastic toys, freezer pops (the kind that come in plastic sleeves), and maybe some food coloring or sparklies, once the cube is partly frozen. As the final party activity, give each child a cube to melt while he waits for his ride. (Have heavy-duty plastic freezer bags available to hold freed treasures and any remaining ice for taking home.) A mister for each child makes a much-appreciated extra favor. Obviously, this activity is easiest at an outside party, but you can do it inside if you put the cubes in a plastic kiddy pool or individual dishpans.

Treasure Ice

As the ice starts to crystallize, stir in various objects that can be released as the ice melts. Try plastic figures, sequins or other sparklies, frozen fruits (like strawberries), and natural objects (like flowers, leaves, pine cones).

Bucket o' Beans:
AN INDOOR SANDBOX

Buy at least three bags (four or five is better) of dried beans. Choosing a variety of colors and sizes will add to the fun. (In my experience, split peas do not hold up well, but lentils are passable.) Store the beans in a heavy-duty container with a tightly fitting lid to avoid spills or uninvited pests. Be sure to keep the play beans separate from your food supply.

The beans can be played with in a variety of places and ways. Make cleanup easier by putting a mat or cloth under the container. Some containers to try:

- a washtub or tray on the table
- a large plastic bin or cardboard box that your child can sit in

- the plastic wading pool lugged in from the garage
- a plastic cloth on the floor, bordered with blocks, pillows, cereal boxes, or whatever to make a clear edge

Then, give your child some props to stimulate different kinds of play. Some suggested themes and props:

- *Cooking* Scoops, funnels, measuring cups, wooden spoons, pots, plastic bowls, and plastic tea party sets for serving
- *It's a Jungle in There* Plastic animals or dinosaurs, rocks, tree branches or sticks, blocks
- *Treasure Island* Pirate guys and ship, rocks, coins, beads, toy gems
- *Magnet Magic* Wand-style magnet and several metal objects that your child can bury and find magically by stirring with the magnet
- *Earth Movers* Toy bulldozers, dump trucks, cement mixers, and so on, set out on a plastic floor cloth

TRY THIS!

Even dried beans that are several years old will still germinate. Split open a couple of beans and look at the tiny baby plant (called an embryo) inside. Then take some whole beans and place them in a small jar (a baby food jar is great). Use a rolled-up damp sponge to hold the beans against the walls of the jar. In just a few days, the beans will sprout, sending a root down and seed leaves up. Very cool. Transplant the seedlings, if you'd like, and grow a good prop for playing Jack and the Beanstalk.

SAFETY ZONE

Dried beans can pose a choking hazard. Keep them away from younger siblings—we often played with them during the little guys' naptimes. Also, because even children old enough to know better "forget," you should frequently remind your child never to put beans in his mouth, nostrils, or ears.

This activity was hands-down all three of my children's favorite (and mine) during their preschool years. It encouraged high-quality imaginative play, soothed ruffled nerves, and promoted relatively smooth cooperative play.

Play-Dough Pizzazz:
NEW FUN WITH AN OLD FAVORITE

Preschoolers love play dough, but a few new ideas can boost interest and lengthen playing time.

Mix In Interest

Let your child knead stuff into the dough to give it an interesting texture, scent, or appearance. Try used coffee grounds, glitter (make a "well" in the dough, pour in the glitter, cover it over, and give the dough a good squish, so loose glitter doesn't end up in anyone's eyes), unsweetened drink mix, a couple of drops of contrasting food coloring, drops of flavor concentrates like vanilla or peppermint, sawdust, sand, tiny shreds of construction or other paper, fish bowl gravel, leaves, petals, grass, or other natural materials. The mixing-in process alone will occupy most kids for a considerable period of time, and playing with the new material they've created adds still more focused time.

Cut Ups

Many preschoolers can cut ropes of play dough with safety scissors before they can manage cuts in paper. Pre-make a series of snakes for your child to cut "to smithereens" to keep him occupied. Older preschoolers will also enjoy experimenting with different cutting tools on slabs and ropes of play dough. Try pizza cutters, plastic knives or butter spreaders, spatulas, cookie cutters, toothpicks and Popsicle sticks, toy saws, or other pretend tools. Extruders, whether commercial or adapted (like a garlic press) make good hair or grass to trim. If your child has trouble operating these (and many do), pre-press a large quantity.

Dough Boy

Shape a big gingerbread-like person, using as much play dough as possible. You can make it flat or give it some dimension (like a rounded belly or a stick-out nose). Supply your child with materials to "finish" his ungingerbread guy (or gal). Try buttons, pieces of cloth, contrasting colors of dough, bits of fabric trims, hardware, play gems, yarn or string, pasta, toothpicks, pipe cleaners, natural materials. You can also make dinosaur or animal shapes, monsters, buildings, vehicles, bugs (try a series of balls for a caterpillar guy), etc. The fun is in embellishing them. This project works well with a small group.

Dough as Canvas

Roll out a thick slab of dough and let your child use it as a background for making a temporary collage. The beauty of dough over paper is that you don't need glue or paste—just push the materials in. Anything you might use for a paper collage will work. My kids also liked using the pegs from pegboards or LiteBrite to make designs.

Dough as Landscape

Give your child a tray and enough dough to cover it. Show him how to make mounds to represent hills or mountains, channels to be rivers or roads, and depressions for lakes or caves. Add natural materials or small toys for making additional features, and give him some figures or vehicles to play with on his "set."

TRY THIS!

Commercial play dough is great, but expensive, and it comes in such small quantities. This recipe is my personal favorite because of its consistency, scent, and quantity. It will keep for months in a tightly covered container.

- 3 cups flour (plus more for kneading in—the amount seems to depend on humidity and the consistency you prefer)
- ½ cup salt
- 2 packages dry unsweetened drink mix (like Kool Aid)
- 2 cups boiling water
- 3 tablespoons oil

Combine the dry ingredients in a heatproof bowl (your child can help with this step). Pour in oil and boiling water (an adult job only). Stir until mixture forms a ball. Let cool slightly, then knead on a well-floured surface, adding flour until the mixture is smooth and has the consistency of bread dough or commercial play dough. (We always set aside a small amount for the kids to knead themselves. First, we flattened it to increase surface area and speed cooling, then checked the whole lump to make sure it was cool enough to handle safely.) Cool until it can be handled comfortably, but it's great while it's still kind of warm.

Snack-tivities:
MAKE IT-EAT IT PLAY

These are good activities for when you are busy, since it bothers most adults to watch the process.

Lincoln Logs

Your child will enjoy assembling stick pretzel cabins with a little peanut butter cement. Give her a bowl of pretzels, a blob of peanut butter, and a piece of waxed paper on which to assemble her creation. Use graham crackers for the roof. Show her how to assemble her building Lincoln-log style. Younger children can just dip each end of the pretzel in the peanut butter, but older kids can try using a plastic knife or Popsicle stick to spread a little on the ends. Another easier approach is to coat a small milk carton with peanut butter, and let the kid stick the pretzels to it. Provide mini-crackers, other shapes of pretzels, raisins, dry cereal, and so on, for decoration. Goodies like animal crackers, teddy bear graham crackers, or gummy guys may spark pretending play before eating.

Edible Jewelry

Children enjoy stringing cereal O's on a stiff cord, pipe cleaners, or, for an edible cord, a piece of shoestring licorice. If you use different colors or flavors, you can demonstrate how to follow a pattern, like AAB (e.g., pink, pink, green). Fruit Roll-Ups and similar products can be cut with a plastic knife and twisted, stuck, and shaped into rings or bracelets.

Sandwich Canvas

Your child can paint or print on bread (boring white works best) with paints made from a tablespoon of milk and a drop or two of food coloring. Use pastry brushes, new paintbrushes, or stamps cut by a parent from veggies (carrots work well and can be eaten afterwards). Encourage the artist to go easy, or the "canvas" will get wet and tear or be too soggy to eat. Dry and set the paintings by lightly toasting the bread. Condiments, like catsup and mustard, also work for printing, and can be used on slices of American cheese as well as bread.

Paper Plate Mosaics

Give your child a plain paper plate and an assortment of small foods to create a portrait or landscape masterpiece. Try foods like raisins, cereal, chopped veggies (carrots, broccoli, alfalfa sprouts, celery, brightly colored peppers), banana circles, other fruit slices, and crackers (whole or crushed). You can provide a little edible glue (peanut butter or cream cheese) if needed. Many children will spend a long time arranging and rearranging their creations before eating them.

Potion Play:
MAKING A SORT-OF-CONTROLLED MESS

What preschooler doesn't love making a mess? Potion play lets your child indulge his passions for dumping, mixing, and glopping while keeping the mess relatively contained. And while he's having fun, your child is also learning skills he'll need later for cooking and chemistry.

 MORE TO KNOW
Although some parents worry that letting children play with their food will lead to all sorts of bad habits and manners, in my experience sanctioned food fun leads, if anything, to a greater willingness to try new foods and to respect usual mealtime manners.

Potion Lab Set-Up

Give your child some clear plastic containers, an assortment of edible liquids, powders, and other ingredients, and a variety of tools for transferring ingredients to his containers (like eyedroppers, measuring spoons and cups, funnels, tongs, paper packets, tweezers, garlic presses, etc.)—and I'll bet you can have an hour of free time. Minimize the later cleanup by setting everything inside plastic bins and by covering the tabletop and floor with plastic. Or, save this activity for an outside day and just hose down the mess. I also recommend sticking to measuring tools that hold only very small quantities. This is even fun in a miniature version, using dollhouse cooking equipment or bottle lid cauldrons.

Always review safety rules before this kind of play. Your child should be reminded that he may not add any ingredients besides those set out. Also, unless all the ingredients are edible, he should not taste the potion without first checking with you.

Ingredients to try:

- Water—the main ingredient—with food color or a little packaged drink mix for color
- Drops of other liquids, like milk, juice, pickle juice, vinegar, or cooking oil
- Tiny amounts of dense liquids, like honey, molasses, catsup, or corn syrup
- Small quantities of sugar, salt, flour, baking soda, cornstarch, or cocoa
- Pinches of spices like cinnamon or nutmeg
- Stale, broken, or crushed stuff from the pantry (like crackers, bread, cereal)
- Leftovers/garbage, such as vegetable and fruit peels, crusts, dollops of sauce or gravy, or over-ripe bananas
- Bottom-of-the-package crumbs, salt, or sugar sprinkles
- Ice chips

MORE TO KNOW

If you set out vinegar (or other acid liquid, like lemon juice) and baking soda at the same time, be prepared for a potentially messy chemical reaction.

Imagination Boosters

Add fun props, like a toy cauldron, wizard/witch's hat and cape, magic wand, cool ladle, and a "book of spells." Encourage your child to concoct a recipe to cure warts or a love potion. But be sure to remind him that his potion is pretend, and he shouldn't taste it without double-checking with you.

Or, deck your child out as a chemist. Give her safety glasses, an old white shirt as lab coat, and a clipboard to record results.

Follow up with simple science experiments and concoction creations like those found in *Super Science Concoctions* by Jill Frankel Hauser or *The Ultimate Book of Kid Concoctions* by John E. Thomas and Danita Pagel.

Concocting Color:
PLAY WITH COLORED WATER

These activities were much loved by preschoolers when I taught daycare. The teachers loved them too, because they had a soothing effect on the whole room. As a bonus, they're educational! They nurture the fine motor skills that preschoolers will need for writing, encourage kids to use a scientific approach to experimenting, and teach color concepts.

Colorful Drip Drops

Assemble the following supplies:
- Water
- Food coloring or watercolors
- Tools for transferring drops: an eyedropper, pipette, small piece of sponge, a drinking straw, or even a tiny spoon (like those for feeding an infant)
- Containers for each color: yogurt cups, muffin tins, margarine tubs, clear plastic cups, Styrofoam egg cartons
- A "canvas" to color: ice cube trays (the best are the white mini-cube trays), paper towels or coffee filters, waxed paper, even a soap suction holder (put droplets on each of the cups—arrange them in patterns or pictures)
- Something to protect the work surface: plastic mat or cloth, trays or bins
- Optional: paper and crayons to record results (also, soothing music to work by such as Handel's *Water Music* or Bach's *Brandenburg Concertos)*

Give your child four colors to start—clear water and water you've colored red, blue, yellow. (You can also offer a little milk as an opaque white.) Show her how to use the tool(s) to transfer drops of water from one of the bigger containers to a smaller one (such as one of the ice cube trays). Or, she can scatter a few drops over a paper towel or the surface of the waxed paper. Then have her see what happens if she adds a drop of a different color to that one. Clear water will also create changes. Each of the different tools and canvases has its own appeal, so be sure to vary your materials for different sessions.

TRY THIS!

At first, many preschoolers find it tricky to use an eyedropper correctly and parents may have trouble finding eyedroppers to use. Eyedroppers can be recycled from infant medicines—just clean them well—or purchased at pharmacies, craft stores, or school supply stores. For safety, stick with plastic ones. Look for one with a bulb that isn't too stiff. Most preschoolers can learn how to use an eyedropper with just a little instruction. Have your child squeeze the bulb *before* she puts it in the liquid. Explain that this pushes out the air, leaving an empty space that wants to be filled back up. Dip the tip in the water, and slowly unpinch the bulb. The liquid will come up to fill the empty space created when she pushed the air out. (But if she unpinches it in the air, air will go back in to fill up the empty space.) Have her repeat, "Pinch. Dip. Unpinch."

The Big Swirl

Provide your child with a couple of tall clear containers filled with water (like drink pitchers or pop bottles) and small cups of only one or two colors. Have her watch what happens to color drops added one at a time. Experiment with warm versus cool water. Or float a half-inch of oil (vegetable or baby) on the surface. The drops will slowly diffuse through the oil and then "explode" when they hit the water. The oil also will not change color like the water does. This activity definitely benefits from music.

Magical Milk

If this weren't wasteful of milk (and we didn't constantly run out of it), I would prefer it to the main activity. Pour just enough milk to cover a shallow container like a pie plate. Add drops of full-strength food coloring here and there over the surface. Take a toothpick and poke it in the color drops. Nothing much happens. Put a drop of liquid soap on the tip and dip it again. Wow! You can keep dipping again and again—just stick the tip in areas where the color swirls seem concentrated. Take care not to get too much soap in the milk or it will ruin the fun.

No Muss, No Fuss—But Art!
A SMORGASBORD OF GRAB-AND-DO, NO-MESS ART ACTIVITIES

You can set up these projects without missing a beat in your phone conversation:

- *Coloring books and crayons* The old-fashioned kind. Still fun.
- *Beads or tubular pasta* String them on pipe cleaners.
- *Colored pasta* Put food coloring and a little water in a plastic bag with the pasta. Let your child mush it around to his heart's content. Then he can spread the noodles on newspaper to dry. String them on pipe cleaners when ready.
- *Foil sculptures* Just tear off lots of strips of foil and crumple and twist them to get the kids started.
- *Rubber stamping* Only got a date stamp? Show your child how to stamp the images in patterns like stars or fans.
- *Chalk on construction paper* Dip chalk in a bowl of water (or better yet, sugar water) for making pictures with rich, sparkly colors.
- *Drawing with markers* There are a million varieties and you probably own one or two from every possible set. (Look for smelly, stamping, or color change markers, fine versus wide tip, crazy tips, sparkle ones, blo-pens, and more.) Some of the ones you have may still have ink. If not, provide water so your child can dip the tips of water-soluble ones. Instead of paper, put out

coffee filters or paper towels. Your child can drip water on his pictures to make the colors spread and change.

- *Refrigerator magnet collages*
- *Glue sticks, paper, stuff*
- *Bingo markers* Use them to make dot designs on paper.
- *Stamp pad, paper, fingers* Use a marker to make the fingerprints look like mice or other little "guys."
- *Etch-a-sketch, Magna-Doodle, chalkboard*
- *Cookie cutters, pencil and paper* Stencil designs.
- *Paper, colored pencils, ruler* Make lines in all colors, criss-crossing everywhere.
- *Hand, pencil, paper* You trace around your child's hand. She adds rings, watches, fingernails, other embellishments.
- *A pushpin, cardboard, paper, design, or page from coloring book* Put paper on top of cardboard. Put design or picture on top of that. Have child poke around the outline to make a "pokey-picture." Best for older preschoolers.
- *A mural picture* Roll out a long strip of paper on the floor or tape it to a bare stretch of wall. Provide pencils, markers, or crayons and let your child be. Or children, which is even better.
- A *sticky picture* Tape a sheet of contact paper, sticky side up, to the table. Let your child stick on tissue paper, feathers, and other scraps to make a collage.

Bubble Up Fun:
THINGS TO DO WITH SOAP AND WATER
FOR KIDS WHO DON'T LIKE TO WASH

We do most of our indoor bubble play at the kitchen table, and I use basins or deep trays to keep the wet mess confined. For simplicity, we mostly just use a few squirts of Joy or Dawn dish detergent in some water. Adding a few drops of corn syrup or glycerin will make the bubbles last longer. You can also use commercial bubble solutions.

Bubble Buildings

Give your child a deep container (like the largest-size margarine tub) and a plastic straw. Practice blowing through the straw—try moving around a wad of paper—until you are sure she understands the difference between blowing and sucking. Then, place about a half-inch of water in the bottom of the container, and add a good squirt of dishwashing detergent. Tell your child to blow as tall a tower of bubbles as she can. This activity will captivate a young child for a long time, if you encourage her to experiment with the process and play with the suds. Try different straws or give your child Styrofoam peanuts to ride up a bubble elevator.

Bubble Tray Play

Pour a small quantity of bubble solution onto a plastic tray. Provide a variety of blowers. Good blowers for this activity include straws or funnels. Add some small objects to insert inside bubbles, such as mini-cars, marbles, or a pencil.

Show your child how to dip the end of the straw or blower into the puddle of bubble solution and then blow bubble domes that lie flat on the tray. If he wets the end of the straw in the bubble solution, he can carefully insert it in the middle of the bubble and blow some more. Even more magically, he may be able to blow a second bubble inside the first. This takes practice; caution your child not to get frustrated too quickly.

Similarly, your child may be able to drive a little car inside a bubble without popping it. Or poke his finger or a pencil into it without harming it. The secrets? Wetting the object well with bubble solution first, poking a "fresh" bubble, and going slow. This amazing feat, once mastered, bears much repeating and further experimenting. Have him try blowing bubbles next to each other or on top of each other, as well as moving the bubbles around with his straw. Can he get the bubbles to "swallow" objects on the tray?

Crystal Bubble Balls

If you can get your hands on some of those wire candle holder stands (we often find these at dollar or discount stores), you can show your child how to make a "crystal" bubble ball. Dip the circle part of the holder into the puddle until it is coated with bubble film (this is interesting to examine in its own right). Slowly blow one large bubble. Quickly use the circle end to recapture the bubble and then set it down on the table. Observe how the skin of the bubble gets thinner and thinner until it pops. You can do insertion tricks like you did with the bubble domes—or just pretend it's a crystal ball and make predictions of the future.

Barbershop Quintet:
FIVE GROOMING STUFF ACTIVITIES

Young chimps and gorillas enjoy grooming play, and your little monkey will, too. These activities were much–requested by my kids and their friends. I endorse them wholeheartedly, even though some are a tad ookier than I'd normally prefer, because they are especially effective in keeping kids busy and contented.

LITERATURE LINKS

A Drop of Water by Walter Wick (the talented photographer of the I Spy series) has beautiful photos of soap bubbles, interesting information on bubble science, and ideas for more advanced bubble play.

Shave...

Shaving cream is marvelous stuff (though a bit messy, and I'm not fond of the smell of the cheap stuff). Set your preschooler up in front of a mirror (in a room that wipes up easily, like the bathroom or kitchen). Have her lather her face like Dad does (avoiding the eye area), then shave it off with a Popsicle stick. Preschoolers also enjoy shaving other body parts, like arms, legs, or bare bellies. This is a good pre-bath activity—have her sit in the empty tub. Make it even more soothing by warming the shaving cream by floating the can in a basin of warm water for several minutes.

...And a Haircut

These words strike fear in the heart of every parent who has ever seen the handiwork of barber-wannabes. You can actually reduce the likelihood of their really cutting hair by providing a pair of pretend scissors that don't actually cut and/or giving them an acceptable alternative to trim.

Make pretend scissors from a Styrofoam fruit or vegetable tray. (Avoid ones from meat to prevent food poisoning.) Trace around a pair of children's scissors, drawing each blade separately. Cut out the two pieces and assemble them by poking a brass paper fastener through the spot where the real scissors are fastened. These no-cut scissors will open and close in a satisfying way.

Or have your child cut "not-hair." Alternative hair can be made from the following substances: paper from a shredder (glue lots of it to a paper plate face); grass grown indoors in a pot; play dough squeezed through an extruder and attached to a dough head; or cold cooked spaghetti.

Shaving Cream, Part II

Let your child fingerpaint with a mound of shaving cream on a tray or cookie sheet. A little food coloring will make pastel shades. Provide some interesting tools, like a hair pick, items to stamp, or cardboard cut with different edges. Your child can create and erase repeatedly. Warn your child that he will be in deep doo-doo if he leaves the table and fingerpaints the carpeting.

Hair Stylist

This is not for every parent—it is a bit sticky. Mix up a little sugar water (the sweeter it is, the better it will work). Pour it in a plastic bowl. Give your kids some of those little black barber combs and a mirror or two. If they dip the combs in the sugar water and then comb their hair, they can style it in all sorts of interesting "dos." Their hair will be stiff and hard to comb once it's completely dry, but it sure stays put. It's cheaper than real hair gel and poses no chemical risks. It also shampoos out readily. This is obviously best to save until just before a bath or when you're looking to shock fussy Great-Aunt Agatha.

Mani-Cured

Keep your child busy decorating fingernails and toenails. Naturally, you will *not* want to give him real nail polish. Young preschoolers may be content spreading hand cream with a Q-tip or a small paintbrush. Older preschoolers can create faces, bugs, and interesting designs with water-soluble fine-tipped markers. If they don't like what they make, they can wash it off and try again.

Pretendables:
THEMES THAT ENCHANT

Pretending is one of the best activities for occupying young children. The themes listed here can be used with many of the described activities. Or, you can simply set out appropriate toys or props to engage your child.

Most preschoolers tend toward being either "acting-out" (also known as "dramatic play") pretenders or miniature world-creator sorts. Follow your child's lead (but keep in mind that miniature world play is often easier for children playing on their own). Most of the following themes can be adapted for either style.

Real-Life Play Themes

- *House (or family)*—cooking, housework/laundry, baby care, family routines
- *Work or school*—office, repairs/building, money management, driving
- *Community helpers*—garbage hauling, firefighting, police officer, military, post office, library, doctor, dentist
- *Restaurant or store*—fast food, supermarket, bakery, shoe, toy, pet, bank, cleaners
- *Transportation*—airport/plane/helicopter, depot/train, bus, car, hot air balloon, rocket/space shuttle, ships/submarines
- *Vacation*—beach or pool, sightseeing, camping
- *Museum, amusement park, circus, theater*

- *Snow play and other pretend weather*—hurricane, snowstorm, or thunderstorm
- *Holidays*—birthdays, religious, Halloween, Valentine's Day, tea party

Animal Themes

Types of animals to consider include farm, zoo, wild, pets, dinosaurs, other reptiles, bugs, birds, fish and other sea creatures, imaginary (dragons, unicorns, etc.), and characters like Pooh Bear or Clifford the Big Red Dog. Favorite types of play include veterinarian/animal hospital, animal families, being animals, visiting or working in animal places like farms and zoos, animal aggression, danger, or rescue play, and acting out a familiar animal story like "The Three Little Pigs."

Fantasy Themes

Witch/wizard; good guys vs. bad guys; magic carpet and genie; space aliens; royalty; ghosts and other Halloween-inspired scary guys; pirates; olden days and time travel; mer people; enchanted forest (giants, fairies, ogres, gnomes, elves, and other magical beings); fairy tales; wild jungle worlds; and superheroes.

Tips for Encouraging Pretending

In general, I've noticed that the highest-quality miniature play comes from a combination of a multipurpose material (like blocks, pieces of fabric) and figures or objects that can be "animated" and given lines and personalities. I recommend staying away from figures of television show characters. With those, children tend to regurgitate episodes they have seen rather than invent something new. (And, depending on the show, those characters may lead to more violent themes.) For dramatic play, "real" props are a plus.

If your child is not a natural pretender, get him started (and keep trying). Move the little figures and make them talk in different voices. Set up a conflict. Then step back and let your child take over.

Order in the Court:
SERIATION AND SORTING PLAY

Some children really enjoy lining things up or sorting objects into groups. This activity will have strong appeal for those kinds of kids. Give them a good assortment of objects to arrange and discuss the kind of order they'd like to put them in.

Good Objects to Sort or Arrange

- toy cars or animals
- coins
- pantry items like cans or boxes
- their Halloween candy
- colored paper clips or other office supplies
- books
- holiday greeting cards
- marbles or glass beads
- buttons
- action figures or dolls and their accessories
- sticks and other natural materials
- craft supplies like beads or crayons
- blocks
- playing cards or dominoes
- hair accessories

Ways to Sort

- size (Put items in order or categorize them as big or little.)
- color
- category (e.g., meat eaters versus plant eaters, cars versus trucks, nickels versus pennies)
- beauty (Put items in order from most to least beautiful or classify them as pretty versus ugly.)

- shape (e.g., box versus cylinder)
- preference (most favorite to least)

More Ways to Use

- Make patterns or pictures.
- Use as measurement unit (e.g., how many car lengths is the hallway?).

Tips

Make sure you have enough objects to keep your child busy for a good chunk of time. Sorting is also easier for many children if they have clear places to put the items of each category. Try providing bins, cups, place-mats, or even circles fashioned from loops of string or hula hoops. If your child is lining things up, you might want to mark off a nice line with a piece of tape on the floor, "draw" one in plush carpet with your finger, or use a natural line such as a floorboard, a yardstick (or two), or an empty stretch of baseboard.

Tub Ball:
BOUNCY BALL RACES

This game was invented years ago by my oldest son. It remains a staple alone-time activity in my family to this day.

To play, your child needs three containers like shoeboxes, an assort-ment of small bouncy balls (avoid anything choking-size with children who might put things in their mouths), and an empty bathtub. Label one box with a smiley face and another with a frowny face. Place all the balls in the remaining box.

Now your child is ready to start. She should select two balls and hold them against the sloping side of the tub at the end farthest from the drain. She lets go of the two balls at the same time and watches them bounce around the tub until one settles in the drain. That ball is the winner and goes in the smiley-face box. The poor other ball is the loser and goes in the frowny box. After all the balls have had turns, she dumps the winners into the empty box and races them in pairs against each other, putting them in the correct box after each race. She continues the races until an overall winner emerges.

My kids like to make a fuss over the day's winner. It gets a name (and a personality) and is displayed in a place of honor (often in an inconvenient spot in the bathroom). Very strange game, but, as I said, endlessly appealing to the kids.

Other Racing Games

Anything that can be rolled or slid can be raced. Show your child how to construct ramps with various materials like rulers, books, manila folders, wrapping paper tubes, and on and on. Commercial sets, like marble runs or racecar ramps, can be used, too. Races can be decided by speed (who finishes first), accuracy (who ends up closest to a predetermined marker), or distance (who continues the farthest). The possibilities are endless.

These Activities Make Cents:
EASY PENNY GAMES

Preschoolers are fascinated by money, which probably accounts for some of the appeal of these games. I like them because I always have pennies on hand, which makes them a breeze to set up. If you have a handful or jar of mixed coins, your child can sort the coins by denomination as a warm-up activity.

Penny Drop

You need a tall container with a wide mouth (like a half-gallon to gallon pitcher), a small metal jar lid or tiny glass cup (like a shot glass), and a whole mess of pennies.

Place the jar lid at the bottom of the container and fill the container three-quarters full with warm water. Tell your child to drop the pennies in one at a time. How many can she get to land in the jar lid? It's harder than you'd think. Have her try holding the pennies flat versus on edge, dropping them from a height versus close to the surface, and so on. What ways work best? When she is done, she can fish out the pennies and try to beat her record.

Pitching Pennies

For this, you need a section of wall that you won't worry about (like cinderblock in the basement) or a big piece of cardboard to tape up and protect the wall; a line (use a string or a yardstick); and pennies. The object is to toss pennies at the wall and have them bounce off. Those that land between the wall and the line are losers; the others win.

A variation is to set up a number of cups or jar lids, an open egg carton, playing cards, or other small containers. Your child stands a marked distance away and tosses the pennies, trying to get them to land in the cups or on the cards.

Penny Table Games

If you tape cups at each corner and ones in the middle of each long side of the table, you have instant penny pool. How long does it take your child to get ten pennies into the cups? Or scatter nine quarters over the table. Have him grab his wood (a pencil) and play nine holes of penny golf. (Making the penny hit the quarter counts as sinking the ball.) Can he get a hole in one? (We just tee off from the previous hole.)

Tips for Penny Games

Any of these games can be played with other "balls" or "pucks." Try larger coins (easier to hit), small balls made from a wad of paper and taped together (these can be "shot" by blowing through a straw), beans (which slide a little better), or even an ice cube, if you don't mind the wet.

Telephone Treasure Chest:
A NEST EGG FOR DESPERATE TIMES

Keep an opaque box near the phone or your work center. Stuff it with cool toys or items that are normally off-limits. Save it for really special occasions, like long-distance contract negotiations.

What might you put in it? It is completely up to you and your child's interests, but here are some suggestions that have been popular in my family:

- Office supplies, like sticky note pads or a mini-stapler
- Pristine art supplies, like an unopened can of play dough or never-used crayons
- Cosmetic jewelry and an ornate hand mirror
- Assorted out-of-date (and thus interesting) toys from yard sales or flea markets
- Face-painting crayons
- Scarves in assorted fabrics and sizes or pieces of beautiful material
- Anything wrapped like a present
- Single-serving "treat" foods, like a lollipop or package of fruit snacks
- Stickers, a roll of tape, or bandages just for "decoration"
- A button jar
- Trinkets to examine—foreign coins, broken jewelry, tassels, or old keys
- An assortment of locks and keys that will work them; also key chains
- Paper clips for making chains
- A ball of string or yarn
- Magnets and objects to test
- Doll-play supplies, like pretend food, clothing accessories, or play diapers

- Almost anything from the dollar store
- Mini play-sets, such as little bears and some furniture
- Coins for sorting and stacking, maybe an interesting piggybank or coin purse
- Hardware, like springs, screws, nuts and bolts

Making It Work

Bring this out *only* when you need a chunk of time, and put it away promptly afterwards. If you can't enforce these limits, don't bother with this activity. It works only to the extent that it is forbidden—or at least novel—fruit.

Consider having an assortment of objects in the box, to minimize the "I'm not in the mood for *that*" complaints. Periodically, fill the box with new things or at least add surprises. Increase the "specialness" of the box by decorating it, scenting it with a sachet, storing individual items in fancy containers, having the box lock with a key, or bringing it out for other unusual circumstances, such as when someone is sick or injured.

CHAPTER THREE

"It's Not Fair!"
but Siblings
Squabble Anyway

Even though I should have known better—after all, I have two sisters, a brother, and several degrees in psychology—before my second child was born, I fantasized that my kids would basically get along. Oh, I knew there'd be some of those cute moments when the first one asked if we could please send the baby back, and later occasional bickering about who got the last ice cream sandwich. But it was with a kind of shock that I'd watch my three-year-old stroll past the baby, who was innocently chewing on my old slipper and not bothering anyone, and give him a little *whack*. And the baby, equally shockingly, would grin and gaze up at his big brother with a look of unfettered adoration. Until he learned how to talk and discovered tattling. And got another even smaller sibling whom he could whack.

Preschoolers have all the sibling rivalry issues that older kids have, plus poorly developed skills for dealing with them. This means tears. And pinching. And saying mean things like, "You can't come to my birthday party!" (Which is such a powerful threat in the under-six world that my children have gotten carried away and used it on me. Successfully. When I forgot for a moment that I hate birthday parties for four-year-olds.) And, of course, a constant background refrain of "*It's not fair!*"

That's why you have to do lots of teaching and supporting and putting ice on the pinched places. And saying the most important phrase that anyone who works with kids needs to know: "Use your words, not your body." (I think I've already said it more than 7 trillion times. And that is not the world's record.) And agreeing that yes, it is so not fair.

Actually, what is now most surprising to me is that despite the unrelenting competition, teasing, and whacking that is the norm in my household, my three kids basically *do* get along and love each other. There has been endearing proof of this, like the time we moved the youngest out of her crib and, as a transition, onto a mattress on the floor in her own room. About a half-hour after everyone was tucked in that night, my husband and I heard a loud scraping noise coming from upstairs. Alarmed, we dashed upstairs in time to see the big brothers coming to help their little sister drag the mattress from her room to the one the boys shared. Finally, they explained, they could all sleep together in the same room. Which they did for the next three years—my daughter on a mattress squeezed between the boys' twin beds. So that's why this chapter may not have answers for obliterating teasing and whacks on the head, but it does have some activities aimed at promoting the kind of sibling relationship that could make them want to *share* a room. And if nothing works and the kids won't stop bickering, you can always try, "I won't let you come to my birthday party!"

Sibling Bonds without Handcuffs:
ACTIVITIES TO PROMOTE CARING RELATIONSHIPS

These are activities you can introduce that may seem designed just for fun, but that have the bonus of making siblings stay a little nicer to each other. Kindness, just like whacking your brother, *can* become a habit.

Secret Pals

This activity is often used in elementary schools or scouting troops to encourage friendships and a sense of community.

Pick a week when not much is happening. Have each person in the family draw a name of another family member out of a hat. Even infants can participate, provided they have an adult helper. (You can also feel free to rig the matchups.)

The chooser becomes that person's secret pal for the next week. Each day, he must perform a kind deed or leave a small gift for his pal. For example, he might do a chore for his pal, put fresh flowers in her room, leave a sweet next to her dinner plate, let her pick the story to read that evening, or admire her new outfit. You will, of course, be available to help support or bankroll each kid's altruistic ideas.

On the last day, everyone guesses who his pal was. Naturally, each participant will have been trying to "trick" the others by letting them "catch" him appearing to do kind deeds for them. Pals can tell about their kind deeds, and recipients will, of course, express their appreciation.

Sibling Sleepover

In my family growing up, we always had sibling sleepovers on special occasions like Christmas

LITERATURE LINKS

Extra! Extra! Read all about it! Sister is kind to her brother!

Books can provide quarrelsome siblings with models of better (but still realistic) relationships.

Our family's favorite was *Dogger* by Shirley Hughes. In this picture book, big sister Bella sacrifices to help her brother Dave retrieve his beloved stuffed dog. The line, "And then Bella did something kind," is such an easily recognized allusion in our household that we whisper it as praise to a child who is observed doing something nice for a sibling.

Other recommended picture book titles are *Julius, the Baby of the World* by Kevin Henkes; *A Birthday for Frances* by Russell Hoban; and *An Evening at Alfie's*, also by Shirley Hughes.

Ask your librarian for additional recommendations.

Eve or birthdays. My children have happily continued the tradition. Sleep-overs are especially effective with siblings who do not share a room, but those who do can share the other sleepover activities, then switch beds or use sleeping bags. Be sure to help the kids enjoy all the activities that have traditionally made sleeping over at a friend's house fun. Treat the host sib as a proper host, planning the evening with her and making a big deal of her contributions.

Good activities include a video and popcorn, board games, a special snack (perhaps in the bedroom as an extra-special treat), a pillow fight, grooming activities like hair or nail fussing (okay, this tends to be a sexist girl thing), sleeping in sleeping bags on the floor, staying up a little later than usual, and talking and giggling after lights out.

Please Stop!
PREVENTING SIBLING ABUSE

If you have more than one child, there will be a power imbalance between them. One is bound to be bigger, stronger, or more persuasive. (Of course, the others may try to compensate by being trickier, cuter, or better tattlers.) Regardless, whenever there is a power imbalance, there will be opportunities for one child to abuse the others. Prevent, or at least minimize, abuse with the following strategies:

Please Stop!

While they are still young, introduce this technique to empower weaker children. Teach them that the phrase, "Please stop!" has absolute authority to end an abusive (and in some cases merely bothersome) action by another. For example, if an adult is teasing a child, and the child says, "Please stop!" then the adult *must* stop immediately. Similarly, if one child is teasing another by singing an annoying song repeatedly, he must stop when told, "Please stop!" Parents can also direct the phrase toward children for dangerous or bothersome behaviors.

This phrase is most effective when you can teach everyone to say it in a calm but firm voice. That's why you need to begin young. You will also have to enforce compliance many times before it catches on.

Clarify rules for acceptable and unacceptable uses of the magic phrase. For example, one child cannot order another to please stop playing with a toy so that he can take it over. Similarly, he cannot order another to please stop engaging in a harmless, acceptable activity, like ordinary singing or talking. For those situations, the offended party can be encouraged to go in another room or find a way to distract himself.

Outlaw Abusive Behaviors

Again, "use your words, not your bodies," should be a refrain in every family. Children who use physical means to express frustration or get what they want must be stopped, *whether it is the older or younger child.* Children who are old enough to know better should have consequences for physically hurting another, such as removal from play or loss of a privilege like television. They should also be required to apologize to the child they have injured before resuming play and to make restitution when appropriate.

Verbal abuse can be just as damaging as physical abuse and should not be tolerated either. Ban words that belittle, frighten, or deliberately annoy. My oldest son picked up the charming phrase, "*Yoooo idiot!*" from a well-known children's video, and was soon applying it to his siblings at every opportunity. And paying a fine, in the form of lost privileges (and, later, allowance). Verbal habits like this can be hard to break, but for the sake of all children involved, you must work at it.

Help Children Who Are Frustrated, Angry, or Scared

Children tend to lash out when they lack the skills or resources to solve their problems. Teach them more appropriate words to say, help them obtain needed privacy or protected space, and give them physical affection or reassurance when they need it, and you will prevent many problems from spiraling out of control.

Choosers:
GAMES FOR PICKING "IT"

Who gets to go first, who gets the window seat, who chooses the biggest piece of cake, who gets to be "it"—all of these are important issues to children (and especially to siblings). Try some of these time-honored methods of picking winners impartially:

Drawing Straws

Break a dried spaghetti noodle into unequal lengths. State whether the longest or shortest piece will win. Have the adult arrange the lengths in his hand (out of sight of the choosers) so that they appear to be equal. Each child carefully removes one piece. For the "straws," you can also use lengths of drinking straw or toothpicks broken off in different places.

Counting Out or In Rhymes

Be sure to state at the outset whether you are counting *in* (first one "out" is "it") or counting *out* (last one remaining is chosen). You can use fists, bodies, fingers, or feet as the counting unit.

Eeny, meeny, miney, mo.
Catch a tiger by the toe.
If he hollers, let him go.
My mother said to pick the very best one
And that means you are "IT!" (or out)

Bubblegum, bubblegum in a dish,
How many pieces do you wish?
(Child chooses a number)
One, two, three, four, etc.

Entry, kentry, cutry, corn.
Apple bush and apple thorn.
Wire, briar, limber, lock.
Three geese in a flock.
One flew east, and one flew west.
And one flew over the cuckoo's nest.

Engine, engine number nine,
Running down Chicago line.
If the train should jump the track,
Do you want your money back?
(Child answers "yes," "no," or "maybe so.")
(Spell out answer) *Y-E-S, and that means you are IT!* (or out).

One potato, two potato,
Three potato, four.
Five potato, six potato,
Seven potato, MORE!

One, two, three, four
Don't go through the bathroom door.
If you do, you must rush,
How many times will you flush?
(Child responds with a number—less than twenty, please!
(Count to specified answer)
and that means you are IT! (or out).

Other Choosing Games

Put slips of folded paper in a bag. One is marked as the winner. Let the children draw them out and open the slips to see who is the winner.

Flip a coin (best for just two children). Specify in advance whether the coin must be caught or will just land on the ground. You can also specify in advance best two out of three (or whatever).

Even-Uppers:
HANDICAPS FOR FAIR PLAY

Explain the concept of handicapping. For example, a poor golfer may get to subtract a few strokes from his score when he plays against better golfers. A really fast racehorse may have to carry extra weight on his saddle. These adjustments make it fair for all players to try their hardest and give everyone a reasonable chance of winning.

You will probably have to be creative in devising appropriate handicaps for many of your children's games, but here are some suggestions to get you started.

Races

Provide different starting lines. Or, give the slower child a head start (have the ref count to a specified number). Or, aim for different ways of moving. My husband always runs backwards against the younger children. My son used to skip while my younger daughter ran full out.

Target Games

Adjust the distance to the target and/or the size of the target. Use a larger missile, such as a bigger ring or a larger ball. Allow more tries.

Charades

When younger children are in the game, stick to pantomiming simple objects, actions, or well-known nursery rhymes or fairy tales. Appoint an independent consultant to give tips on how to act it out. Work in pairs, matching stronger players with weaker ones. Similarly, for games like Twenty Questions, stick to solutions the younger child will know, and spot her several questions.

Group Games

Adjust teams so they all contain a mix of weaker and stronger players. In tag games, adjust the rules to compensate for differences in speed.

Allow younger players to have safety bases. Or require older players to use a two-handed touch. Or have them use a less-efficient way of moving, such as galloping or skipping. Give younger players extra hiding time and/or a helper for hide-and-seek games.

Board and Card Games

Stick to those where winning is determined by chance instead of strategy or skill. War and Crazy Eights are good card games. Board games that rely on luck include lotto-style games, Chutes and Ladders, Heigh-Ho Cherry-O, and Candyland. Older preschoolers may be able to play some skill games like checkers, if the more skilled player starts out down a few pieces. The card game Concentration, at least in my household, requires a reverse handicap. We find that younger players outperform older, too easily distracted ones, and so we spot the old guys like me a few pairs.

Parting Tips

Involve the children in determining fair handicaps. They may have a better sense than you do of the magnitude of the difference in their abilities. Also, remember to adjust handicaps over time. A long string of wins by one player suggests that the handicaps need fine-tuning.

Tease-Ease:
TEASE-PROOFING YOUR CHILD

Teasing, whether by siblings or peers, is inevitable during childhood. The way a child responds to teasing can influence how likely he is to be teased again and can affect both his self-esteem and the quality of his relationships. Help your child survive being teased by teaching skills like these:

Laugh It Off

Children who respond to teasing with humor seem to have the easiest time. Unfortunately, a funny response does not come easily to many children. Thus, you will need to teach your child some things to say if he gets teased. A joke "insult" may be an effective response, especially if it is unexpected. Preschoolers can make up and remember a variety of these, like, "Oh, you're just being an old broccoli nose." Teach them to smile and even start laughing when they say these things—you don't want them to respond to hurting with hurting.

Help them learn the difference between *teasing*, where the intent is to hurt, and *joking*, where being silly is the point. (In reality, a little bit of both may be the intent, but it's to your child's advantage to presume it's joking *even if it isn't*.) Often a child may be able to turn a tease into a joke, simply by agreeing with it and adding to the "game." For example, a child labeled a baby might say, "You're right—I am a baby. Goo-goo, ga-ga. Change my poopy diaper, please!"

Sticks and Stones

The classic line, "Sticks and stones may break my bones, but words will never hurt me," has stuck around to this day, despite being fundamentally untrue. What the line does, though, is shift power from the teaser to the teased. Another, more modern variation is, "I know you are, but what am I?" My favorite version is a mouthful for preschoolers, but enough fun to say that it's worth the practice it takes to learn it: "I'm rubber and you're glue. What you say bounces off of me and sticks to you!"

Whenever you have opportunities to observe groups of children playing together (like on the playground), keep your ears tuned for other child-culture responses. Teach these to your preschooler, especially if teasing by older children is a problem. Lines like, "He who smelt it, dealt it" (for when someone accuses another of passing gas) typically provoke laughter and lessen the hurt feelings and conflict between children.

Tune It Out

Learning not to react to teasing is often the most effective (though not easiest) response. Show your children how to plug their ears, turn away, or go into a different room. Or, teach them to imagine that they can put up a force field or wear special armor that keeps teasing from getting into them.

Or, they can mentally hop on a flying carpet and go someplace where people are kinder to them.

Squabbling siblings stuck in close quarters, such as a vehicle or a shared room, may benefit from together-breaks. Let them listen to tapes with headphones (be sure the volume is turned low), busy them with separate activities, or even throw a lightweight blanket over each, like you'd do to a bird in a cage, being careful to make it a joke.

Un-Tattle Tales:
TECHNIQUES FOR MINIMIZING TATTLING

A certain amount of tattling is inevitable with preschoolers. Often they lack the skill or power to resolve social problems, and tattling is a way of asking for help. Nonetheless, tattling can easily get out of hand, driving a wedge between siblings or making a child unpopular with his peers. Try these techniques to minimize tattling.

Telling versus Tattling

Allow telling and ban tattling. *Telling* is when your child reports a situation where someone is getting or could get hurt or something significant is broken or endangered. *Tattling* is pretty much everything else. But, as you have undoubtedly noticed, it can be difficult to distinguish between them. You will need to play "What if" to teach the difference, which varies from family to family. "What if your big sister put on a cape and said she was going to jump off the deck?" "What if your little brother won't let you play with his new beanie baby?" "What if you see your friend sneaking candy?" As your child learns to tell the two apart, you can stop her mid-tattle/tell and ask, "Is this tattling or telling?"

Make It Expensive

Often, even when a child knows that something is tattling, she still feels driven to tell you about it. That's when you offer her the choice of tattling—for a price. We know a family that charges a dollar to tattle, a fee that their children sometimes decide is worth it. Our family has resorted to this method at times, too. Another option is to give everyone three tattles per day. When your tattler starts in, stop her and ask if she really wants to use one up right now. (Often she'll decide to wait until later.)

Solitary Confinement

Whenever your child comes tattling, separate the children for five minutes. Do this very calmly, nodding your head and saying something like, "Sounds like you two need a little break from each other." If they can't be physically separated (like in the car), enforce five minutes of silence. Make sure you do it every time. Separation is generally the last thing the kids have in mind.

Mm-Hmm

Often your child just needs to tell you about the injustice, and you are not required to act. Listen sympathetically, nodding and clucking if it seems appropriate. End with a dismissing comment like, "Okay." If your child wants to know what you are going to do about the problem, you can tell her, "I've made a note of it." You could also ask for her ideas about how she might work it out, or help her consider the other person's point of view. Go ahead and offer suggestions about how your child might solve the problem, if she can't figure any out herself, but avoid stepping in to be the policeman.

Toy Story:
"ONCE UPON A TIME, THERE WERE SIBLINGS WHO LOVED TO SHARE"

Now that's a fairy tale for you! Even kids who willingly share with friends, neighbors, and perfect strangers will balk at sharing a broken toy they haven't used in a year with a brother or sister. You can't eliminate the problem short of having only one child, but these strategies have minimized the shrieking in my household and, even more amazingly, have sometimes led to sharing—grudgingly, perhaps, but sharing.

Communal Property

Make big-ticket, high-interest toys family property rather than individual possessions. This often means that stuff like home playground equipment, games, even many ride-ons belong to all children in the family, even if some are not yet technically big enough to use them properly. We also make most construction, craft, or add-on sets (toys like Legos, play dough, Playmobil, etc.) communal. If one kid gets a package as a gift, it's his to use first—to assemble or play with the first day or two; then it gets added to the communal container and made available for general use. This approach has generally met with little protest. The kids, of course, still quarrel over who was using what first or who has rights to claim something not yet in use, but shared property makes it easier for the supervising adult to impose turns.

There Is Enough for All

One of my favorite novels when I was a school-age kid was *Rabbit Hill* by Robert Lawson. In the book, the owners of a country home coexist happily with the ravenous pests that other farmers battle simply by growing plenty of food—enough for all—as a sign in the garden attests. While it would be neither practical nor effective to have multiples of every toy (the kids would just find different things to fight about while your house collapsed under the weight of too many playthings), duplicating the most popular toys can help lessen the intense competition inherent between siblings. At a minimum, take care that *all* kids have their fair share of toys that are desirable to their siblings, so that it isn't always the younger kids coveting their older sibling's possessions.

King for the Moment

One family we know uses the calendar to decide disputes: each child has one day a week when *he* gets to choose which seat he wants in the minivan or be last to brush his teeth or whatever. Knowing that he will have a regular chance to be king seems to minimize the disputes that originate from a kid's determination to prove that *he* is special. (This family only has three kids, so that leaves four days for normal opportunities to fight, in case you think the kids are being deprived of that wonderful learning experience.)

Protect and Serve

When kids know that you'll help them protect their most treasured possessions, they are more likely to respect others' property rights as well. Even the smallest family members should have a box, shelf, or other storage place for things that are their special possessions—and that cannot be used by *anyone* else without permission. The same rules should apply to adults, too. It is not greedy to have a few items that you prefer not to share willy-nilly—doubtless you do not offer to let every casual visitor borrow your favorite vase that belonged to your great-grandmother—and for preschoolers, it is necessary to have that feeling of complete ownership before they can learn to share willingly.

The Golden Rule

In our family, Rule Number One is *Treat other people the way you'd like them to treat you.* Preschoolers are just beginning to develop empathy, but you can see the beginnings of this ability in what they choose for your birthday present (probably something along the line of action figures or ballerina fairies). You will naturally model sharing for them, letting them have a taste of your ice cream or use your pen in the restaurant, while remarking, "Of course I'll be happy to *share* with you." (It's much easier for kids to learn sharing as the recipient of the kindness, of course.) And teach your kids reminding phrases (for themselves or their siblings) like, "A turn for you, a turn for me, that's the way it's supposed to be," and "All for me and none for you wouldn't be a very kind thing to do."

These reminders will not solve the issue instantly or permanently, but gradually the concept will start to become embedded in the kids' psyches. By the time they're in their twenties, they'll probably be willing to share with each other occasionally.

Non-Binding Arbitration:
MEDIATING SIBLING SPATS WITHOUT TYING ANYONE UP

"Let the kids work out disagreements themselves." This is the standard advice from most parenting experts. The problem: it doesn't really work, especially with young kids. Preschoolers lack the experience, verbal skills, and physical strength to prevail in fights with older siblings, and their immature approach to solving problems may cause them to hurt or terrorize younger ones. The preschool years are when *you* invest time and patience in teaching the kids how to work out their problems. You'll be happier if you take on the role of Argument Coach rather than Family Court Judge (because face it, can you really tell who is right?). Here is an approach for coaching young combatants in problem resolution, followed by a list of quickie justice ideas that kind of work.

Step One: *"I Have the Potato Now!"*

To settle a dispute peacefully, the two parties have to listen to each other—which means taking turns to speak. Preschoolers will do better with a physical prop to remind them when it's their turn to speak—so grab anything handy, like, say, an Idaho potato, and let the kids take turns holding it and saying their pieces. (This technique is often used in preschools at circle time.) You may want to set a timer for the maximum time allowed. We sometimes require the holder to speak into the prop, as if it were a microphone. Sometimes, this silliness diffuses the problem before everyone even has a turn to speak, and sometimes I get to hear impassioned speeches made into a potato. Either way, it's more entertaining than just listening to everyone screeching at me. Often, too, just getting a chance to air their grievances is enough to end the dispute.

Step Two: *Repeat after Me*

If it doesn't, the next step is to have the participants repeat what the other said. Again, you may need to be more active than you would be with older kids—your preschooler may genuinely not understand his sibling's point of view. Use a soft, respectful tone, and help to diffuse the anger. Let the kids know that they may both have legitimate concerns.

Step Three: *The Solution Solution*

Finally, teach the kids to brainstorm a variety of ways to resolve the dispute. Be active in helping them evaluate solutions—ones that make both parties happy (or unhappy, as the case may be) are more likely to be accepted. After receiving a couple of good suggestions from each, you can either assign numbers to them and draw the winning number from a hat or have the participants vote on their preferred solution.

Young kids have a limited attention span. Frequently, the two fighters will simply get bored or distracted during this process and wander off to do something else. And that's fine, isn't it? Over time, though, they may pick up enough of the approach to be able to try it themselves.

Drive-By Justice

The above approach does work, but it obviously takes time, energy, and patience—resources often lacking when siblings are fighting. So, here are some quick strategies to distract or deflect the strong feelings.

- *Us versus Them* Focus the combatants on hating you instead of each other. My mom used to assign us all chores when we couldn't work out our problems without fussing at her. I've read about several families whose preferred chore is having both kids wash opposite sides of a glass door or window—it's hard to stay mad at each other when you're making faces. The other option is to make both kids losers in the dispute (e.g., the toy is removed from both). If you do this calmly and consistently, the kids will be more motivated to try to work it out.

- *Cool Your Heels* Both kids get benched—sent to their rooms or to sit on different steps or chairs quietly until the timer rings. If the fight resumes immediately, parole is revoked, and both go back in the cooler a little longer.
- *Pick a Winner* Use one of the Chooser methods (see page 66) to decide who is right. It's impartial, if not always accurate, and doesn't put you in the position of always siding with a particular child.
- *The Five-Minute Warning* Good for property disputes. When a child comes to you complaining that his sibling is hogging a communal toy, etc., issue a standard-length warning (five minutes was agreed on in our family) to the current user, set a timer, then give the other kid a turn. Of course, the new user can have the five-minute warning applied to him, too. It's not completely fair (since the first kid may have had the toy longer), but since the warning starts at the moment of desire, we agreed it would work. Mostly it did, too. (Sometimes we adjusted the length of the warning, depending on circumstances.)

Baby Games:
THINGS YOUR PRESCHOOLER CAN DO WITH THE BABY BESIDES POKE HIM IN THE EYE

The average preschooler is remarkably effective at entertaining younger siblings when you are busy. Here are some games that children can play with older babies. For a discussion starter, read the attractive picture book, *101 Things to Do with a Baby* by Jan Ormerod.

Peek-a-Boo Games

Most preschoolers will need a little bit of feedback from you the first time. Show them how to get the timing right (hide too long, and the baby gets bored; too quick or too close, and the baby gets overwhelmed), exaggerate their voice and expression, and use props, like a blanket or big box to hide inside. For safety, encourage them to hide their own faces, not the baby's.

SAFETY ZONE

Preschoolers must have an adult nearby when they are playing with babies. Young children lack the judgment, skill, and strength to protect a baby for even a few minutes. In addition, young children tend to misjudge or "forget" how easily a baby can be hurt and may injure him unintentionally.

High Chair Follies

What does a baby in a high chair like to do? Bam the tray and/or throw things over. Both these activities make adults cringe. Preschoolers, on the other hand, are delighted to join in the play. Give your preschooler a variety of objects for the baby to bang, trying for ones that will make different sounds. Show her how to take turns and how to do demonstrations for the baby. Or, give the pair a basket of soft objects for the baby to grasp and release or throw.

Ticklers

Avoid these with a rough older sibling. Others, though, will be proud of their ability to get the baby to chuckle. Show your older child how to give the baby's tummy a "Zlerbert"—a raspberry tummy kiss. You can also teach her to play tickley games, like "This Little Piggy Went to Market" with the baby's toes. Or try this one:

Knock on the door.	(Softly knock on the baby's forehead.)
Peek in.	(Gently raise the baby's eyebrow.)
Lift up the latch.	(Push up on the baby's nose.)
Walk in.	(Creep fingers up to baby's mouth.)
Tickle, tickle under the chin.	(Stroke the baby's neck.)

Watch Me!

Stow the baby safely in a highchair or infant seat. Direct your preschooler to perform antics that will amaze and delight the little bundle of incompetence. Somersaults, hopping or jumping, crawling around and barking, silly dances, and so on will make even a cranky baby laugh most of the time.

Toddler Games:
GAMES FOR PRESCHOOLERS TO PLAY WITH ONE- AND TWO-YEAR-OLDS

LITERATURE LINKS

A preschooler with a little baby care experience under his belt will enjoy the antics of the family when they try to comfort the unhappy baby after Mom goes to bed early in *What Baby Wants* by Phyllis Root. And the book *Kate's Box* by Kay Chorao addresses baby-jealousy, and the power big kids have to delight babies and little guys with games like peek-a-boo.

Nothing pleases a toddler more than getting to hang with a big kid. And, since most preschoolers get a kick out of being top dog, this pairing is often successful, especially in small doses. These games are likely to satisfy both age groups.

Fingerplays

Because both toddlers and preschoolers have big appetites for repetition, your preschooler is the perfect candidate to play these games. Here are two favorites. You can find more ideas in the book *Clap Your Hands: Finger Rhymes* by Sarah Hayes.

Five little monkeys, swinging in a tree,
   (Hold up five fingers and swing them side to side.)
Teasing Mr. Alligator, "Can't catch me!"
   (Waggle finger and shake head.)

But along came Mr. Alligator,
   (Open and close hand like a mouth, moving it closer.)
Quiet as can be. . .
   (Make "shhh" sign with finger to lips.)
SNAP!
   (Clap hands.)
Four little monkeys, swinging . . . (Repeat.)
   (Hold up four fingers.)

Five green and speckled frogs
   (Hold up five fingers.)
Sat on a speckled log
   (Use finger from other hand to be the log.)
Eating some most delicious bugs.
   (Pluck imaginary flies from air and eat.)
Yum, yum!
   (Rub tummy.)
One jumped into the pool,
   ("Jump" one finger up and down, tip first.)
Where it was nice and cool.
   (Pretend to swim, frog-style.)
Now there are four green speckled frogs.
   (Hold up four fingers.)
   (Repeat, continuing to "All gone!")

SAFETY ZONE

Toddlers are better than babies at protecting themselves when playing with big kids, but you'll still want to be nearby and ready to step in if either child is getting too frustrated or needs help.

Crash Down

It understandably drives older children crazy when their little siblings keep wrecking their constructions. However, when wrecking is the point, the activity suddenly becomes fun for both. Explain that the toddler may not be able to wait until the building is finished because it's just so exciting. For safety, provide sponges, cardboard blocks, or commercial foam blocks for building. Pillows or cushions also make exciting building blocks, and your preschooler can strut his superior strength.

LITERATURE LINKS

Books featuring nice relationships between preschoolers and their toddler siblings include *Alfie's Feet* by Shirley Hughes and *Best Friends for Frances* by Russell Hoban.

Pretending 101

Preschoolers will benefit from taking on pretending apprentices— before long, they'll have trained some good playmates. Good pretending themes for beginners include play cooking and eating, being dinosaurs or other growly animals, toy vehicle play, pet play (for safety, use only pretend leashes and collars), baby care with the big kid as baby and the toddler as parent, and other real-life imitation.

Big Guy Games:
PLAYING IN THE BIG KID LEAGUES

Hockey superstar Mario Lemieux credits some of his success to his childhood determination to keep pace with his older hockey-playing brothers. His efforts did not come without tears and tantrums, though, and neither will your child's attempts to be included with the big kids she knows. But, the following activities *may* help your child find a niche without shedding quite so many tears.

SAFETY ZONE

Preschoolers tend to be pretty sturdy, as well as expert tattlers, so it's easy to think you can relax when they're in "the care" of bigger siblings and friends. Beware, though, of young children's willingness to take risks, physical and otherwise, when they are trying to impress or keep up with kids who are stronger, tougher, or more savvy than they are.

Pretending

A younger child who is willing to take on some of the less desirable roles (like baby or pet in "house," student in "school, "or the bad guy in rougher play) may find he is readily included by older children. Even with a less easy-going child, a preschooler may find he is willingly added to games where a cast of thousands is desirable, and where physical or verbal skill is not at a premium. Play with "little figures," like Playmobil or action figures, is successful with preschoolers and older siblings, though expect the older child to act as director.

Slightly More Difficult Board Games

Games like Sorry, Bingo, or Connect Four can be played with an older sibling who is willing to act as a mentor and help with any reading or high counting needed. An even slightly patient older child is often a more effective teacher of the skills needed to play these games than a parent is.

Neighborhood Games

Many outdoor games for groups can expand to include younger children, especially if a few modifications are made to allow for their lesser skill. Hide-and-seek games work well if younger kids are paired with an older partner (preferably *not* a sibling) or given hiding tips (like "Don't keep hiding in the same place," "Be quiet as a mouse," and so on). It helps to have several younger children playing; when there is just one, that child is likely to be teased or singled out. Other fun games for a big mixed-age group include Ghost in the Graveyard, Kick the Can, Tag (many varieties), and Capture the Flag.

Audience and Apprentice

Younger children make good audiences for children who want to show off or who need practice with emerging skills. You may squirm through your first-grader's forty-seventh halting version of *Go, Dog. Go!* by P. D. Eastman, but there is a good chance that your preschooler will be delighted with the attention from an older sibling who reads to him. Similarly, he may be glad to watch an improvised puppet show with no discernable plot or endless repetition of questionable magic tricks.

Many older children also enjoy teaching younger children how to do the things they have learned recently. Provide props and opportunities for school-like instruction, musical-instrument demonstrations, or other teachable skills. Encourage older children to coach younger children to tell jokes or ask riddles, repeat rhymes, or perform tricks. Off-color jokes are favorites. Praise both teacher and student for good performances (though you can also raise your eyebrows a bit if the story includes farting or poop). Here's a poem my boys learned from their older cousin and in turn delighted in teaching to their little sister:

Birdy, birdy in the sky,
Dropped some whitewash in my eye.
Gee, I'm glad that cows don't fly.

LITERATURE LINKS

Frustrated younger siblings will enjoy stories where the little guys get the upper hand. We especially enjoyed the stories about Max and his bossy big sister Ruby by Rosemary Wells, and the classic Marjorie Flack story *Wait for William*.

CHAPTER FOUR

Rest for the Leery

Adaily rest time is essential. A nap is even better. But your child won't care what you want to do. She will want you to stay up and play fairy princess with her.

This is the part where I get to be an old geezer and complain about what the world is coming to. When I was a preschooler, which back then was called "a little kid," preschoolers napped. Every day. In their beds, shoes off, shades down. Or at kindergarten and preschool, which back then was called "nursery school," on little mats. (Or in my case, a slightly frayed green towel with my older sister's name crossed out and mine written just below it.) Some of us didn't sleep even then—that's why I remember that green towel so clearly—but millions did. And it was a Good Thing. Because those former nappers are now healthy, productive members of society who floss their teeth and scrub their toilets regularly or at least put that blue stuff in the tank so it looks like it's clean. The non-nappers are mass murderers and people like me who wish flossing had never been invented and whose bathrooms are at times only slightly less disgusting than port-a-johns.

So why don't little kids—I mean "preschoolers"—nap nowadays? Because they don't, you know. According to the research I've seen, American preschoolers are unlikely to nap regularly past the age of three, and many have stopped well before that. Unless their parents make the mistake of trying to drive anywhere in the car after 2:00 in the afternoon. Then the kids will fall into a coma for five hours, wake up in a mood that makes Hannibal Lecter seem like a sweet old gentleman, and bounce on your stomach until 4:00 in the morning asking could you please, please, please play fairy princess some more?

The unpleasant demeanor of post-nap kids may explain the demise of daytime sleeping. The daycare teachers I know say they are under pressure from parents to limit or eliminate naps altogether because parents don't want to spend the evening with Hannibal Lecter or wait until 4:15 A.M. to get started on laundry and making the next day's peanut butter sandwiches. And probably the American push to grow up earlier and earlier (except in the area of potty training) plays a part, too. How can you squeeze in a nap when dance class is at 1:00 and then you have to dash to soccer practice before the Art for Little Tykes class at 4:30? Plus, napping ties caregivers down, forcing them to schedule their days around Junior's nap and miss the chunk of time when the mall is relatively empty because the walkers have strolled home and the teens and tweens are still stuck in school.

Okay, I'll stop ragging on everyone. But I'm still going to encourage you to schedule a nap or rest time for your child every day possible. Because she needs it. To learn how to play fairy princess *all by herself.* And to recharge her batteries. And to grow up to be the kind of person who flosses regularly. Besides, your child doesn't have to be Hannibal Lecter after her nap and it is possible to structure her rest so she will go to sleep *more* easily at night—in the long run, overtired kids actually have a harder time sleeping.

And, guess what? You'll learn to like it too. Wouldn't you like a short snooze, a few minutes to read a book, or just a chance to change the thing that turns the toilet water blue?

Settle-In Strategy:
HELPING YOUR CHILD UNWIND

Just as bedtime goes more smoothly with a routine, so does settling down for a nap or rest. The naptime routine, though, can be much shorter than the bedtime one. Try an approach like this for a quickie wind-down (about ten minutes).

Visit the potty first, wash your child's hands and face, and remove his shoes. Say something like, "Now your body is ready to rest." If you do this consistently, the routine will soon trigger an automatic relaxation response.

Read one or two poems, and save longer stories for bedtime. Good poetry anthologies include *The Dragons Are Singing Tonight* by Jack Prelutsky (and any of his other anthologies), *Where the Sidewalk Ends* by Shel Silverstein (and any others by him), and *You and Me: Poems of Friendship* with incredibly cool fabric sculpture illustrations by Salley Mavor.

Dim the room by turning off lights and closing curtains. Not dark enough for your child? Create greater darkness with heavyweight room-darkening shades or drapes. You can also help your child to imagine darkness. A flashlight without batteries can be called a "flashdark." Your child can "shine" it on himself to create a pretend dark place to sleep in. You can also describe a soft darkness tucking itself around him like a light-weight blanket.

Use white noise to shut out sounds of the busy world. Fans, tapes of nature sounds, or even just a radio tuned to static are effective white noise makers. Tell your child, "Now your room is ready for rest."

Give your child his special "nap kiss" (which should be different from his bedtime kiss), and depart the room. Tell him, "Before you know it, it will time to play again. You'll feel refreshed and happy after your rest."

If your child dislikes having his door shut (but won't stay put), put up a baby gate, so he can still see out.

Timing

Aim for a consistent naptime. Most children will go down most easily soon after lunch. When the start of naptime edges into late afternoon, you can expect naps to start to interfere with bedtime. At that point, transition to giving your child an after-lunch rest instead of a nap. Avoid letting your preschooler sleep more than about two and a half hours.

Connections

Separation is one of the hardest parts of the transition to napping, and feeling connected to family in the period just before sleep helps many children drift off. Parents who are away can develop a habit of calling just before naptime to read a poem and give a kiss. Won't be available at the usual time? Prepare a tape (audio or video) to substitute. A picture of his family or favorite pet taped next to his bed to gaze at may help a lonely napper as well.

Rock-a-Bye-Bye:
HELP FOR INSOMNIACS AND STRUGGLERS

If your child nearly always fights sleep or finds it unusually hard to

 SOUND BITES

There are dozens of recordings of nature sounds available (try the *Echoes of Nature* series), and you can also buy machines or clock radios programmed with a variety of soothing noises. You can also find a number of soothing musical options, from traditional lullaby recordings to New Age instrumentals to Gregorian chants (one of my favorites—try recordings by Voices of Ascension, conducted by Dennis Keene on the Delos label). Not sure what suits your child's taste? Preview options on the internet at Amazon.com or one of the Napster alternatives like AudioGalaxy.

shift from active to quiet, chances are she also has trouble with bedtime and waking up, as well as other changes that require her to shift energy level and alertness. Children do not choose to have this difficulty; it is the way their bodies are wired. Try this technique to teach your child how to ready her body to sleep. It is also good for children who are giving up pacifiers or thumb-sucking.

Step One: Prepare Your Child

Tell your child that you have noticed that it is hard for her to settle down for a nap. Explain that she has a body with lots of energy, but that she still needs a good rest every day to help her body grow well. You are going to teach her how to make her body settle down and be ready to rest.

Step Two: Finding a Steady, Rhythmic State

You want your child's breathing, brain activity, and muscle tension to slow down and become rhythmic. For thousands of years, parents have rocked their infants to help them attain this state. Preschoolers with spirited bodies may still need this help.

After potty and wash up, devote five minutes to a rhythmic physical activity before you settle your child down. You can snuggle her in a rocking chair or try slow, gentle movements: swinging, spinning (try a Sit 'n Spin type toy), a short wagon or stroller ride, a *short* car ride (you don't want her to actually fall asleep), a rocking horse, forward rolls if she knows how, or bouncing on a mini-trampoline. Talk to her about how good the steady movement feels, how you notice her breathing becoming rhythmic, and so on. *Note:* Five minutes may feel like a long time. At first, though, your child needs that long to adjust her body patterns.

Step Three: The Countdown

Settle your child in her bed in a dimmed room, shoes off. Tell her to close her eyes or have her focus on something like a picture taped on the ceiling or an interesting nightlight (like a lava lamp or spinning picture lamp). She should keep her mind on your voice and let her body sink down into the bed.

Keeping your voice low, quiet, and slow, tell her to picture that she is lying in a hammock hanging high in a bright, sunny sky. Way down below is a beautiful place where it is dark, starry, and peaceful. You are going to count backwards from five to one. As you count, the hammock will swing gently back and forth and the ropes will gradually stretch longer and longer. By the time you get to one, she will be rocking under the stars and fall asleep.

Start counting very slowly. Between numbers, talk about the rocking of the hammock, the smoothness of her breathing, the peaceful feeling in her belly. Let yourself relax, too.

Don't worry if this doesn't work at first. Learning to relax may take a couple of weeks. Praise your child for trying and for any progress you see. In time, you want her to be able to do the countdown herself.

Pterodactyl Nests, Hidden Caves,
AND OTHER SPECIAL SLEEPY SPOTS

An imaginative approach to napping can make the experience much more appealing to youngsters who are reluctant to stop playing and rest. A new locale may also help your child to distinguish naptime from bedtime, which is useful if his naps are often too long. (Just don't make it too exciting or he won't be able to wind down.) Your child's current passions may suggest some good sleep-coaxing themes, or try these inviting pretending games and places.

Pterodactyl Nests and Hidden Caves

Fluff up a nice soft blanket nest for your little pterodactyl to nap or rest in. Pterodactyls like to have you sing a lullaby like "Swing Low, Sweet Chariot" as they float off to sleep. Another option: Drape a cloth over the dining room table to create a cave in which your now-happier camper can spread his sleeping bag. He'll appreciate a flashlight to check out the bats hanging from the underside of the dining room table while you read Janell Cannon's *Stellaluna*.

Be sure to set a restful scene, helping him visualize the sparkling stalactites in his sleeping cave or the soft down lining his warm nest in the swaying tree. A story or song that targets the theme will make the experience vivid.

A Little Babying

A turn in the baby's crib is fun for a big kid. Rock your former baby in the rocking chair and give her a few cootchy-coos before winding up the music box or singing a classic lullabye like, "Hush Little Baby, Don't You Cry." Don't have a baby in a crib? Conjure up a make-believe nursery to tuck your baby in. Read some favorite interactive books from her baby days, like *Pat the Bunny* by Dorothy Kunhardt or *Good Night, Sweet Mouse* by Cyndy Szekeres.

Dream Boats

Rocking gently in a hammock aboard a schooner will lull even the most reluctant napper to sleep. Hear the soft slap of the waves and feel the warm breeze brushing your faces. Create the scene with a blanket spread over your child's carpet, a fan on low, and some nice New Age water music, ocean sounds, or a tabletop fountain running nearby. The perfect snuggle-time reading for a watery fantasy nap? The poem "Wynken, Blynken, and Nod" by Eugene Field. Look for the version illustrated by Johanna Westerman, with soft watercolors that mirror the tranquil text.

Or, put your little mermaid to bed in a silky-smooth oyster shell and float strands of seaweed to cover her beneath a starfish-studded seascape. Use a satiny blanket or nightgown to fashion her sleeping shell, and stick paper stars on the walls or ceiling. A goldfish in a bowl or a sea creature stuffed animal makes a perfect sleeping companion. Sing one of the many catchy tunes from Disney's *The Little Mermaid* video, or "Baby Beluga" from the recording of the same name by Raffi.

Sleeping Beauty in the Enchanted Forest

Many children enjoy an outdoor nap in pleasant weather. Settle your sleeping beauty on a blanket in the shade of a tree or in a play tent.

Sprinkle a few blossom petals over her as the bad fairy godmother's spell takes effect. (But wave your wand over the young princess, ensuring she'll wake in just an hour or two.)

Napster:
TUCK-IN MUSIC

Avoid arguments about heading in for a nap by singing instructions to your child. Use of a consistent melody will make the song prompt your child to relax automatically.

The following rhymes are sung to the tune of "London Bridge Is Falling Down," but you can use any tune or lyrics you'd like. Sing something like this:

One o'clock and time for rest,
Time for rest, time for rest.
One o'clock and time for rest,
Let's go upstairs.

First go potty and have a drink,
Have a drink, have a drink,
First go potty and have a drink,
It's time for re-est.

Wash your hands and wipe
*   your face,*
(Etc.)
It's time for re-est.

Take off your shoes and
*   snuggle up,*
(Etc.)
It's time for re-est.

I love you, I'll see you soon,
(Etc.)
When you're rested.

(You can have a puppet or stuffed animal sing the song and tuck it in for a nap with your child, too.)

Tired Tunes

Play soft music to help your child settle down. (Don't fret if your pre-schooler prefers to hear the same song every day.) Play energetic music as she wakes up.

Taped Timer

Make up several tapes of peaceful music that last for varying periods of time. Select the one that fits with the period you're allotting for your child's nap. Tell your child he can get up when the music stops. If he wakes too soon and hears the music, then he knows to let it help him drift back to sleep. At a minimum, he needs to stay in his room until the music ends.

Wake-Up Tunes

Have a child who's hard to wake? Fifteen minutes before wake-up time, come in your child's room and turn the volume up a bit. In five minutes, increase the volume again. Continue to increase the volume at five-minute intervals until wake-up time. At that point, the volume should be slightly louder than comfortable. Show your child how to turn it down to a pleasant level. This activity will force him out of bed.

Here We Go Again!
INSTANT GAMES TO WARD OFF THOSE WAKE-UP BLUES

Two of my three kids were decidedly not cheery sorts after their naps, and I dreaded the days when I had to rouse them and move onto another activity, like fetching a sibling from school. Eventually, I figured out that I could often shorten the growly after-nap period if I played the right sort of game as they revived. I hope some of these ideas work with your child, too.

Happy Hunting

Hide two or three objects in your child's room just before you wake her. Make one easy to see from her bed and hide at least one that she will have to get up to find (but still keep it fairly easy—this is not a good time for frustration). Wake her whispering, "Bunny is hiding and wants you to find him. Look and see if you can." Snuggle and rub her as she wakes and whisper hints if needed. Then urge her to find the other object(s) hidden in her room. You might hide her shoes and get her to look for them. As she finds them, help her put them on.

Finally, encourage her to hunt for something you have hidden in the bathroom (so she'll take care of her toilet needs) and another in the direction of the next activity. This might be an item for her snack or something related to what you'll be doing. If you need to go somewhere, hide something in her jacket or the car. Give plenty of easy clues and make a quiet fuss over her successes.

Return Trip

If you used a rhythmic activity like a wagon ride or swinging to relax your child before her nap, try the same activity to help return her to alertness. Or, if you used a counting down technique to quiet your child, count back up to wake her. Sit next to her and say gently, "I'm going to count from one to five. As I count, you will leave the dark and stars and swing up to the light where we will (do the next activity). When I get to five, you will open your eyes feeling relaxed, refreshed, and ready to (do what's next)." Kiss your child when she opens her eyes, and help her to go potty and put her shoes back on.

Wake-Up Stories and Songs

Narrate your child's waking up as an interesting story or a participation song. Say something like, "Once upon a time, there was a sleepy little girl with beautiful dark curls. (Stroke her hair and face.) Suddenly, a silly old walrus bent down and gave her a kiss. (Kiss your child.) His whiskers tickled her so much. (Brush your hair across her arms or face.) The little girl stretched just like this (Make loud groaning noises and stretch out your arms—if she doesn't follow suit, stretch out her limbs too.), and she yawned like this (Give a big yawn.). She fluttered her pretty eyelashes, and woke right up! The silly old walrus gathered her in his flippy, floppy flippers and smooched her all over. Then, he put her shoes on her sweet little feet, and he tied the laces just right to look like butterfly wings. The walrus and the little girl flopped and hopped off to the potty." Continue to narrate and act out the story, throwing in lots of humor and/or fantasy.

Or try singing waking-up directions to the tune of a familiar song like "The Farmer in the Dell." Sing "(Child's name) wakes up! (Child's name) wakes up! Heigh ho, the derry oh, (child's name) wakes up!" Continue with verses like, "And then she gets a kiss," "And then she yawns a bunch," "And then she puts on shoes," and so on. Throw in an occasional silly verse and handle your child gently and lovingly.

Holding Tanks and Isolation Booths:
RE-ENTRY ZONES FOR THE CRABBY

Some kids, no matter what you do, wake up in a bite-your-head-off mood. (Unfortunately for their parents and caregivers, these tend to be the same kids who have a hard time falling asleep.) These guys need time and/or space, and nothing else will do. I have noticed, though, that a few "adjustments" like these below can make the process a little smoother or at least more predictable. Meanwhile, just keep telling yourself, "This, too, shall pass." It will.

Holding Tanks

Lead or carry a cranky waker to an officially designated Holding Tank. This could be a soft chair or a corner padded with pillows—any place where you and your child can cuddle comfortably out of bed. The idea is to have a slow, gentle transition time. Use your own breathing, posture, and activity level to lead your child slowly to a higher level of alertness.

Make up a routine for the Holding Tank time. For example, first snuggle and hum a quiet song like "Twinkle, twinkle little star." Then hand her a cup of juice to sip while you read a short book (try an interactive book like *How Many Bugs in a Box?* by David A. Carter). Finally, sing a move-around-and-wake-up song like "The Wakey Pokey." Sing:

You wake your eyebrows up, you wake your eyebrows down.
You wake your eyebrows up and wiggle 'em all around.
You do the wakey-pokey and I give your nose a kiss.
That's what it's all about!
> (Continue with other verses, ending with waking your whole self up.)

Other possible activities include:
- grooming activities like gentle hair brushing or putting on lotion
- tickling or stroking that progresses to knee bouncing games like "Ride a cock horse"
- stretching various body parts in turn
- kissing different body parts good afternoon

Just be sure to have a ritual activity that clearly signals the end of the holding time and the return to play and work.

Isolation Booths

Some children wake in such foul moods that they will hit or kick you if you try to touch them or even talk to them. These children need a transitional *non-punitive* "isolation booth" where they can be alone out of bed while they wake up. Clear out a closet and stock it with cushions, a mirror or pictures, a few books, and cuddle objects. Place a drink by the entrance when you rouse your child or hear her get up. A large cardboard box can also be made into a little alone room. During an alert time, enlist your child in helping make the place be just what she needs.

Another alternative is to lure the crabby kid out of bed and cover her with a blanket or laundry basket. Comment that she is a turtle who is waking up slowly and isn't ready to come out of its shell. That's okay;

some turtles need time to feel happy again. You'll check back soon to see if she has started to come out of her shell.

Visit the turtle every few minutes and check nonjudgmentally on its progress. Leave a cup of juice or milk near the shell on one of the visits. You can certainly comment on the fun activities the turtle will be able to join once she's ready to lumber back to her family.

Happy Wake Up To You!
A BREATHE-UP GAME

You'd think one of those basic, essential functions like breathing would automatically fine-tune itself. But, as any physical therapist, exercise instructor, or other health worker can tell you, often it doesn't. For young kids, switching from sleep-breathing to awake/alert-breathing can make a big difference in mood and energy—and take a surprisingly long time. Here are some breathe-up techniques that may ease the change.

Happy Wake Up to You!

Adding a birthday motif to almost anything makes it more appealing to a preschooler. (I've even tried it with moderate success on hated dishes like meatloaf, as in, "Blow out the candle and have a slice of birthday meat-loaf!" Hey—it got the kid to try a bite.)

Sit by your child's bed and hum "Happy Birthday to You!" As he stirs, gather him up in your arms and carry him to the kitchen table singing, "Happy Wake Up to You!"

Set him in his chair in front of a snack (something that can hold a birthday candle, or place a candle in a holder next to it). Light the candle, and urge your child to make a wish and blow it out. Watch the pretty smoke patterns that swirl upward. If your child would like, re-light the candle and let him blow it out again. In fact, repeating the activity a few times often improves its success rate.

More Blow-Me-Up Play

Other blowing games work too. Wake a child from an outside snooze with dandelion puffs to scatter. Or bring a jar of bubble soap to his room (try the mini-blowers to minimize mess). Sit near your child and blow a few bubbles. Talk about what you are doing and seeing. Ask him to pop a bubble that floats near him. Have a wand ready for him to blow, too.

You can dangle a feather from a string near your child. Can he blow it hard enough so that it bumps your nose? Can he blow the whole thing out of your hand? Try resting a scrap of tissue paper over his lips. Can he blow it up in the air and sit up before it floats down again?

Or, use a squeeze bottle or turkey baster to blow soft puffs of air onto your child's closed eyes, cheeks, lips, neck, hands, and so on. When he gets up, let him blow puffs on you, too.

Taking a Breather

Play other games that affect your breathing. Put on quiet music and have your child breathe in rhythm to it. Then play something boppier, and have her adjust her breathing to match.

Or, give her some different things to sniff. Compare different flowers you've cut in the garden, smell the rain or snow outside, or inhale some of the spices you're planning to add to the evening's dinner.

Cat Naps:
GIVING-UP-NAP TIME

I'm not sure whether giving up naps is harder on kids or parents. The only good advice I have to help parents cope during the transition is to keep telling yourselves that no nap means an earlier bedtime. Oh, plus drink more coffee. These ideas, though, may help your child manage his change in lifestyle with minimal pain and suffering for him.

Un-Napping Readiness

How do you know when your child is ready to give up his nap? Most American children stop napping regularly between the ages of two and four, but there is huge individual variation. Watch for these signs:

- He goes down easily and sleeps well but becomes groggy and out-of-sorts after his nap for the rest of the day.
- His naptime has gotten later and later. You're now waking him for dinner. And he isn't ready for bed until ten or eleven.
- He resists going down and now can't fall asleep.

The next issue is how to help him give up the nap habit. This process may take several weeks and your child (and you) may be unusually cranky during this period. Here are some ways to help both of you muddle through the transition.

Trade a Kid-Nap for a Cat Nap

Explain to your child that he is now old enough to give up kid naps and take catnaps instead. What's the difference? Cats nap near people, instead of off in their own rooms. They settle down by themselves without anyone helping. They sleep for just a short time—but they still wake up full of energy and ready to play chase-the-jingle-ball.

Make up a kitty bed for your child to take his catnap in. (Try a sunny spot in a room other than your child's bedroom.) The first few times, help him stretch and yawn like a cat before curling up. After an hour or so, make sure there is enough household noise nearby to start waking him. Curl up near him, mewing and purring to help pull him back awake.

And, of course, be ready for a romping game of chase-the-jingle-ball once he finishes his cat stretches. A little kitty kibble (cereal served in a bowl on the floor) is also a welcomed wake-up. You can also extend this transition with a little extra quiet time by using some of the activities suggested below for rests.

Slice and Dice

Slowly trim the amount of time that your child spends sleeping in the middle of the day. Put him down five or ten minutes later than normal. If necessary, wake him five or ten minutes earlier than usual. (Do not let him sleep past his normal waking time, or you will be defeating the purpose.) Each week, put him down a little later and wake him a little earlier. Within a few weeks he should be down to a very short nap. If he is genuinely ready to give up his naps, he will be able to stop altogether at this point.

Early to Bed, Early to Rise

Or, keep moving naptime a little bit *earlier*. Although a later naptime seems to make more sense, late naps only interfere with bedtime and are harder for your child to give up. Put him down five minutes earlier each week until his naptime is forcing him to have an early lunch. Because he is not as tired, he probably won't sleep as long.

If This is Tuesday, It Must Be Nap Day

Put your child on an occasional napping schedule. Let him nap on high activity days when he is very tired, but shoot for keeping him busy and awake on the other days. Plan a slightly earlier bedtime on those days. And—very important—do not go anywhere in the car if you don't want him to nap!

No-Dozers and Rechargers:
METAPHORS FOR SLEEPLESS SURVIVAL

Undoubtedly you are familiar with the feeling of fighting sleepiness when driving, staying up late to finish work, or reading a bedtime story. You probably have tricks to help you stay alert like rolling down the car window, munching crunchy snacks, or enlisting your kid's help in smacking you when you doze off in the middle of your 645th repetition of *Where the Wild Things Are* by Maurice Sendak. Those elements—cool fresh air, food, a little physical jolt—will help preschoolers too. But you can also try these kid-friendly approaches.

The No-Dozer

Drowsy child who needs to stay awake? Have no fear! The No-Dozer is here! Turn your fingertips into a magical bulldozer that can push all your child's sleepiness into a pile. A steam shovel (your other hand) can then scoop it up and deposit it into a paper bag or cardboard box to save for later.

Have your child show you where on her body she feels sleepy. Examine that place, for example, lifting up her sleepy arms. Comment on how they feel very heavy. Obviously, they are completely coated with sleepiness. Put the No-Dozer to work, using your fingertips to shift every bit of the sleepiness to a mound on her belly or on the chair. Sound effects, reversals, difficulty shifting big rocks of slumber, and so on will help the activity grab your child's attention. (The transfer should also be more tickley than relaxing or your plan might backfire.) Afterward, check to make sure all the sleepiness has been scraped away and that her arms now feel light, loose, and refreshed.

Continue working at all the sleepy spots your child notices. Scoop up the sleepiness and store it next to her bed for the evening. Or save it up for a night when she needs it.

Rechargers

Use the metaphor of fresh or recharged batteries to revive your preschooler's flagging energy and turn a crabby kid into a happy kid. Point out batteries that can be recharged after they are used up. After recharging, they are as good as new. Your child is probably also familiar with how putting fresh batteries in an electronic toy makes it work again.

Choose a theme that taps one of your child's interests. For example, if he is into dinosaurs, pretend to turn him into a battery-powered allosaurus. Or he could be a robot or a run-down spaceship. After you transform him, he is ready for all his parts to be recharged or batteries replaced. Continue as above, identifying body or brain parts that have run out of juice. Pull out his used-up batteries and insert new ones or use your magic vibrating finger rechargers to make his batteries work again.

SAFETY ZONE

Use this opportunity to remind your child about the potential dangers of real batteries and electricity. He should never touch electrical appliances or outlets without your help. Explain that he could get badly shocked or burned. Similarly, batteries contain acid that could burn him if he put them in his mouth or handled one that was leaking.

Cuddle Up at the Snuggle Inn:
SNUGGLY NO-SLEEPS

A quiet time each afternoon will benefit you and your child. Even if you can't do it every day or for very long, a regular shared cuddle time will help teach your child how to slow her body without sleeping—and create some special times to refuel you both. During the period when your child is giving up her nap, though, you will want to provide enough stimulation that she does not fall asleep. Try some of these snuggle-up-together activities.

Cuddling Down Memory Lane

With busy lives, many families find it hard to make time to look at all those photographs they take, watch the videos they shoot, or tell family stories. Take a half-hour or forty-five minutes each week to cuddle with your child and revisit special memories. Simply look through an album or box of pictures, watch a video, or examine artifacts (like old baby clothes or grampa's tackle box). If you have a little more energy, walk through the past topic by topic. For example, one week, you can focus on birthdays. Check out photos from your child's birthdays. Talk about how you celebrated when you were a child. Tell her about memorable birthday celebrations of other family members or famous people. The next week you can devote to a different topic, like cars that people in the family have owned, or pet tales.

Seasonal Sensual Pleasures

Take the opportunity to enjoy the quiet treats of each season. For example, during the winter, share a cup of cocoa in front of the fire and let your child play with scraps of yarn or fabric while you do needlework. In the summer, spread a blanket in the shade and sip lemonade while misting each other with an atomizer. In the fall, you can bundle up in stadium blankets and sip cider through a straw, while reclining on chaise lounges to watch the swirling autumn leaves. On a rainy spring day, listen to *Appalachian Spring* by Aaron Copland and use a magnifying glass to examine the forsythia you've forced or a bouquet of daffodils.

Cuddle Kits

Too busy to cuddle a needy child? Or, is your child with another caregiver during afternoon rest time? Use a cuddle kit to substitute for your presence. Prepare a kit in advance, so you or your child's caregiver can pull it out easily at rest time. Your child can get settled on the sofa or your bed with her kit—and cuddle herself! You can pack up the materials in an old pillowcase and tie it closed with a pretty ribbon. What should you put in it? Almost any assortment of soothing luxuries will do, but here are some suggestions to get you started.

- *A blanket or pillow* A flannel or satiny receiving blanket is nice.
- *A cuddle companion* An unfamiliar stuffed animal, doll, puppet, or small figure.
- *A quiet-time toy surprise* Maybe wrap it up like a present. Try a coloring book and crayons, a box of cheap dominoes to build and arrange, plastic animals, and other novel, inexpensive toys that can be used in a variety of ways.
- *Music or story* A tape, CD, comic, or wordless book, especially something new.

- *Sensory treat* A single-serving drink, a small snack like a box of raisins, a potpourri sachet to sniff, hand lotion, a hot water bottle or cool washcloth, an eye pillow (see page 160).

Story Snuggles:
LOVE-LY LITERARY LOUNGING

Reading to your child as a quiet activity is hardly original—but it is probably one of the easiest and most satisfying ways to structure a rest together. Add a touch element and themes of revival to make the most of your reading rest.

Cozy Caterpillar Cuddles

Read some favorite tales of metamorphosis. Try *Gotta Go! Gotta Go!* by Sam Swope, *The Very Hungry Caterpillar* by Eric Carle, and *The Caterpillar and the Polliwog* by Jack Kent. Then gently wrap your own little caterpillar in a blanket cocoon (keep her face free and the blankets loose—or simply form a cocoon with your arms). Hold her and let her sink into your body as you talk softly to her about all the marvelous ways she is growing and changing. Then let her stretch and squirm out of her cocoon. She can lie in the sun for a moment while her wings dry, flutter them a few times, then fly off to enjoy the rest of the day.

Baked Babes

Read "The Little Red Hen," "The Gingerbread Man," and James Marshall's appealing version of *Hansel and Gretel*. Then turn your child into a tasty dish. Try making her into a loaf of the Little Red Hen's piping hot and delicious bread. Have her lie down on the sofa or carpet. Add the necessary pretend ingredients (flour, water, a little sugar, yeast, maybe some cinnamon and raisins) into her as a "bowl." Use your fingers to gently stir the ingredients into a nice ball of dough. Knead the dough all over, being sure to squeeze out any air bubbles. Cover the dough with a clean cloth and narrate how it's rising in a nice warm place. Then punch it down, shape it into a loaf, and bake it in a hot oven. When it's done, ask, "Who will help me eat this bread?" No volunteers? Gobble it up yourself! Make this last step vigorous and silly, so your "crumbs" will be ready to resume playing.

Other fun foods to make: a gingerbread man (let him "run, run as fast as he can" after he's baked), a sandwich, a wedding or birthday cake (spreading the frosting is fun), an ice cream sundae (great for a hot day), and tossed salad.

You can let your child cook you up next if you both need a little longer break.

More Reading Rests

Set aside of pile of picture books on the same theme. For example, for a "pig-in-a-blanket" rest, cozy up in a quilt and read a couple of versions of "The Three Little Pigs" (try *The True Story of the 3 Little Pigs* by Jon Scieszka, *The Three Pigs* by David Wiesner, and *The Three Little Wolves and the Big Bad Pig* by Eugene Trivizas) and another book or two featuring pigs as main characters like *Toot & Puddle* by Holly Hobbie. Use toy animals to act out the dialogue on your child's belly or lap. At the end of the session, put away the books and props and choose a fresh set of both so you'll be all ready for tomorrow's reading rest.

All's Quiet on the Resting Front:
RESTFUL ALL-ALONE FUN

If your child has given up his nap, you may still need some all-alone time in the afternoon. Also, children who are introverted by temperament or who get overstimulated easily will benefit from a period of solitude. The answer is the all-alone rest, in your child's room or some other separate space. Try these tips to help your child rest alone contentedly.

Rest Routines and Rules

Even if your child isn't going to sleep, she needs help to slow her body into a resting rhythm. Follow a routine similar to the pre-nap one. Plan on toileting, washing up, removing shoes, and spending a short settle-in time together. Help your child make a plan for her play before you leave the room.

One important rule is that your child must remain in her room until rest time ends. Have a clear understanding about exceptions (e.g., urgent potty needs, significant injury or illness). If your child won't stay put, try imaginative containment strategies first. Have her pretend she is a pony latched in her stall, a dinosaur corralled by a deep earthquake fissure, or a fairy who cannot leave the enchanted forest until her fairy mother figures out how to break the spell (in an hour or so). If those measures fail, use a baby gate to restrain her. Ban loud, wild, or dangerous play.

Finally, be sure your child can communicate with you if she needs you and reassure her you will notify her promptly when rest is over.

Restful Play, Playful Rest

Rest time will be best for everyone if your child finds it both relaxing and enjoyable. Activities like drawing, quietly pretending with stuffed animals or miniatures, working puzzles, looking at books, listening to story or music tapes, or building with small construction materials are all suitably restful. Materials that are relatively "easy" for your child will be less likely to provoke frustration and cries for help. Try the following to add interest:

- *Novelty or Specialness* Occasionally trot out a new material (try reserving some gifts for first use at rest time) and/or have a cache of high-appeal toys that may be used only during rest.
- *Fun Themes* For example, plan a horse rest, with toy horses to pretend with, books about horses to look at, a large cardboard box outfitted with a blanket to serve as a stable for your little pony, and a horse snack of carrots, oats (granola bar or oatmeal cookie), and water. Other popular themes: pretend parties or holidays, construction sites, prehistoric play, school, other animals like dogs or turtles, camping, and fairy tales.

- *A Snack* You may get more time if you let your child have her afternoon snack alone in her room. Obviously, stick to easy-cleanup foods. Designate an eating site in the room, and be sure it is adequately protected. Serve water in a water bottle. Consider letting your child use a big-kid lunch box, toy picnic hamper, or doll dishes for serving.
- *Play Stations* Most preschoolers cannot stick with a single activity for the sixty to ninety minutes you'll want them to rest. Anticipate this problem by helping your child arrange a series of "stations" with different activities. Be creative about the placement of the stations. For example, you might want to set up a puzzle on the floor of her closet and a book to read in a cardboard box.

Wet Rests:
PLAY BATHS AND DRIBBLE-DRIPS

Water is the ultimate soother. Try a wet rest for an overwrought child who cannot relax, an extroverted child who needs company while he recharges, or just for a nice change of pace.

The Play Bath

Fill the tub with warm water and trot out the bath toys or a jar of bubble soap and blowers. Dress your child in her bathing suit—or her birthday suit if she prefers. Just leave the soap and shampoo behind. This bath is all play and no business. (If you need play ideas, see the bath activities in Chapter 8.)

Enhance the restful mood by piping in quiet music or nature sounds, dimming the lighting, and shutting your child in the tub.

Bring in supplies to make the rest period productive and/or relaxing for you, too. Bring a portable phone or turn on the answering machine. Make yourself comfortable with pillows or a beanbag chair and a cup of tea. Or use the time to clean the rest of the bathroom. Your child can scrub the tub before she gets out.

Dribble Drips

Out-of-the-bath water play soothes well, too. Sit your child at the table with a bucket of warm water and a plastic bin or washtub; on a plastic mat on the kitchen floor with the same material; or on a no-skid stool or high chair at the kitchen sink.

Provide materials for dripping and dribbling water. You can punch holes in various patterns into items like plastic pop or water bottles and old margarine tubs to make "rainmakers." Some of our favorites are an all-over pattern in the bottom of a margarine tub for a heavy shower or a vertical row of holes up the side of small (twelve ounce or less) bottle. (Watch how the water shoots out farther from the lower holes because of the greater water pressure.) Also try poking a single small hole in the bottom

 SAFETY ZONE
Use a clear shower curtain or glass doors. NEVER leave a preschool child alone in the tub or in the supervision of a slightly older child.

of a pop bottle. Fill the bottle with water and put the cap on tightly. Hold up the bottle and watch how the water slows to a few drips. Untwist the cap slightly—what happens? This activity bears much repeating. Other good dripper materials include squeeze bottles, turkey basters, funnels, and sponges.

Add props for imaginative or additional sensory play. Small figures (maybe with toy umbrellas) and plastic buildings or cars can lead to rainy-day theme play. Give your child flat rocks or waterproof blocks (try Duplos) to stack and create an imaginary waterfall. Let him rearrange the pieces and watch what happens to the flow patterns. Or give him an assortment of materials to drip water on and notice the different sounds they make or the changes water makes in their color or texture.

CHAPTER FIVE

Putting the "Great" in the Outdoors

Every October, I optimistically lug a few of my summer pots of geraniums inside to brighten my windowsills. And every January, I give up and toss their spindly pale green carcasses onto the frozen pumpkin mush on the compost pile. Because no matter how sunny the windowsills might seem, the light and air in my house simply cannot compete with the stuff provided outside by Mother Nature. (It probably doesn't help that I can never be bothered to water the plants once I can't do it with the hose.)

But the point of all of this is that living things need fresh air and sunlight—or at least some of the low cloud cover that we settle for here in Western Pennsylvania. And young children need space and opportunity to move their limbs vigorously. Plus some sprinkling with the hose. So I hereby command you to take your preschoolers outside every single day. Excused absences will be granted for Category Four hurricanes, tornado warnings issued by the National Weather Bureau, and hail larger than golf balls. Also lightning or major flooding. And plagues of locusts. But those should be rare events. And if they're not, I suggest you move.

You don't have to make outside time into a Major Production. (Except for the getting outfitted part—that just *is* a Major Production, so I've included some ideas to help with that.) A short romp daily will suffice, especially if you allow the kids to jump in puddles or collect things like worms and chunks of asphalt while you're out. I've included some strategies for dealing with common outdoor play problems, like how to keep kids from transferring all the sand into their underpants and coping with folks who insist on walking up the slide instead of the ladder. I've also listed some ideas for yucky weather play, because when it's cold or rainy it can be a little trickier to entice kids away from the VCR and their Barbies (and you away from your magazine or even the dirty oven).

In addition, this chapter has ideas for coping with outdoor bothers like boo-boos. And, of course, dealing with the number one preschooler outdoor problem: bugs. Even the toughest tough guys can be reduced to hysteria by a harmless fly, especially since it happens to sound like that true horror for the preschool set: the buzzy bee. I am a particularly well-qualified expert in this area because all three of my kids went through *looooong* periods of Bug Terror. My oldest resolved his bug fears by declaring war on creepy crawlies, lisping as he "'tepped and 'tomp, 'tomp,'tomped on all the 'cary bugth" in our neighborhood, but the younger two, who had unfortunate encounters with buzzy bees, were not so easily cured of their phobias. I had not noticed how many bugs there are in every square inch of our yard until my daughter took up obsessive bug-spotting for several summers. What eventually worked for my scaredy-bugs was getting to know some harmless "friend bugs," as Sara called them. Unfortunately, these lovely creatures then had to come live in mayonnaise jars on the kitchen table. But it's worth a slug or two at the breakfast table to get to go outside and spray paint an old sheet or simply to avoid cleaning the oven. So take a deep breath of that fresh air, throw out the geraniums after the first frost, and have fun!

Caddy Land:
GET ORGANIZED TO STAY OUTSIDE

I promised some tips to make getting ready for outside play less of a Major Production, so here they are. The first step is to assemble your supplies in a semi-permanent fashion, so you don't have to do it all over each day. I know from experience that if you have to be running inside every five minutes to hunt for sunscreen and bubble soap, before you know it the whole outside thing is going to seem like too much trouble. Try these ideas to get organized for fun.

Outdoor Supplies

A well-stocked "Outside Play Caddy" can save you many interruptions and enable you to deal promptly with common problems. I actually store most of my outside supplies on shelves in the garage (and add refills or perishables as needed before play), but if you don't have an easily accessed garage or shed, keep your supplies in a plastic caddy or backpack and just lug it out with you when you go.

Your Outside Play Caddy should include the following:
- Soap, hand wipes, or water-free cleansers (like Purell) to clean hands and boo-boos
- First aid supplies, especially bandages, no-sting spray (like Bactine), antiseptic cream, and tweezers
- Washcloth and small towel
- Sunscreen (SPF 30 or higher, child-friendly formula), lotion, and petroleum jelly
- Timer and/or watch
- Cordless or cell phone, paper and pencil for messages, and a list of emergency and frequently called numbers
- Healthy snacks (raisins, crackers, dry cereal, etc.)
- Sunglasses, hats, and extra clothing
- Plastic bags for collecting treasures, holding muddy clothes, etc.

You'll also need to have available:

- Water for drinking (individual water bottles or insulated jug and cups—colorcode the cups by child or tape names on)
- Water for washing (fill milk jugs and set in the sun to warm, or have a hose handy)

Fun Stash

Store much-used play supplies where you and your child can access them easily. In addition to bigger items, such as ride-on toys, a climbing structure, sandbox, kiddy pool, or playhouse, you might stock:

- Sidewalk chalk
- Bubble soap and items for blowing different kinds of bubbles
- Hula hoops
- Jump ropes
- Magnifying glasses, binoculars, periscopes, and other "lookers"
- Child-sized gardening supplies
- Picnic blanket, old sheets, cushions, old towels
- Spray bottles, soaker "guns," sprinklers, watering cans
- Paint brushes (all sorts and sizes)
- Bins, tubs, buckets, plastic bottles, cups, and trays (assorted shapes and sizes)
- Vinegar and baking soda (for making volcanoes)
- Kites, pinwheels, streamers, mini-fan, other air/wind toys
- Sand-play toys (old cooking gear, sieves, diggers, vehicles, and small plastic animals and figures)
- Pretending supplies (short lengths of old hose, housekeeping toys, fabric squares, hats and helmets, and other props for your child's current passion)
- Junior sports equipment (balls, tee for t-ball, soccer net, hockcy sticks, skates or blades)
- Cones (or plumber's helpers, which can serve the same purpose)

Unpressed but Dressed:
OUTDOOR PLAYWEAR

Suit up your child to match the weather and her activities—and thereby increase her fun and decrease your distress.

The Mud Suit

Designate one of your child's outfits as a messy play suit. Don't forget to include socks and "puddle shoes" or boots. Store the clothes in a bag and hang them on a low hook near the door. Keep an adult's old T-shirt handy, too, for a "cover-up-quick" smock. Be sure to change the mud suit with the seasons or as your child grows.

You'll also need a designated changing area. I stripped down dirty kids in the basement laundry room (accessible through my garage), but any area protected with a tarp or newspaper will do. Have your child stuff muddy clothes into a plastic bag, a bucket, or the utility sink. Rinse or soak clothes prior to washing (to prevent making the rest of the load a muddy mess), but don't worry about new stains. Instead, point them out to your child so she will understand why you want her to change into her play outfit before stomping in puddles—and remember to praise her for making the mess on the right clothes!

TRY THIS!

Look for inexpensive easy-on, easy-off clothes among hand-me-downs, yard-sale finds, and stained-beyond-repair clothes. For footwear, try your child's just-outgrown shoes, yard sale specials, or washable rubber boots.

Playable Play Clothes

Your child's clothes should permit him to play safely, comfortably, and without excessive worry about keeping clean and tidy.

Look for play clothes with the following features:

- Comfortable, durable, easy-care fabrics (Save "cute" outfits for special outings.)
- Do-it-myself styling (elastic waists, slip-on tops, Velcro fasteners)
- Sneakers, sandals, or boots with normal-thickness rubber soles and secure straps and fasteners

Some clothes have features that are unsafe or impractical, including:

- Cords and loops (Remove them if necessary—they pose a choking hazard.)
- Dresses (They can be a safety hazard when climbing, and they tend to limit a girl's ability or willingness to participate in active play.)
- Platform shoes, floppy sandals, hard-soled shoes, and cowboy boots
- Unsafe costumes or accessories, such as masks, jewelry, and capes that fasten around the neck
- Bare feet (most of the time)

Boundary Basics:
SHOWING YOUR CHILD THE LAY OF THE LAND

Clearly understood boundaries will prevent accidents, ease your supervisory duties, and increase your child's independence.

The Warning Track

As much as possible, restrict your preschooler to playing in the backyard or other areas away from the street. When he is out front, make or designate a warning track. For example, tell him that the strip of grass between the sidewalk and the road (if your yard has one) is off-limits. Or, chalk a line dividing the width of the sidewalk in half, or use a rope, flags, cones, lime, or even spray paint to mark where the lawn ends for him. You can also plant a flowerbed or simply spread a strip of mulch to delineate the end of the road for your child. Explain that baseball players use their warning track to keep from smashing into the outfield fence. Your warning track will remind him to stay out of the street. Your child should slam on his brakes when he hits the warning track, even if his ball, pet, or whatever keeps going.

Also, set up a barrier to prevent your child from running into the road at the end of the driveway and to prevent vehicles from entering during playtime. Some of my neighbors park their cars blocking the entrance to the driveway. We used plastic cones to mark the entrance as "closed."

The No-Fool Rule

Your child is *never* permitted to leave his home or yard without telling the supervising adult. Period. Make sure to impose memorable consequences for violations of this rule. Role-play different scenarios if your child doesn't seem to understand.

The Swing Zone

Create and mark a safety zone around swings and slides to help keep kids from straying into the paths of moving swings or stepping in front of kids who are zipping off the end of the slide. The average preschooler won't remember to "watch out!" on his own and is a very poor judge of distance. He will, however, be happy to help you determine where to mark the lines, by swinging or sliding repeatedly while you set the boundaries. Once the boundaries are marked, remind kids that no one may enter the danger zones without stopping and checking that it's safe to do so.

Don't Jump Off a Giant

Establish a maximum height from which your child can jump. I used my children's heights as a guideline. Before they could jump off something, they had to stand next to it. If their feet would be above their heads—no go. If the surface wasn't cushioned, the maximum height was lower. You can set similar limits for climbing. Finally, you may need to adjust these guidelines to suit your child's ability.

SAFETY ZONE

Children are individuals, and environments vary in how safe they are for young children. What works for most children of a given age may not be appropriate for your child. Impulsive or highly active children may require tighter boundaries (because they're bound to violate them), and some timid children may feel more secure with them. If, however, you notice that your boundaries are consistently tighter or looser than those used by other parents around you, stop and evaluate. Perhaps you need to adjust your own comfort zone.

Let Boundaries Stretch with Age and Ability

In general, a three-year-old can walk next door to the neighbors while you watch him. A four-year-old can go next door with your permission. A five-year-old may be able to venture farther, so long as he doesn't have to cross any streets.

Frozen Fun:
SNOW BALLS AND ICE SPICE

My kids love winter. It's their favorite season. I hate winter. That's because I feel like I invest way more effort in dressing, undressing, and dealing with wet clothes than we do having fun. These activities, though, may encourage everyone to stay outside long enough to tip the balance more in favor of fun than drudgery. Plus, these activities are little-kid-sized fun, so *you* won't have to get a hernia making snowmen. Maybe you can even just wave to everyone out the window while you sip your hot chocolate and read your magazine.

Make a Snowballman

Show your child how to pack a snowball. Then have her stack up two or three snowballs and decorate as usual. Use a baby carrot for the nose and raisins for facial features. Dress the figures in doll hats and ribbons for scarves. Stop with just one or make a whole family. Or, make other snow-ball figures, such as Snow Ants (three balls in a row, with stick legs and antennae) or Snow Pokey-pines (decorate an elongated snowball with pine needles and seed-pod eyes).

Snow Portraits

Preschoolers delight in making the classic snow angel (lie down, wave arms and legs, stand up), but turning their imprints into portraits will keep them busy and happy much longer.

Instead of making a snow angel, your child can lie down and make an impression of a pose. Suggest that she try positions like Muscle Man (legs hip-distance apart, arms flexed to the sides), Jumping Jack, (arms extended overhead, legs spread wide apart), or Princess (wave legs as for a snow angel, but have one arm down by "skirt" and the other raised in a royal wave). She can then decorate her prints for extra pizzazz. Have her "paint" areas of color by misting the print with spray bottles (fill with water mixed with food dye or *very* diluted tempera paint). Or, she can clothe and adorn the figure using branches, pine needles, rocks, old clothing, and so on. Arrange objects in interesting patterns to fill in large areas and create some wacky outfits.

Popsicle Courses

Make mounds or scoop out holes for your child to scramble over or hurdle as she dashes around a wintry obstacle course. Include a target to hit with a snowball, a place to make an angel, a spot to somersault, and other of your child's favorite snow-play activities. Wrap up with a refreshing drink—or even a Popsicle (your child will probably feel hot)!

Simple—But Sensational: Ice Experiences Preschoolers Love

- Fill a disposable or freezable container with water. Set it outside when the temperature is below freezing. When the ice is solid, bring it back inside and again observe what happens. Then put it back outside. Repeat endlessly.

- Freeze different things. Try a different liquid like juice, milk, or pudding. Hang wet fabric up to "freeze dry." Also freeze chipped pottery (fill it with water—which may expand and break the container), old plastic toys (observe how they get brittle and break more easily), lettuce leaves, or a few leaves from a houseplant.

- On a super-cold day, take a mister outside and spray it into the air. Watch the ice drops fall to earth. Or mist your snowman and watch how he changes. Or, blow bubbles outside. The warm air from your breath will make them soar quickly. They will freeze from the bottom up in interesting crystalline patterns and leave a filmy shell when they pop.

- Find a frozen puddle and walk on it. Find puddles with a thin "skin" of ice.

- Break off an icicle and examine it. Pick a baby icicle and watch it grow. Hang a string from a tree limb. Keep dripping water down it, and make your own icicle.

That Blows Me Away!
ACTIVITIES FOR WINDY DAYS

Preschoolers usually consider blustery days to be pretty exciting. As long as everyone (that means you, too) is dressed warmly enough, you can have a great time outside with activities like these.

Fly a Kid Kite

One of the easiest and most satisfying kites for a small child is made from a plastic grocery bag. Have your child staple some streamers (or a more traditional tail with bows) to the bottom of the bag. Tie the handles together with a length of string at least as long as your child is tall. Let your child run and fly his kite.

An ordinary balloon on a long string, pinwheels, crepe paper streamers (tape or staple them to a dowel or paper towel tube), flags, windsocks (shape paper into a tube and attach streamers), and long scarves to flutter will also delight preschoolers on windy days.

SAFETY ZONE

Always supervise young children when they are playing with string, which can pose a strangulation hazard.

ON THE WEB

There are many websites where you can view beautiful kites or get directions on making them. Two with easy pre-school-level instructions are www.molokai.com (click on "Big Wind Kite Factory" and look for "20 kids, 20 kites") and www.sound.net/~kiteguy.

Sail a Boat

For an easy boat, take an empty juice box. Poke a hole in the center of one of the large sides (an adult's job) and insert a straw. Cut a sail from construction paper, poke holes near the top and bottom, and thread it through the straw mast. Set it in a puddle or a tub of water and watch how the wind moves it.

Race against the Wind

Hand your child a large sheet of cardboard (about three feet by three feet). Have her hold it in front of her (but make sure she can see easily) and run into the wind. It's hard work! Then have her run again without the cardboard. Much easier! Experiment some more. What happens if she holds the cardboard behind her? Over her head? Sideways?

Make a Pinwheel

Cut a square of paper and crease it lightly to find the middle. Cut four slits, starting from each corner and ending a half-inch shy of the middle. Fold up each point so that the four points overlap in the middle. Poke a tack through all the points and into the eraser of an unsharpened pencil. Blow!

 ON THE WEB

Look for directions for making pinwheels from plastic report covers at www.kidsdomain.com. Click on "crafts," then select "spring" from the seasonal/holiday list.

Take Flight

The Wright brothers chose to test-fly their plane at Kitty Hawk, North Carolina because of its windy weather and high dunes. Combining wind and height will similarly aid your young flier's efforts. Let him experiment with some of these flyable items:

- Paper airplanes
- Foam planes
- Maple keys, dandelion seeds, other wind-blown seeds
- Parachute guys or homemade parachutes (Gather the four corners of a piece of cloth together and tie them with a string. Fasten a weight, such as a washer or other heavy item at the bottom of the string.)
- Bubbles

Help your child release his flying machines safely from a height, such as atop a stepladder, from the top of a climbing structure, or from an upstairs window (open it less than five inches). (You can also do the releasing and have your child watch from below, trying to catch or track the items, if you worry about his ability to handle heights.)

Puddle Jumping and Mud Mucking:
RAINY DAY PLAY

Rainy days used to make me groan. Being cooped up in the house with three high-energy kids stinks. (Sometimes literally, if they decide science experiments will keep them busy.) Then I read that catching colds from getting wet was just an old wives' tale—and I started sending the kids out to play on most rainy days. They loved it! I loved it! And you will too! Keep the playtime short if it's cold or windy, and scurry in if there's thunder or lightning. Afterwards, dry your kid well or soak him in a warm tub.

Take an Umbrella for a Walk

Try some umbrella investigations:
- Hold it upside down—where does the rain go? Why are umbrellas shaped the way they are?
- Try out an oiled paper umbrella. (Look for one at an Asian goods store.) Or make a mini one. Try rubbing a cocktail paper umbrella with cooking oil. Rub another with polyurethane. Let them dry and then take them out along with an un-oiled one on a rainy day. How well do they work?
- Play "Singing in the Rain" and dance like Gene Kelly. Rent the video (or borrow it from the library) and watch clips of some of the dance scenes, especially the rain one, before you play.
- On a warm rainy day, go for a walk under an umbrella. Notice how dry you are. On the way home, close up the umbrella. Which way did your child prefer? Why?

- Try using some found objects for umbrellas. Try a cookie sheet, a newspaper, a piece of fabric, a cardboard box, or whatever else your child thinks might work. Are they as good as a regular umbrella?
- Notice where birds and animals go in the rain. Do they use anything for umbrellas?

Play with Puddles and Rivulets

Have some fun on a wet sidewalk or in a puddly driveway:
- Stomp, splash, kick. Leap over a puddle as well as in it. How high can you make the water go? How far?
- Float natural "boats" like flower petals, leaves, bark, etc. Make up stories about little people, fairies, or animals who might use the tiny boats. Compare the way boats work in a puddle versus a moving stream in the gutter. (Carefully supervise your child near streets.)
- Look for rainbows and reflections in puddles. Where might they have come from?
- Follow the path of rainwater from the roof to the gutters and downspouts to the street and down to the storm sewer. What might happen if the roof were flat? If there were no gutters? No sewers?
- Measure a puddle's circumference with a piece of string, and its depth with a Popsicle stick. Come back later and measure it again. Has it changed? Why?

Mud and Muck

Most of the time, you'll sensibly prefer that your kid stays out of the mud, but once in a while…
- At least once, let your child get completely, utterly muddy. (Just make sure he's wearing his mud suit!) How does it feel? What happens when the mud dries on his skin? If you can find an area

without debris, let him walk in the mud and feel it on the soles of his feet. Take a picture of him muddy and another after he's cleaned up. Hang them side by side. Read *Mud* by Mary Lyn Ray for a celebration of this glorious substance, or test the recipes in *Mud Pies and Other Recipes: A Cookbook for Dolls* by Marjorie Winslow.

- Make mud parfaits. Layer pebbles, mud, sticks, grass, and other objects in a clear container.
- Collect muddy clay soil, if you have it in your area. Shape it into a bowl or a ball and let it harden completely. (These mud creations are remarkably durable—I still have a six-year-old "teapot" my son made this way.) Or spread the muddy clay in a shallow box, cut it into small rectangles and let the whole thing dry. (You can mix the clay with grass for extra strength—that's how adobe bricks are made.) Later, try building with the mini-bricks, using fresh mud for mortar.

Hot Day Cool Downs:
WARM WEATHER WHINE COOLERS

Heat and humidity certainly make me cranky, so it doesn't surprise me that kids' tempers run as high as the thermometer. Fortunately, keeping cool can involve fun stuff to do. The key to enjoying those hot dog days is prevention—once you let the kids get overheated and crabby, you might as well head for the air conditioning. Here are some of our favorite ways to keep our cool.

Misty Moisty Mornings

Or afternoons. We always have misters available on hot days (we take one on outings, too). Spray mist into the air and let it drift onto your child's skin for the gentlest cooling. One great idea I spotted around my neighborhood: Someone bought a bird mister attachment (it's a copper tube that attaches to the hose and is suspended someplace in the garden for spraying birds who prefer being misted to splashing in the birdbath—look for them at nature stores or pet supply stores). She hung it from a tree branch for the kids and wildlife to zip through while they play. Recently I spotted a similar hose attachment at Sears for spraying people with a gentle mist. (It's a stiff rubber coil that sits on the ground or a table.)

Cool Headgear

A wet paper towel or washcloth tucked under a sun hat feels wonderfully refreshing. One scorcher day we stuck ice water in a freezer zipper bag and put that under our hats. Ahh! Wet towels can also be worn as cool capes or fashioned into some tight-fitting evening gowns.

Rehydration

Keep water *in* the kids as well as on them. Those big jugs with push button spigots are very appealing to kids—they'll even drink plain water from them. Just watch out for their preferred drinking method (mouth open under the spigot).

Crushed ice is fun to make and eat. Put the ice in a zipper freezer bag and squeeze out as much air as possible. Stick the bag inside several other plastic or paper bags. Then let the kids whack the whole thing with a hammer. Open the bag and suck on the chips.

Water Colors

Wet an old white sheet and use ropes tied to the corners and then to trees or other structures in the yard to stretch it for use as a painting canvas. Dilute tempera paints or use food-coloring water to paint the sheet with misters, brushes, sponges, hands, and so on. Your child can paint herself while she's at it. Not satisfied with her masterpiece? Hose it down and try again. Another option is simply to give kids buckets of water and paintbrushes and let them paint the town wet. Most kids will be content to paint anything handy, but you can keep them at their "work" a little longer with some ideas like painting faces all along the driveway and watching them evaporate. Or painting a tic-tac-toe board and playing quickly before it disappears. Or have a contest to see who can "paint in" a square or other shape first.

Learn to Siphon

You need a bucket, a wading pool, and about a yard of plastic tubing (available at hardware stores—we just use those corrugated "noisemaker" tubes that you spin to make "sing"). Fill the bucket with water and place it on a chair next to the pool. Place the tube in the bucket and fill it with water. You can do this by submerging the whole tube (and waiting until the bubbles stop) or sucking on the end like a straw (which is sort of gross, but if you're using all clean materials, it should be okay). When the tube is full, pinch it closed or hold your finger or palm over the end.

Quickly lower the end into or near the pool (making sure the other end stays submerged in the water in the bucket) and release the water. If you've managed to create a partial vacuum—which may take beginners a couple of tries—the water will flow from the bucket into the pool. This is very cool to young kids (and grownups like me). You can also use the siphon to "vacuum" up small objects like marbles (provided the diameter of the tube is big enough) and shoot them into the pool.

Blasting Out of Sand Traps:
SANDBOX PROBLEMS AND SOLUTIONS

Sand is one of those basic materials, like water and play dough, that most preschoolers seem driven to play with. Unfortunately, like water and play dough, sand also comes with its share of safety and mess issues. These ideas may minimize the problems while promoting maximum fun and soothing.

Problem: *Sand gets in the eyes.*
Solution: *Repeat after me. Endlessly. "Sand stays in the sandbox."*

Show children who throw sand the effects of their behavior. If they won't stop, shift them to another activity. Warn kids against rubbing eyes with sandy hands, and keep a soft towel nearby to brush sand off faces. To get sand out of eyes, encourage the child to blink repeatedly. You can stretch the upper lid over the lower lid and hold it for a few minutes to encourage tears. These methods will usually wash a grain or two of sand to the inner corner of the eye where it can be removed easily. Or, have the child lean over a very full cup of water and blink into the water. This method is better if there is a lot of sand in the child's eyes.

Problem: *Sand ends up in the house.*
Solution: *Provide duplicate toys.*

Have duplicate toys (like play dishes, vehicles) for the sandbox, so kids are less tempted to bring the sand toys inside. And, remind kids of the "sand stays in the sandbox" rule yet again.

The other way that sand tends to come in the house is on kid's skin or in their clothes. It has always been a mystery to me how kids can walk around for hours with their underpants loaded with three pounds of sand. These tips won't solve that mystery, but they may reduce the transfer of sand to the house.

Put the sand in a raised container, like a sand table or a wheelbarrow, or one too small to sit in (like an old baby bathtub or a plastic bin). This will cut *way* down on how much sand comes in.

SAFETY ZONE

If a child who had sand in her eye continues to complain that it is watering profusely or hurts severely, or if you notice that the child's nose is suddenly running on the same side as the injured eye, she may have a grain embedded or a scratched cornea. Call your doctor.

It is also important to keep outside sand covered to prevent contamination with animal feces. Be sure to have your child wash his hands when he finishes playing.

Encourage sand play in bare feet or have a policy of removing shoes outside (and away from the doorway) after sand play.

A sprinkling of cornstarch makes it easier to brush sticky grains off skin. You can also fill the sandbox with something like aquarium or pea gravel that is easier to brush off.

At the beach, we keep a dishpan of water next to the door (and a bathmat just inside). Kids are encouraged to step in one and on the other before heading in.

Finally, you can also teach your kids to do an after-sandbox cheer like this one:

Brush, brush, clap, clap!
Off my hands and off my lap!
Shake and stomp and jump and flap!
Now I'm clean, just like that!

Problem: *The kids are bored with building castles and sifting sand.*
Solution: *Suggest some new and interesting ways to play with sand.*

Some of our favorites:

- ***Wet Sand*** Use wet sand to mold some different landscapes. My kids liked making prehistoric landscapes for their dinosaurs. They collected rocks of varying sizes, sticks, bits of bark, shallow dishes to make lakes, and, with my help, small flowers or leaves from ferns and other lacy plants. They then sculpted an exciting landscape with deep fissures (from earthquakes), mountains of varying heights, rain forest areas, and stretches of barren desert. The pièce de résistance was a volcano made by mounding up sand and hollowing out a hole for a plastic bottle. This they filled about one-third full with diluted vinegar colored with red food coloring. They populated the landscape with assorted dinosaurs. Finally, they added a twist of paper towel filled with baking soda to the plastic bottle. *Ka-boom!* (Or, more precisely, ooze!)

- *Zen Garden Play* Very soothing and fun for artistic children. You need a piece of cardboard or a spatula (to smooth the sand), forks or small rakes for making patterns, beautiful rocks (preferably crystals), flowers or small plants, and a few ornaments or figures to complete the arrangements.
- *Treasure Hunts* Hide twenty pennies or other small goodies in the sand. Let your child use a spoon to hunt for them.

But It's Wet!
DOUSING WATER WOES

Playing in the sprinkler or kiddy pool is one of the joys of childhood—except some kids *hate* water, especially in their eyes. And some make a colossal muddy mess of the lawn or won't share the hose or take turns running through the sprinkler. And some won't get out of the pool to take their baths. Here are some ideas to ease these common water fusses.

But It's Wet!

This was the response from a neighbor kid when I suggested he play in the sprinkler with the other kids one day. He was right—it *was* wet, and there wasn't anything we could do about that. But we lured him in by turning the water *way* down. And using the sprinkler that sprayed in a continuous pattern rather than alternating. These two tactics—making it small and predictable—make it easier for timid kids (and those who detest water in their eyes) to enjoy water play. Goggles help some kids, too.

And Cold!

My middle kid is a polar bear and would swim happily in the Arctic Ocean in January, but the other two turn blue in a warm bath. Because of them, I've learned lots of tricks for heating up kiddy pools. The easiest strategy is to fill the pool as soon as you get up and let the sun take care of the problem. But if you're impatient like us, and you have a utility sink in the garage or basement, you may be able to hook up a hose—most utility faucets have threads for attaching hoses—and fill the pool directly with warm water. (I put this obvious idea in because it took me years to realize it.) Or, fill pails of water in the sink or tub with the hottest water possible, dump them in the pool first, and add cold hose water until the water feels comfortable. If you think ahead, you can also heat water in jugs inside a hot vehicle.

TRY THIS!

One family we know had a plumber add a hot water tap next to one of the existing cold water ones outside. They used a "Y" hose attachment to mix hot and cold water. Then they had warm water available for filling kiddy pools or washing cars.

Wet Mess Taming

Move the kiddy pool daily and shift the sprinkler to new spots frequently to avoid killed grass and mud puddles fit for a pig. (Mark spots, set the timer, and put the kids in charge of moving the hose.) We often put the pool in the driveway or on the deck, which also forced us to empty it daily (and that also helps avoid bacterial contamination). When you empty the pool, you can set up a bucket brigade with the kids to water the garden and go easy on the lawn.

Another low-mess strategy is to rely more on a water-table (like preschools and daycares use) than the kiddy pool. Don't have a water table? You can purchase one through www.childcraft.com (they offer a wide array of sizes and prices), and major toy stores sometimes carry smaller sand/water tables during the summer. Or, simply set large bins of water on a low table or wall.

"It's *My* Turn for the Hose!"

Those are the shrieks we can all do without. Options: only grownups use the hose (good idea if you're conserving water), use a timer to create equal turns, or buy a Y-attachment for the spigot and hook up two hoses—then duck.

Sneaky Clean Strategies

Once in, my kids never wanted out of the sprinkler or pool, so I just snuck in some bathing while they played. Younger preschoolers may happily undress altogether, but older ones can wear a bathing suit to accommodate their growing modesty. Warn your child that soap will make everything more slippery—he should sit down as he does in the tub. Use Ivory soap (which floats) or liquid soap to avoid losing the soap on the bottom of the pool. Rinse your child with the hose (if he doesn't mind the cold), a watering can, a milk jug studded with holes—or try a camp shower, usually available for less than $20 where camping supplies are sold.

Turn-Taking Unscrewed:
BACKYARD ETIQUETTE

Ahh, the sounds of children playing. "It's my turn on the slide!" "He squirted me!" "She took my swing!" "He ran into me with the Cozy Coupe!" And so on. Isn't it delightful? Try some of these tips to tame the chaos and conflict that often define outdoor play.

Swing Timers

I have never yet found a backyard play set with enough swings. No matter how many you put up, at least one extra kid will come to play. Unfortunately, it's hard to hear the stove timer from the swing set. We've used a variety of other timers to structure turns. Here are some ideas that work for swings, ride-ons, and other equipment:

- *Improvised Sand Timer* Set a strainer or funnel on top of a bucket or other container. Use another container to add a *big* scoop of sand. When all the sand's in the bucket, it's time to switch swingers. (Use several scoops per turn if necessary—the non-rider can scoop.)

- *Sing Timer* We sang a made-up dorky swing song when the kids were babies, and it just became an unofficial swing timer. When the song ended (or sometimes after the second or third round), the swinger got off, and the next kid got on for his version of the song. You can make up or choose your own dorky song, but ours went like this (sung in rhythm with the swing):

> *Swing, swing, swing, swing.*
>   *(Child's name) can swing, swing.*
> *Back and forth, and up and down,*
>   *(child's name) can swing, swing.*
> *Swing, swing, swing, swing.*

Told you it was dorky.

- *Three More Pushes* This gives kids a warning that the transition is coming and is easier for them to grasp than "two more minutes."

Slide Rules

You know how playgrounds always post rules about no walking up the slide? Well, kids love to do that. But you don't have to be a genius to see that some spectacular accidents are waiting to happen if some kids are going up and others are coming down. Plus the whole "whose turn is it?" thing gets messed up. We had a rule that you could travel on the slide however you wanted if you were alone, but if there was a group we announced "regular" or "backwards" (climb up) slide times. To avoid the tendency of bigger kids pushing littler kids out of the way, we also had everyone match up with a slide buddy—your turn always followed the same kid's.

Squirts Who Squirt

"Ask before you squirt." That's a good rule, especially if you are trying to read the washer repair manual. "Aim for the tummy or lower" is another good rule, but it will be broken constantly. Even better is getting the kids focused on squirting *things* rather than each other. Try squirting a beach ball to make it move, targets like a bucket on its side, or a picture drawn with chalk to erase it. Grownups in my household find that household mister bottles set on "spray" work fine and are less likely to cause tears in the squirt-ee, but naturally the kids prefer the giant mega water blaster things, at least until *they* get squirted.

Ride-On Traffic School

No ramming. That's my number one rule. Also, no Cozy Coupe car-jackings. Pedestrians, especially of the toddler variety, *always* have right of way. If you act like a police officer and hand out tickets for infractions, you can enforce safety and sharing rules with a little humor—and that makes the lessons more effective. Using chalk or paint to mark lanes or roads and crosswalks also seems to reduce road rage, as will timers for turn-taking.

 TRY THIS!

Mix sand into latex exterior paint for a decent driveway paint if you want your road markings to be more permanent. While you're at it, paint some parking spots for all the vehicles. Turn everyone into valet parking attendants at the end of play, and kids may actually stow their vehicles cheerfully.

Bug Zappers:
KEEPING CREEPY CRAWLERS AT BAY

Worrying about bug bites, stings, or bothers may completely ruin your child's (and your) enjoyment of the outdoors. Keep your little snuggy-bug protected outside with these strategies.

Buzzy Bee Chant

Even children who have never been stung may panic when a bee flies near. Teach your child to stand absolutely still, close his eyes, and chant

MORE TO KNOW

Honeybees die when they sting. That means that the bee will only sting when it feels its life is in danger. If your child doesn't bother the bee, it won't want to bother her.

I'm still as a statue, can't you see?
So buzzy bee, fly away from me!

This chant forces the child to stay motionless (which reduces the chance that he'll anger the bee and get stung) and creates a delay—by the time he opens his eyes, the bee will probably have disappeared. It also gives the child a feeling of control over the bee—and increasing control is a sure-fire method for reducing fear.

The Shoe Fly Shuffle

Flies, whether biting or merely annoying, are the opposites of bees—they are more likely to bother you when you're still. Show your child how to dance around, waving her arms, as she sings the classic:

Shoo fly, don't bother me,
Shoo fly, don't bother me,
Shoo fly, don't bother me,
For I belong to somebody!

Dress—and Scent—for Success

Wearing white or light-colored clothing and avoiding floral prints and hair accessories will make your child less attractive to bugs. Also, encourage your child to wear shoes or sandals to protect her feet from stings. In the woods or tall grass areas, she should wear long pants (tucked into socks) and long sleeves to guard against tick bites, chiggers, and biting flies.

Avoid having your child use scented lotions, soaps, shampoos, and so on during bug seasons. Especially avoid sweet and fruity scents—you don't want your child to smell like a flower or food! Other scents seem to repel bugs. Burning citronella candles will reduce mosquito attacks at night. Adding garlic to your child's diet may make her stinky to mosquitoes and many other bugs.

More Ways to Keep Bugs at Bay

- Empty standing water. (It's a breeding ground for mosquito larvae.)
- Apply DEET-free bug repellents (or use those formulated in child-safe concentrations). Some people recommend Skin So Soft bath oil by Avon as an effective repellent.
- Make a sign designating your yard a "No Bugging Zone" and threatening violators with removal from the premises. (It won't really work, of course, but it will make your child feel more in control).
- Near play areas, plant basil to check mosquitoes (and avoid planting bee-attracting flowers).
- Use yellow bug lights to keep evening bugs away.
- Check play areas regularly for webs, hives, and bug nests and remove them.
- Avoid using bug zappers (recent research suggests they may actually attract bugs) or strong pesticides (which may harm young children's rapidly developing bodies and brains).

The Ants' Picnic
AND OTHER WAYS TO BEFRIEND BUGS

Making friends with a few bugs is one of the best ways to get kids over their creepy-crawly fears. And what better way to make friends than to invite them to a picnic? While your child is preparing this miniature meal for his new buddies, he can also fix a snack for himself.

Suggested Menu

- peanut butter and jelly triangles
- chips
- cake with frosting
- juice

Ingredients

- three slices of bread
- peanut butter and jelly
- one potato chip
- a tablespoon of confectioner's sugar
- one-quarter teaspoon of water
- one teaspoon of cream cheese (optional)
- a few drops of juice
- a rolling pin, plastic knife, and a bottle cap

You Also Need

- cloth napkin, bandanna, or other square of fabric for a picnic cloth
- miniature doll dishes (like for Barbie or G.I. Joe) or natural "dishes" like acorn caps
- small leaves, shells, or seed pods
- a paper napkin
- a paper drink parasol (optional)

- a small sign announcing "This Way to the Ant Family Picnic" (also optional)
- a large magnifying glass for close observation

Have your child roll two slices of bread flat with a rolling pin. He should spread a thin layer of peanut butter on one and jelly on the other and put them together. Then he can cut a narrow strip off and slice it into a series of triangles. Next, have him break the chip into tiny pieces, and place the mini sandwiches and chips on plates.

To make the cake, your child can cut two circles from the third piece of bread, using the bottle cap as a cutter. Help him combine the confectioner's sugar with a few drops of water (and cream cheese if you have some), mixing it to a frosting-like consistency. (He can add barely a drop of food coloring if he'd like tinted frosting.) Have him spread some of the frosting on one bread circle and top it with the other. He can then frost the entire outside of the cake. If he'd like, have him decorate it with a few cake sprinkles or a teaspoon of granulated sugar mixed with just a drop of food coloring. Put the cake on another plate (cut one slice out for appearance if desired). Ants love this cake, and they don't care if it looks a bit lopsided or the frosting is runny.

Lay the picnic cloth outside, preferably near an anthill or existing "trail." Arrange all the food on the cloth. Use an eyedropper to put a little juice in doll cups or acorn caps. Help your child cut a strip along the fold of the paper napkin and divide it into several tiny napkins for the ants, and place them under the plates. Set up the parasol and sign. Then, have your child eat his own picnic (of the leftovers) before the ants come! Check the picnic every fifteen minutes or so for activity. Once the ants arrive, examine their behavior with the magnifying glass.

Roly Poly Races

Roly polies (also called pill bugs, sow bugs, potato bugs, and armadillo bugs) are favorites of young children because they do not bite, are easy to catch, and are relatively difficult to squish. Look for them among decaying

MORE TO KNOW

Pill bugs are more closely related to lobsters than to ants. In fact, they are the most numerous land crustacean. Children love to examine their overlapping plates of armor with a magnifying glass. Another fun observation: Put a drop of water near a pill bug. When it's thirsty, it will dip its bottom into the water to drink! For more on these interesting bugs, read about keeping them as pets in *Mudpies to Magnets* by Robert A. Williams, Robert E. Rockwell, and Elizabeth A. Sherwood. You can also learn about them on the web at www.udel.edu/msmith/pillbugs.html.

plant matter (under logs or rocks, on the compost pile). Once you've collected several, you're ready for a race! Cut a circle from a piece of paper. Examine the bugs for distinguishing features (color, size, etc.) and have everyone pick a favorite. Place all the bugs in the center of the circle and watch what happens. The winner is the first to leave the circle. Replace the bugs where you found them after the race.

Did your bugs just curl up and stay put? Then you have pill bugs rather than potato bugs. Pill bugs curl into a ball to protect themselves. Their nearly identical cousins, the potato bugs, make a break for it. You can tell the difference between the two by checking their butts—potato bugs have little spiky things sticking out from theirs.

Taking the Sting out of Stings
AND THE BITE OUT OF BITES

If your child does get stung or bitten by a bug, prompt first aid will help him feel better, minimize the reaction, and lessen the chances he'll develop a lasting fear.

Stings

Honeybees leave a stinger behind in the skin. Remove it by scraping a dull knife, credit card, or fingernail across it. Do not use tweezers—squeezing the stinger will only force out more venom. Wash the area with soap and water. Apply ice to the area, give your child an oral antihistamine like Benadryl, and observe her for signs of a serious allergic reaction. Ease the pain and itch further by applying calamine lotion, a paste made from baking soda and water, or some antiperspirant. (Really! These work on all bites and stings.)

Wasps, hornets, and yellow jackets do not leave stingers but may sting multiple times. Treat all the sting sites as you would bee stings, and again, be sure to watch your child for allergic reactions.

The biggest problem, though, is likely to be your child's reaction to the experience. See the next activity for suggestions on coping with her pain and distress, and "Bug Zappers" above for dealing with her ongoing fears.

Tick Bites

If you find an attached tick on your child's skin, remove it promptly. Grasp the body with tweezers and pull away from the attached end. Do not use a match to make it "let go." It doesn't work, and you might accidentally burn your child, adding to his troubles. Clean the area with rubbing alcohol and keep an eye on the site for signs of Lyme's disease (bull's eye rash, fatigue, flu-like symptoms).

Ticks, chiggers, and other blood-sucker guys gross out kids. Plus their parents. But playing up the black humor aspect actually seems to soothe some kids (especially boys). For example, try cracking jokes about the bug "vanting to suck your bloooood" or fake-scolding your child for inviting so many little friends to have "dinner on him" without first asking your permission.

Mosquito Bites

Typically the only problem with these is that they cause itching. Often the bites will bother your kids more early in the morning and at bedtime.

Try After Bite, an ammonia-based "stick," as soon as possible after the bite occurs. (You can also just apply a little household ammonia with a cotton ball or swab.) Other techniques to soothe itching include applying ice, calamine lotion, or cornstarch paste or, for numerous bites, an oatmeal bath (grind quick oats in a blender and add a cup to the bath or use a commercial preparation like Aveeno). If your child runs a fever following bites and encephalitis or West Nile virus has been reported in your area, check with your child's doctor.

SAFETY ZONE

Signs of a severe allergic reaction, whether to a bite, sting, or some other allergen, can include severe swelling near the site or of the affected limb, tightness in the throat or a swollen tongue, shortness of breath, vomiting, and collapse. These indicate a medical emergency—call 911.

ON THE WEB

There are many excellent websites with current information on first aid for all kinds of bites and stings, as well as other childhood injuries. Two excellent general sites are www.kidshealth.org and www.mayoclinic.com. One of my favorite starting sites, though, is www.healthynj.org, which has a great listing of up-to-date links.

All Better Now!
TAKING CARE OF BONKS AND BOO-BOOS

Whatever the injury, a few strategies will make your first aid more effective. First, examine the boo-boo if your child is concerned about it, no matter how minor it seems—your looking at it is respectful and reassuring. If the injury requires treatment, tell your child you will help her feel better, but it may sting for a few more minutes. Talk to your child about each step, and warn her about how it may feel. See "First Aid (and Later Aid) for Feelings" on page 141 for more ideas on minimizing emotional upset.

Cuts and Scrapes

Wash the area with warm water and soap. A squeeze bottle will help you aim (and rinse out dirt more forcefully). Apply some liquid soap to a cotton ball or pad and wash the area gently. (This may hurt.) Rinse the soap off, pat the area dry, and apply an antiseptic cream or spray. Many children find Bactine soothing on scrapes. Neosporine and similar antibiotic creams are available in formulas with painkillers. They may, however, take several minutes to start working. Treat mouth cuts with Popsicles.

The sight of blood freaks many children out. Reassure your kid that she has plenty of blood, that her body can make new blood, and that her skin will grow back together. Nonetheless, many children will feel better if they cannot see the blood, so finish up with a bandage if desired. Or, better yet, *lots* of them. This goes even for those cuts visible only with a magnifying glass.

Bonks and Bruises

How you handle these depends partly on the incident and partly on your child. Some preschoolers need soothing after minor collisions with fast-moving molecules; others brush themselves off and keep going after accidents practically worthy of a 911 call.

Most minor accidents can be treated with some quick reassurance and a kiss. Say something like, "You're okay. It will just hurt for a minute. You can go play again." Humor helps some children, too—say something like, "Oh no! Did you bonk your boodle again?" Encourage your child to brush herself off and even to kiss her own boo-boos (you can give a kiss, too)—it's important for her to learn how to soothe herself.

Bigger bumps and bruises may need some ice. A bag of frozen peas makes a perfect ice bag. Wrap it in a dishcloth or pop it in an old pillowcase, so it doesn't come in direct contact with your child's skin. Most bumps will feel better well before the peas get mushy. Another good option is a baby's cold teething ring. Bruised areas can also be soaked in Epsom salts. (Follow the directions on the package.)

Splinter-Ease

Soak the area first to soften the skin and possibly loosen the splinter. If an end is protruding, use tweezers to grasp the end and pull it out.

SAFETY ZONE

When does a boo-boo need medical attention?
Call your doctor if:

- You think your child may need stitches. (The edges of the wound are gaping and won't stay closed; you can see white tissue underneath; bleeding will not stop after you apply pressure for several minutes.)

- You suspect a sprain or broken bone. (There is rapid or severe swelling and bruising; your child is not able to bear weight or use the limb after several hours; there is severe localized pain.)

- A child who has bumped his head loses consciousness, vomits, complains of dizziness or vision problems, or is pale or sleepy.

- A wound shows signs of infection (redness, oozing, ongoing pain) or fails to heal in a reasonable period of time.

For small splinters, you can try applying a dot of white glue (like Elmer's), letting it dry completely, then quickly peeling it off. Some people find that duct tape or a sticky bandage will also remove a small splinter. These last methods seem to work best for those super-fine, nearly invisible splinters.

If no end is sticking out, sterilize a needle with rubbing alcohol and use it to gently push back the skin around the splinter. This will hurt, so it helps to have someone hold your child firmly but kindly. Acknowledge that it may hurt sharply for a minute or two, but it will then feel better.

Methods that make your child feel like he has some control can lessen the pain. Give him choices like where he sits, or whether to try to numb the area first with ice or Bactine (though pre-numbing seems to be only moderately effective in my experience). You can also instruct your child to count to three or say "Now!" before you pull. Let him hold a magnifying glass or the tube of first aid cream. Finally, older preschoolers may be able to remove some splinters themselves.

Distraction may also aid removal. Call your child's attention to something around her and talk briskly about it. Give her something to eat and talk about how it tastes. Put on some peppy music, or seat her in front of a favorite video or a mirror to make faces.

First Aid (and Later Aid) for Feelings:
EMOTIONAL CARE OF BOO-BOOS

For most boo-boos, the first aid is pretty straightforward. Wash cuts with soap and water, dab on antibiotic ointment, and cover with as many Band-aids as possible. Put ice on bonks and bruises. Administer kisses for everything. But taking care of boo-booed feelings can be a bit trickier. These ideas may speed recovery and lessen the chance that your child will overreact to minor injuries.

Feelings First Aid

- Let a distressed child "borrow" your calm.
- Speak quietly in a low voice.
- Hold her firmly and close.
- Talk through what you are doing to help her feel better.
- Reassure her that the pain will soon stop, and that her body will heal and feel better.

MORE TO KNOW

Many children hyperventilate when they are scared—they actually breathe in too much oxygen and exhale too little carbon dioxide. This will make them feel dizzy and like they can't breathe. Have your child breathe into her cupped hands or a paper bag if you suspect she is hyperventilating. This will force her to re-breathe some carbon dioxide and restore the proper balance of the gases. Talk to her about what is happening in her body and what she can do to make it better herself. Praise her for her efforts.

- Allow her to cry, but encourage her to take deep breaths in and blow slow breaths out.
- Stroke her and urge her to loosen her muscles and go floppy like a beanie animal. (When she tightens her muscles, it makes the pain greater.)
- Praise her for her efforts to be calm and "brave" or "tough."

Later Aid

After a sting or major (to her) accident, your child will need opportunities to relive the experience and to talk about her feelings. Try some of these activities to help her work through the aftermath.

- Have her color her feelings. She can show how scared she felt with one color, how much it hurt with another, and how angry she was with a third.
- Show her ways to help you understand how much it hurt or how scared she was. She can hold her arms apart at varying distances, or rate it on a one-to-ten scale (compared to other hurts she has had).
- Use humor, if that suits your child. Ask her if the sidewalk is dented now or if that bee has learned its lesson. (Be careful not to belittle your child's real pain—not all children like this humorous approach.)
- Share similar experiences you have had and describe how you got better.
- Let her tell the story of the incident to sympathetic others, like grandparents.
- Help her act out the incident with small figures or draw pictures of what happened. A doctor kit may let her reenact the aftermath, too. Playmobil makes nice hospital/doctor figures and props, as well as a dentist set-up. They're relatively expensive toys, but the investment may be worth it for a traumatized child.

- Examine the wound daily and note the changes that show it is healing.
- Praise her for her courage and for coping with a difficult and painful experience.
- Keep in mind that most children will need to talk about stings or big injuries on repeated occasions.

LITERATURE LINK

Children who have been stung by bees often enjoy reading about Ferdinand the Bull's encounter with an angry bumblebee in the classic *The Adventures of Ferdinand* by Munro Leaf. (It is also reassuring to them to see that Ferdinand is able to return to his favorite spot under the tree without being stung again.)

CHAPTER SIX

Arsenic Hour
Antidotes

The first time I heard the phrase "Arsenic Hour" I knew instantly what time of day it must refer to. At the time, I had several children—wait, it was just one kid, but it seemed like several—and Kyle turned into a beast precisely at 5:32 every evening. Exactly the time when I emerged from my study, where I was trying to finish my dissertation, paid the sitter, and scrambled around trying to make an appealing dinner from leftover chicken and a bag of freezer-burned broccoli that Kyle wouldn't touch with a ten-foot pirate sword. Let's just say it was not a pleasant time of day. By the time my husband arrived home many hours later at 6:30, he probably wished he hadn't, but he was careful not to say anything because he didn't want to get ripped to shreds by his snarling wife and child.

For a time, I tried relegating my little beast to telly limbo with a *cup-oo,* as he called it, of apple juice and a few graham crackers. All right, it was a whole package of them. Still, this approach sort of worked. He sat quietly in front of the television with *Mr. Rogers* and *Reading Rainbow* while I puttered and nibbled in the kitchen. The problem was that by the time my husband got home, Kyle was zooming around on a TV and sugar high, completely uninterested in any food with nutrients, and I was more starved for companionship than dinner, having done a fair bit of taste-testing while I cooked. Dinnertime remained unpleasant.

The article that called this time of day "Arsenic Hour" had lots of suggestions for combating it, all of which involved spending Quality Time on the floor with your kid, and none of which helped get dinner on the table. So I went back to the drawing table. Many years, several kids, and much experimentation later, I have developed a rough formula for Arsenic Hour antidotes, of which, fortunately, there are a variety that work. The primary ingredient of mine is a *dollop* of that infamous quality time and/or some soothing sensory activities. The second is a little food—not a package of graham crackers, but some high-quality nutrition, either in small enough quantities just to whet appetites or in large enough quantities to sate them (in which I case I expect the kids to join us at the dinner table for dessert only).

Finally, the key secret ingredient—getting the kids to help with dinner preparations. This ingredient does not work every night, nor in every family. My energy reserves have to be reasonably great, or I just don't have the patience for being helped. (Low afternoon energy is why I insist on quality-time activities I enjoy—for example, I absolutely refuse to play the card game War, having exhausted my lifetime supply of tolerance for that interminable game ages ago—and I join the kids in eating a reasonably nutritious snack.) If I can get myself in the mood to accept help, we tend to have great family dinners—followed by delightful family time and a smooth bedtime routine. I'm not sure why this works, but I suspect it's because I feel less resentful and used when everyone pitches in, and the kids are less likely to complain about the meal when they have helped prepare it. From there, the evening evolves in a virtuous spiral (the opposite of a vicious circle), and life seems good.

You'll probably have to do some adjusting to create the perfect recipe to counteract your own family's version of evening poison, but I hope you find some of the raw ingredients in this chapter helpful in creating some better end-of-day transitions.

Reunion Rituals:
BACK TOGETHER TACTICS

Coming together again is one of the big events of this time of day in most families. Although we tend to think of reunions as happy, many pre-schoolers melt down when faced with the transition. Simple rituals give structure to the return, so your child knows exactly what to do or say when you come together again. Try some of these rituals to make your hellos happier all around.

Pick Up Lines

Have a consistent phrase to say when you greet your child—and make sure she has a stock reply for you. An exchange like, "Where's my Sweet Petunia?"—"Here I am, Daddy, ready for picking!" may seem syrupy sweet, but most young kids find these exchanges funny and comforting.

One family we knew used riddles to make good-byes and hellos easier. The dad asked his son a riddle every morning at drop-off. At pick-up, the son supplied the answer if he could and the dad shared his intended answer. Knock-knock jokes work too.

Pocket Surprises

What kid doesn't like to hunt through pockets for a surprise? Obviously, you don't want to make hellos expensive, greedy affairs—so focus on surprise rather than stuff. You can hide a piece of a puzzle in a pocket daily and let your kid gradually assemble the whole thing. Pieces of other put-together toys work too (Legos, Tinker Toys, blocks). Or hide something from your day—a natural object you found, an office supply that can be reused, an object that sparks a story. You can also hide a small toy day after day in different pockets—"Where's Tiny Teddy today?"

Show and Tell

Have your child get in the habit of showing you *one* thing from her day and telling you about it. Art projects are a natural for this activity, but she can also show you items in her classroom or on the playground.

Welcoming Committees

What could be better than being greeted by a herd of wild things? Probably peace and quiet, but if you wanted that, you shouldn't have had kids. Teach your kids to recognize signs that a parent is arriving home (mine listen for the garage door opening) and then assemble for a vigorous welcome. When they were small, each of the boys attached himself to one of Dad's legs (sitting on his foot), and my daughter got carried. Dad then Frankenstein-shuffled over to the steps, where everyone unloaded. Many kids like to be in charge of turning on outside lights, getting the newspaper, or doing other "Father Knows Best" kinds of rituals to greet a returning parent.

MORE TO KNOW

If you are picking your child up from a caregiver, she may act angry or aloof. Some kids dawdle or delay maddeningly. These are normal reactions, so don't panic—your child still loves you. She's just been saving up feelings for you, her safety net. Or, she may just need help handling the transition.

Find Me!

Hide-and-seek games make kids feel in control, and are fun and exciting. Preschoolers often like to hide in the same place every day. My daughter used to hide in my husband's closet so he could discover her when he went to change out of his suit. Then he'd throw her on the bed and tickle her.

Attention!
A MINUTE IN TIME SAVES NINE

A few minutes of undivided attention can refuel a young child enough to make it to dinner, so it's worth delaying meal preparations to share a five- or ten-minute togetherness ritual every evening. Schedule it for a consistent time, and treat it like a major meeting with your boss—no interruptions, no excuses, no delays.

Game Time

Begin an ongoing daily tournament. Choose a short game to play each day, play a portion daily of a longer game, or flip a coin to decide who gets to choose from a list of acceptable choices. If necessary, adapt the game to make it shorter (for example, play War once through the deck and then count cards for a winner or play a game for five minutes and see who's ahead). Some children may enjoy keeping a running score and watching how the numbers mount up over time.

Color-Talk

Put out crayons or markers and either plain paper or coloring books. Sit side-by-side and work on your own masterpieces. Use the time to talk about your days or problems that are bothering either of you. (It is often easier to have a discussion with a child when he is half-focused on another task.)

Pretend-ercise

A good stretch and five minutes of brisk calisthenics or dancing may revive you both. Make the exercise child-friendly by using imaginative movements and appropriate music. For example, put on something from the musical *Cats* by Andrew Lloyd Webber. Start by curling up like a sleeping cat, then unfolding and stretching your rump up in the air. Next arch your back like an angry cat. Pretend you are rubbing against someone's leg or rolling in the dust. Claw your way up an imaginary screen door, and stretch to swat at the butterflies overhead. Then sneak after a mouse, pounce, and get chased by a dog around and around the room. Finish up by choosing a patch of sunshine to curl up in for a quick petting before returning to your human form.

Other exercise will revitalize you, too. Have a skipping race, walk around the block, zip up and down the stairs a few times, play tag-team tickle wrestling, jog beside your kid while he pedals his tricycle, or toss a ball outside for five minutes.

Story Minute

Read a picture book each day at this time. Then set your child up with props to reenact or make up a sequel to the story. You could also listen to a book on tape together (try the public library's collection)—you can cook while your kid draws or acts out the tale.

Or, try reading a story from a themed anthology or chapters of short, first chapter books. Books in this genre often have chapters that can stand alone as individual stories and may have simple illustrations on most spreads. Although many preschoolers will not initially have the stamina for more than a page or two, daily experiences with longer text will help them gradually build up their listening "muscles." Look for books like the Riverside Kids books by Johanna Hurwitz, the Pippi Longstocking series by Astrid Lindgren, or the Captain Underpants series by Dav Pilkey.

Snack City:
BEATING THE LOW-BLOOD-SUGAR BLUES

A well-timed nutritious snack may boost your child's mood without ruining his food intake for the day. Here are some ideas for healthy Arsenic Hour snacks.

Small Portions of Whatever Foods You are Preparing for Dinner

- Provide plain pasta with a couple of spoonfuls of sauce for dipping.

MORE TO KNOW

There are several advantages to feeding your child a healthy snack before dinner.

- He may be more willing to try new foods when they are offered as a snack.

- Young children have small stomachs and need to eat more frequently than adults.

- Your child may actually eat more when he is moderately hungry than once he becomes "starving."

- Children may be less distracted at snack time than at family meals, and so eat better.

- Chop fresh or cooked vegetables and offer some salad dressing dip.
- Serve small quantities of cooked meats on crackers.

Cheeses

- Cut some into tiny cubes, matchsticks, or other interesting shapes
- Melt some in microwave on crackers or bread.
- Offer a smorgasbord of several different types.

Other Dairy

- Spoon yogurt into a bowl. Place a dollop of jam in the center. Give child a plastic knife or toothpick to swirl it before eating.
- Mix yogurt with fruit or cereal.

- Combine a half-carton of yogurt, a spoonful or two of frozen juice concentrate, and a little milk in a plastic container (like a peanut butter jar). Give it to your child to shake vigorously, then drink.
- Sweeten milk with a little chocolate or strawberry syrup, instant breakfast powder, or a drop of vanilla extract (just a tiny amount—it contains alcohol).

Fruits and Veggies

- Warm a cup of canned or instant vegetable soup in the microwave.
- Cut apples into interesting slices, or serve with yogurt or peanut butter dip.
- Mix citrus juice (or frozen juice concentrate) with seltzer water for healthy "pop."
- Make banana circles or a banana-peanut butter sandwich (slice the banana in half lengthwise and spread with peanut butter).
- Drizzle precut veggies with low-fat ranch dressing (or other salad dressing).

Other

- Fix teeny tiny sandwiches by cutting a slice of bread into small squares. Serve with a spoonful of peanut butter or chopped lunch meat and let your child make her own miniature sandwiches.
- Pour a bowl of healthy cereal or instant oatmeal.
- Make a tortilla roll-up—put a slice or two of lunchmeat on a tortilla, roll up, and slice into "snails."
- Offer anything nutritious he normally hates.

Hug Bugs:
QUICKIE SNUGGLY, LOVEY-DOVEY GAMES

Irritable children can be transformed by touch. A loving connection can also change the way you feel about your grumpy child. Here are some love-ly touching games that take only minutes during a busy time of day.

Hug Bugs

When you have a crabby child hanging around your feet, start making a buzzing sound. Then say, "What's that noise? I wonder if it's some kind of bug." Continue buzzing and look around the room. Then shout, "Oh no! It's a giant Hug Bug!" Flap your wings and swoop down on your child.

Gather her in your arms and hug her tightly. Hug her arms and legs with firm squeezes. Hug her hands and fingers. Then be careful—a Lovey Bug might swarm in to cover everyone with smooches. Pretend to swat the bugs and return to your work. Phew!

Down at the Kiss Stop

Yell, "Whoo-oo! It's the Snuggle-Up Express. This is the Kiss Stop! All aboard!" Flop down on the floor for a pile-up. Wrestle, kiss, and cuddle every passenger. When everyone has had enough, call, "End of the line! Everybody disembark!"

Instant Kitty

Call, "Here (child's name) kitty, kitty, kitty." Show your child how to purr (make a rolling "R" sound or do raspberry lips) and rub against your legs. Bend down and give her scratches and soft strokes. Rub her cheeks and stroke the velvety fur on her nose. Throw an imaginary ball of yarn into the other room for her to chase. Tell her you'll call her again when you need another kitty fix. This game is good for breaking up sibling squabbles without getting involved—just call in the other child next and treat him like a puppy or pony or other beloved pet.

Touching Requests

Teach your child to recognize when she needs some nice touches. She may notice that she feels tired all over, is making "fighty fists," or has a Grumpy Gus face. Make up family names for different kinds of touches or please-touch-me games. Then she can ask for what she needs. Here are some names to get you started:

- *Tickle-Scritches* Soft, fast scratchy touching—usually on the back or scalp.
- *Squeezer-Wheezers* Quick squeeze and release of limbs or fingers, repeated to cover entire limb or all the fingers.
- *Pinchy-Crabs* Soft fast pinches of the loose skin on the back or arms. Done properly these should feel nice and leave a pleasant

tingly feeling. Gentle hair pulls (a tuft at a time, grasped near the scalp) also feel nice.

- *Karate Choppers* Do a quick tattoo with the sides of your hands up and down your child's back. Then have her reciprocate on you!

Popping Penguins:
GETTING THE JUMPY-JITTERIES OUT

In an open carpeted area, arrange cushions or pieces of cloth (like napkins or placemats) in a line. You can also use hula hoops or loops of string. Space them so the children can jump fairly easily from one to the next. Tell the children that they are penguins and they are going to jump from iceberg to iceberg. They need to take turns, though, because if they push, someone will miss the iceberg and fall in the ocean. Then, the leopard seal will come and get all of them!

When the first penguin reaches the third iceberg (or whatever seems good with your penguins), the next penguin can start popping. When the penguins reach the end of the floe, they zip around to the beginning and get in line again.

Vary the game by increasing the distance between the icebergs, using smaller or larger icebergs, arranging them differently (a side-to-side slaloming path is fun for older preschoolers), or joining in briefly to be the leopard seal. You can also use different themes, such as frogs hopping from lily pad to lily pad, aliens flying from planet to planet, or bees buzzing from flower to flower.

Set out a quiet activity for the penguins to do once they've gotten all their jumpies out.

Leaping Lizards

Jumping from a height repetitively seems not to hurt young joints the way it does mine. Set up an obstacle course of safe things to climb on and jump off of or hop over, like step stools, sofa cushions, telephone books, a certain height stair, and so on.

Popcorn

Pretend your children are popcorn kernels. Put them, curled into tight balls, into an imaginary microwave, and push the buttons. Narrate the heating process, having them puff up just a tiny bit, then Pop! Pop! Pop! Poppity Pop Pop! They can bounce around as long as you need them too. Still jumpy? Eat up that batch and start a fresh one.

Jump-olines

Mini-trampolines and inflatable bouncing cushions intended for young children are commercially available. If you have a high-activity-level child and a lifestyle or climate that forces a good deal of indoor time, consider investing in one. Jumping, because of the level of activity and its rhythmic, repetitive nature, is ideal for relieving tension and frustration. Put on some music like "Sweet Georgia Brown" by Johnny Mercer (it's the Globetrotters theme song), and show your child how to bounce to the beat.

My Little Red Wagon

A favorite of toddlers, the classic song "Bumping Up and Down in My Little Red Wagon" is also enjoyed by preschoolers, especially if you change the lyrics to making them wilder and sillier. Try variations like:

- Jumping up and down in my little red spaceship . . .
- Bopping up and down on my very fierce tiger . . .
- Oozing up and down on my little grey slug . . .
- Crashing all around in my little red racecar . . .
- Rolling round and round in my little brown barrel . . .

Mad about You
AND WHAT TO DO WITH THOSE FEELINGS

Most of the time you want to teach your children to express their feelings directly and deal with whatever the problem is. During Arsenic Hour, wake-up time, and other periods of low energy, though, the unhappy or angry feelings probably stem more from hunger and fatigue than from social issues. Teaching your child to dump, squash, transform, or swallow his overtired grumpies *is* appropriate. One of these techniques may help your child maintain a reasonable mood until his reserves are replenished.

Run the Bad Feelings out of Town

Running enough laps up and down the driveway or around the family room will chase away frustration for most kids. Tell him to imagine he is racing against his grumpies, and he has to run faster and faster so they don't catch him. Or increase interest by having your child be a spaceship blasting off to Jupiter or a racehorse galloping for the gold and leaving his "mad" in the dust.

Draw and Destroy

Have your child scribble his feelings all over a piece of paper (make sure you protect the underneath surface). Then he can tear the feelings into little pieces and throw them away. Or put them in an envelope and mail them to Antarctica. Or dig a hole in the compost pile and bury them so that, like manure, they'll break down into rich soil to help the flowers grow.

Turn a Frown Upside Down

Did you know that turning a somersault can magically reverse a frown? So can the appropriate magic spell. My daughter, though, likes the windowshade technique best. She slowly raises her hand from chin level to the top of her head, transforming her frown to a smile as her hand goes up. Sometimes it takes several tries before the shade will stay up, but it always does eventually.

Gnaw-Gnaw

Get out an old teething toy. Tell your child to gnaw the toy until she has chewed up all her grumpies. She can pretend to be a dog or an ogre that changes into a friendly frog if she likes.

Stomp Till You're Silly

Tell your child to scoop all his crabby feelings onto the floor and start stomping on them. (He might have to pull a stubborn sticky one out of his belly button or pretend-spit out an overlooked one.) You'll know he's cured when he's giggling and acting mighty silly!

Spit It Out

This is for in the bathroom or outside—preferably out of your earshot. Tell your child to go spit out all his grumpy feelings and misbehavior. Give him a cup of warm water so he can rinse and spit to his heart's content into the sink or onto the compost pile.

Grumpy Dolls

Probably you have seen those cute little South American worry dolls that usually come in an oval yellow box. The idea is that a child whispers worries to each of them before bed, puts them under his pillow, and in the morning, his worries are gone. Use a similar technique to rid your child of his sense of injustice. Hand him a pile of beanie guys or other small stuffed animals. Tell him to whisper one way that people are being mean to him to each stuffie. Then he can cram them into an old pillowcase and sit on them until he feels better. I've noticed that the whispering tends to be rather loud and emphatic with this technique, so you might need earplugs.

Whizzers:
BLOW UP YOUR CHILD'S BAD MOOD

Inflate a balloon while your child watches. Then let her hold the pinched neck and let it go. Together, watch the balloon whiz around the room until it falls, empty on the floor. Tell your child she can be a whizzer just like the balloon.

First, she should stand still with her eyes closed. Tell her to imagine that all her grumpies are filling her up and puffing her out, just like the air did to the balloon. (Most children will "expand" themselves, using their arms, legs, and cheeks.) When she is "full," gently squeeze a tuft of hair or "plug" her belly button, explaining that you are pinching her closed, just like you did the balloon. All the grumpies are trapped inside her, making her feel tight and uncomfortable.

Then pretend to release her. Whoosh! All her grumpies come pushing out. The force will send her whizzing around the room in circles and swirls and loops until her grumpies are gone and she just collapses limply on the floor. Narrate the process, and feel free to join your child. It will feel great for both of you!

Here are a couple of variations on Whizzers:

Squeezers

Pick one of your child's body parts, like her hand. Tell her to make a fist and squeeze it as tightly as she can. Have her pretend she is holding a piece of coal and squeezing it so hard it will turn into a diamond. Now she can let go and examine the beautiful diamond she has made. Have her notice too how tingly and loose her hand feels, like a floppy beanbag animal.

Then name another body part and give her images that will help her to tense it. For example, tell her to pretend she is eating a sour lemon. It's so sour it makes her whole face pucker into a tight ball. Then she can take a pretend sip of sweet, cool lemonade, rinsing away the sour taste and letting her mouth and face relax. Experiment with other images and actions like trying to plug her ears with her shoulders, using her knees to grasp a wiggly troll she has captured, or pretending to push the soles of her feet right through the floor and down into the earth beneath the building.

This is an easy activity to direct while you are engaged in meal preparations or other evening chores.

Floaters

Tell your sitting or reclining child to imagine that his arm is very heavy, as if an elephant were sitting on it. He can try to raise it up, but, oooh, that elephant is just too heavy. Then someone comes and pushes the elephant off. Next, he ties about a hundred helium balloons to his hand. Oh my! Now his arm is floating up and up and up because it's so light. Now a bird comes and pops the balloons. His arm settles back down. It feels just right again. Not too heavy, not too light. Aah! Repeat with other body parts.

Soothing Sounds:
TAMING THE WILD BEASTS

Use sound rituals to set the evening mood you want. Look for tapes or CDs of nature sounds, New Age music, or the classics at the public library. Other choices include tabletop water fountains, soft chimes, and rainsticks. If you have a range of choices, you can give your preschooler the important job of choosing the evening's selection. Set the timer for five minutes of Listen-Only Time while you all snuggle, eyes closed, and absorb the peaceful sounds he has selected. Or, try one of these games.

Thunderstorm

While you cook dinner, help your grumpy child create a storm using sounds she makes with her body. Have her sit on a cushion in the kitchen or next room with her eyes closed. In a low, gentle voice, instruct her to make a soft sound with her body like the rising whisper of the wind before a storm. She might try blowing gently while she waves her fingers in front of her mouth or rubbing her hands together. Then tell her that the wind is getting faster and wilder, and have her make a new sound, such as rubbing her hands faster or sliding her feet on the floor. Now the raindrops are starting—slowly and gently at first. Then louder and harder. Finally, the storm is right overhead with pouring rain and booming thunder. Soon the storm begins to pass. Gradually, slow everything down until again there is just a soft breeze. End by having your child make a beautiful sound like a rainbow might make if it were music. With each change, she has to think of a way to produce the appropriate sound and mood.

This game produces physical relaxation in part by increasing tension and then releasing it. Many classical music pieces use the same pattern. Occasionally play a rousing piece like the *1812 Overture* by Tchaikovsky (the cannons are an interesting percussion choice, according to both Calvin from Bill Watterson's *Calvin and Hobbes* comic strip and my middle son) and let your child move her body to it.

Tap Dancing

Tap out a beat with a wooden spoon, tongue clicks, or your foot and tell your child to move to it while you get dinner ready or take care of other chores. Vary the rate and volume of the sound. Compliment your child for adjusting her movements to fit the rhythm. Be sure to finish up with slow, quiet, soft taps. Or tap a rhythm and have your child tap it back to you. Start slow, speed up, then slow down again.

Body Part Ballet

While the evening's quiet music or sounds are playing, have your child move isolated body parts in ways that match or complement it. She can start with a finger dance, add her head, and so on. You can also suggest imaginary sounds or interesting peaceful images for her to create with her body movements. For example, direct her to move single fingers like a bouquet of opening flower buds, her arm like a charmed snake, or her legs up and down like waves.

Bag Of Tricks:
A HANDS-ON REMINDER LIST

Over a period of time, help your child assemble a personal bag or box of special objects that remind him of activities that comfort or relax him. He can also add things that evoke cheering memories or that remind him of big-kid skills he has (like using his words, or taking five when he's tired or overwhelmed). Suggest from time to time that he might like to add a new item to his bag of tricks. Periodically, also help him remove items that he has grown tired of. The bag can contain as many items as will fit, but ten to fifteen choices is plenty for most children. Here are some suggestions for your child's collection.

Things That Suggest an Activity

- Spade or funnel to remind about sand or water play
- Toy animal, doll, or vehicle
- Photographs of children swinging, jumping, running, rocking, spinning, etc.
- Crayon, marker, chalk, or other craft material to remind of easy art activities
- Jar of bubble soap
- Book
- Piece from a building set, like a wooden log or a block
- Item from a collection, like coins, buttons, or stamps

Things That Comfort or Remind about Soothers

- Photograph of him with a special stuffed animal or blanket
- Sachet
- Satin eye pillow (small pillow filled with herbs, meant to be rested on tired eyes—look for them at www.chinaberry.com or in some cosmetic departments)
- Tape of "happy" music or a music box
- Piece of clothing that smells like you or someone else he loves

- Scraps of silky ribbon, velvet, fake fur, and so on
- Small stuffed animal to whisper secrets to
- Photographs of relatives and special occasions

Skill Reminders and Take-Care-of-Myself Items

- Page of writing, a wind-up mouth, or other symbol for "use your words"
- Clock, wooden numeral five, or other symbol meaning "take five" or have a break
- Bandage (for those invisible boo-boos that don't feel better until they're covered)
- Plastic cup to get his own drink of water, or a juice box
- Single serving of a healthy snack
- Pair of dry underpants
- Lotion, lip balm

When your child complains about being bored, is whining, or is fighting with siblings, suggest that he get out his bag of tricks and try to solve his own problem. Older preschoolers may be able to use a poster or scrapbook of ideas instead of a bag of objects.

Prop Master:
A QUICK REMINDER OF GOOD TOYS FOR ARSENIC HOUR

The easiest way to get a child interested in a toy is to get it out and quietly start playing with it yourself. Before you know it, the kid will come take it over. Then you can leave.

Best Bets

- Scarves, ribbons, streamers, etc., for dancing
- Miniature play sets
- Toddler and other "outgrown" toys (Many children regress when they're tired.)

- Basic low-mess art supplies, like paper with crayons or washable markers, paint-with-water books, chalkboard or dry-erase board
- Sand and water toys (away from the eating area)
- Books, magazines, etc. (Try wordless books, comic books, detailed search books, anything with photos, boxes of duplicate photos, and junk mail.)
- Big box or laundry basket
- Collections to sort and examine
- Bubbles (for outside)
- Pattern blocks (Look for these at a school supply store.)
- Dress-up clothes and a mirror
- Dramatic play accessories (e.g., housekeeping equipment, doctor's kit, office supplies)
- Stuffed animals, especially big ones, puppets
- Child's tape recorder, with blank tapes, story tapes, and quiet music
- Sit 'N Spin–style toys, rocking horses, swings, mini-trampolines
- Pillows, beanbag chairs, old cushions, tumbling mats, blankets, or sheets for making simple forts
- Flashlight and accessories
- Felt boards, magnetic paper dolls, and vinyl sticker sets
- Play putty in a noncarpeted area, with colored newspaper (for making copies), small toys to "wrap up" or "dress up," items to impress, and room to bounce
- Large cardboard or foam blocks, bag of dry sponges, soft balls

Worst Bets

- Puzzles (especially ones that are challenging for your child)
- Challenge-level building sets (Most children are clumsier and more easily frustrated when they are tired and hungry.)
- Any art material, like paint, that makes a big mess (You won't want to clean it up.)
- Sports equipment requiring coordination to use properly
- Most competitive board games

- Toys intended for older children
- Electronic or other noisy toys (They'll irritate everyone.)
- Challenging computer or video games
- Television or videos (They seem appealing, but research shows that children are often more restless, irritable, and even aggressive after "watching" activities—if you do opt for this, choose a high-quality participation show like *Barney.*)

Captain Cook:
DIRECTING ALL HANDS IN THE GALLEY

Young kitchen helpers usually need some direction or they are merely a nuisance. During Arsenic Hour, though, my patience is generally in short supply, so I find it hard to calmly direct little people in a nice teacher voice. Fortunately, imagination comes to the rescue, letting me be a bit dictatorial in a polite sort of way—as a pirate captain. So, Captain Cook, put on your plumed hat, unsheathe your sword, and order your hands to their stations in the galley. Be sure to talk in your best pirate voice, throwing in lots of good pirate talk, like "Shiver me timbers" and "D'ya want to walk the plank?" Assign nautical theme chores like these.

Swab the Deck

Give your child a damp paper towel and send her on a search-and-destroy mission for all the sticky spots and dirt marks.

Mind the Prisoners

Your child can be in charge of keeping younger siblings out of trouble. (Try throwing all of them in the brig—i.e., playpen or playroom—together.)

Feed the Croc

Substitute real pets for imaginary crocodiles if you have them. If not, get your child in a cooperative mood by enlisting his help with this pretend task, then slipping in a request for real help. For example, say, "Ahoy there, matey! Feed this (imaginary food) to the croc over there before he comes after my other hand! Then, put this empty can in the recycling bin! And that's an order."

Grog Master

Put your preschooler in charge of getting drinks ready. If you store cups and glasses within reach, she can carry them to the table and put ice cubes in water glasses. An older preschooler can pour water or milk from a small pitcher (which you will probably have to refill for her before she finishes).

Have your child place each glass in a pie tin before she pours. Then, if she does spill, the mess will probably land in the tin instead of all over the floor or table. She will feel more competent, and you will be less harried.

Whistle Up the Crew

A la Mr. Smee in *Peter Pan*, send your child to call "All hands on deck! All hands on deck!" and assemble everyone at the table.

More Themed Helping

Your child will also enjoy helping with meal preparations as:
- *A robot* Program him to do tasks like fetch and carry.
- *A butler* You can be the cook preparing food for the royal family. Your child can polish the silver, set the table, and announce in a stuffy voice that "dinner is served." You can also turn him into a scullery maid, and get some "help" scouring the pots you're soaking.
- *A cowhand* Your child can load up his "chuckwagon" or cart and gallop off to set the table, return ingredients to the pantry, or carry garbage out.
- *An angel* Let her flit about fluffing up the clouds (beating with a whisk) and polishing the harps (drying some unbreakable dishes).

More Cooking Chores for Short Chefs:
EASY AND SATISFYING KITCHEN JOBS

I always felt bad when my little guys wanted to help and I couldn't think up anything genuinely useful for them to do. You might want to photocopy this list and post it on the inside of a cupboard door, so you'll be able to come up with a task on the spot and won't have to live with the guilt of refusing your little darlings' sweet offers.

- Wash produce. (Rinse by hand, scrub with a brush, or rinse in a colander or sieve.) Give a preschooler a potato in a basin of water and she may stay busy for ten minutes. And that will be one clean potato!
- Dry washed produce (with paper towels or using a salad spinner).
- Add ingredients you've measured.
- Scramble eggs, whisk runny batters, stir (as long as it's not too hot or on the stove—use a *large* bowl to minimize spills).
- Dredge meats in flour, bread crumbs, or potato flakes. (Make sure she scrubs her hands when she's done.)
- Shake meats or other foods in a bag of seasonings, sugar, etc.
- Taste-test (unless it's too hot).
- Put ice cubes in drink glasses.
- Hand you the right item from a canister or drawer of kitchen tools, as long as it's not sharp. (Pretend you're a surgeon for this task, e.g., "Spatula, please.")
- Push the buttons on the microwave, blender, or food processor under your supervision.
- Sprinkle salt or other seasonings, sprinkle grated cheese on pizza or pasta.
- Cut dough with a cookie cutter (with supervision regarding placement of the cutter).
- Pick through blueberries or other produce to get rid of the gross ones.
- Peel hard-cooked eggs or tangerines.

- Slice hard-cooked eggs with an egg slicer.
- Cut chives with safety scissors.
- Put dollops of sour cream or whipped cream on foods about to be served.
- Snap snap beans or shell peas.
- Grind pepper.
- Husk corn (and spend hours pulling off the silk threads individually).
- Sift. Probably with help.
- Pack brown sugar down in a measuring cup.
- Line up raisins on the cream cheese stuffed into celery for the classic "ants on a log" snack.
- Shell peanuts.
- Roll lemons or other citrus fruits before juicing them.
- Help to squeeze citrus fruits for juice.
- Squeeze garlic in a press. Maybe. If their hand strength is good.

CHAPTER SEVEN

Don't Throw in the Dish Towel Yet: Winning Food Fights

When I was a kid I hated most food, except for canned green beans, slices of raw cucumber sprinkled lightly with salt, Captain Crunch cereal, and anything chocolate. I particularly despised milk. Although my parents were not Clean Plate Dictators, they did require us kids to eat a reasonable amount of dinner and drink our milk if we wanted dessert. And I wanted dessert.

So, each night after I finished my cucumber slices and green beans, I began my conjuring act. I'd pop a bite of pot roast in my mouth, chew it quickly while holding my breath (so I wouldn't taste it), and then wipe my mouth. With a little sleight of tongue, I deposited bite after bite into my increasingly bulging napkin. However, I could not figure out how to work the same magic trick with my milk. The paper napkins disintegrated after several mouthfuls of milk, dropping wads of incriminating pot roast cud onto the linoleum. Thus, I was stuck sitting patiently at the table until everyone else finished eating and went to do homework or play games. Then I'd sit a little longer, toying with the couple of remaining bites of pot roast until my mother washed the dishes and joined the others. As soon as the door swung shut behind her, I jumped up, poured my milk down the drain, disposed of my loaded napkin, and fetched mom back to witness my finished meal. Ta da! Time for chocolate!

Meals are much more than food. For the young child, they are a prime opportunity for whining. Partly this is because preschoolers like whining, but partly it's because mealtime may tax your child's resources to the max. During mealtime, he must struggle with tricky utensils, carry on complex conversations, sit fairly quietly in his seat, remember arbitrary rules like not talking with his mouth full, and be careful not to make a mess. And food can be an issue, too. He may be expected to screw up his courage and taste new foods. He may have to cope with strong feelings like disappointment about what *isn't* served or disgust with what *is* or simply surprise at *how* it's prepared. Or try to think of ways to make the gross stuff like pot roast and milk disappear magically—and all this when he's hungry (or *not*, but supposed to be)!

No wonder many parents give up on family meals and simply serve peanut butter sandwiches (crustless and cut properly on the diagonal) to the kids before eating their own dinner later. This strategy is fine to reduce stress periodically, but I urge you to persist in having family meals several times a week. Meals present a multitude of well-documented learning opportunities for young children and are a perfect chance for emotional closeness. This chapter has ideas for helping you cope with eaters as picky as I was and dealing with the worst of the dining issues.

Finally, some reminders for memorable meals:
- Focus more on conversation than manners.
- Remember that it is your job to offer nutritious food—and your child's to choose how much or even whether to eat it.
- Offer at least one food you know your child likes.
- Expect children to take one *small* taste of new foods.
- Be calm and matter-of-fact about spills and accidents and let him help clean up.
- Serve chocolate for dessert.

Come to the Table:
CREATING A PRE-MEAL ROUTINE

Even parents who value family meals can find it difficult to schedule them. Keep in mind that the meals don't all have to be dinner. Breakfast and even snack time also give opportunities for conversation and togetherness. And not everyone needs to eat the same thing, or even eat at all, if the schedule doesn't suit appetites. For example, if the adults in the house eat late, it may work best to feed the children early, and have them eat fruit or other dessert while the adults have dinner. But whatever folks are eating, the meal will get off to a better start with a routine that brings everyone to the table ready to dine. Try something simple like this:

Step One: *Warning! Warning! Ten Minutes to Supper!*

A ten-minute warning will give the kids a chance to find a stopping point in their play (and maybe even tidy up a bit, like they do at school) before they pronounce the dinner "Yucky!" I also recommend using a catch phrase, like a stuffy butler's "Mah-dohm, dinner is about to be served!"

Step Two: *Scrub In*

Like a surgeon. (Or you can substitute my lazy approach—passing around a bottle of Purell before the salad.) Actually, this is a good time for a genuine cleaning. Provide some fingernail scrubbers and a little instruction in how doctors and nurses wash up before surgery. Have them get fronts and backs, between the fingers, and under the nails. (My kids also love trying to turn off the faucet with their elbows.) With such conscientious scrubbing maybe you'll have fewer flu germs on the French bread, and not so many black handprints on the kitchen curtains.

While you're in the bathroom, add a mandatory potty stop (prior to washing). Every night for about a year, we'd sit down to eat, I'd get one bite in my mouth, and my daughter would announce, "I have to go potty. Very badly. And I need you to help me, Mommy." You'd think I'd have figured out a little quicker that it would be a good idea to make her go potty *before* we sat down, but my brain doesn't function well when I'm hungry.

TRY THIS!

You and your spouse will appreciate a regular no-kids meal. Schedule a date weekly (it can be lunch or breakfast, as well as dinner). When our kids were small, a sitter was an expensive luxury, so we compromised with Chinese take-out every Friday night after the kids were in bed. And that small luxury sustained me for a whole week of peanut butter and whine.

Step Three: *Sit, Girl!*

Arranging seating so that your kid's feet are supported and he can reach the table easily will make him much less squirmy. Try a kitchen step stool, a low bar stool with a rung for a footrest, or a youth chair for a kid who rejects booster seats (which will be most preschoolers—don't you know that boosters are for babies?). Many kids prefer to perch on their knees while they eat. For those who are constantly popping up and down, a beanie baby in the lap is a good reminder to sit still—or just plan to allow your kid to *stand* near his place.

Most kids like having "their place" at the table, which they will guard jealously. We liked to keep everyone a little flexible about where they sat by playing games that required reshuffling, but I must admit the kids mostly hated them.

Bon Appetit! Now We May Eat!
RITUALS TO START THE FEAST

Use another ritual to signal the start of eating. Otherwise, by the time you sit down your child will be finished and off playing. Keep the ritual short and easy so you aren't tempted to skip it. Here are some ideas:

Cheers!

Look each person in the eye, clink glasses, and say "Cheers!" Making a connection with everybody present is the key part of this ritual. Pick any phrase you like, or let family members take turns choosing what to toast. Other phrases to try:

- "Bon appetit, now we may eat!"
- "To absent friends and family"
- "Skol" ("cheers" in Norwegian)
- "L'Chaim" ("to life" in Hebrew)
- "Salut" or "Salute" ("to your health" in French or Italian)
- "Here's looking at you, kid." (Humphrey Bogart in *Casablanca*)
- "As you slide down the banister of life, may the splinters never point the wrong way." (Irish blessing)
- "North, South, East, West, I wish you all the very best!"

Grace

Even if your family is not religious, many preschoolers pick up this ritual from school, friends, or the media. Give thanks to a higher being of your choice, to the earth, or simply to everyone who contributed to the meal. The important point is to pause, notice your good fortune, and express appreciation. You can fold hands and bow your heads or clasp each other's hands while you say your thanks. Some of our children's favorite preschool blessings:

- "God is great, God is good. And we thank Him for our food. Amen."
- "Thank you for the world so sweet, thank you for the food we eat. Thank you for the birds that sing, thank you, God, for everything."

Pass a Squeeze and the Mashed Potatoes

Have everyone hold hands around the table. One person squeezes the hand of the person next to him, that person squeezes his neighbor's hand,

and so on until the squeeze returns to where it started. You can also pass other gestures, such as a handshake, a kiss, a wink, a phrase like "I love you," a high five, a burp (*just* kidding), or whatever suits your family. Try passing the gesture in one direction, then the other, then across the table, and starting with different family members.

LITERATURE LINKS

For an international smorgasbord of rituals and things to say before eating, see *The Grateful Heart: Daily Blessings for the Evening Meal from Buddha to the Beatles* by M. J. Ryan. For some good Irish toasts, try http://mdds.umf.maine.edu/~donaghue/toasts01.html and read the book *Toasts for Every Occasion* by Jennifer Rahel Conover, for great ideas and a history of toast-making. *Come to the Table: A Celebration of Family Life* by Doris Christopher examines the importance of shared meals in family life and offers tips for preserving the family meal through the teen years and beyond.

Thanks a Lot!

Go around the table, having each person say thank you to another family member for something he or she did that day. Preschoolers will often learn the important things they have to be grateful for from listening to the rest of the family. You can also share the "best thing I did today," the "biggest news" from the day, a poem, a joke, or an interesting question.

Passing the Taste Test:
LIVING WITH YOUR CHILD'S DISCRIMINATING PALATE

To some extent, "live with it" is just what you have to do. Preschoolers are nearly all picky eaters. Their appetites are small, their tongues sensitive (for real), and they're leery of change. The problem is that the neighbor's stories about her little boy who prefers Swiss chard to chocolate will stick to the guilt part of your brain like peanut butter to the roof of your mouth. Although I don't know any magic tricks for getting kids to forsake Ho-Hos for greens, as the mother of three finicky eaters, I have learned some strategies that will encourage them to try—and maybe like—foods outside the peanut butter and sugar groups.

Involve Your Child in Preparations

It's well known that if you let your child help in the kitchen, he's more likely to at least try the meal. What's less well known is that if you let him help in the garden, he's more likely to eat vegetables. I'm not promising miracles, mind you—we're talking three peas, one lettuce leaf—but at least it's a start. Don't forget to let your child help with the shopping, cooking, and presentation as well.

Dine with Adventurous Friends

By the preschool years, peer pressure has become a powerful influence. We tend to forget how positive it can be. Locate a buddy who is willing to eat just about anything and get him to model risk-taking tasting for your child. And don't forget to be a good model yourself.

Serve Tiny Portions

Make it easy for your child to try just a little bite by using plates or containers that are small or have many compartments (muffin tins or ice cube trays will encourage your child to take small portions of many choices). Small portions are less overwhelming to sensitive kids and may prompt them to eat more than they usually would.

Drink-a-Meal

What children drink can dramatically affect the quality of their nutrition. Avoid struggles by making a firm rule that *everyone* drinks milk, water, and/or a calcium-fortified citrus juice with meals. (According to nutritionists, apple juice, grape juice, and "juice drinks" are high in sugar, thereby quickly sating small appetites, and provide few other nutrients.) Flavorings, like chocolate or strawberry syrup, will increase the appeal of milk for most children without adding many calories or otherwise harming its nutritional value. (If you buy the pre-flavored kind, try combining half a serving with half a serving of plain milk.)

Menu Options

By the time my third child was born, I was no longer willing to be a short-order cook. To minimize uneaten meals, I allowed any child who rejected the main course to make himself a bowl of healthy cereal or a peanut butter sandwich in its place. I also minimized rejection by serving meals in assemble-it-yourself form—offering, for example, the pasta with the sauce or other "yucky" ingredients like mushrooms on the side, and the salad as a salad bar.

Serve at Least One Food You Know Your Kid Will Eat

Preschoolers tend to like the bread group, as well as fruit. Many dislike meat—mostly objecting to the texture. (Thinly sliced deli meats may seem more appealing, and chicken is generally liked before other meats.)

Don't Despair

If your child rejects food after trying it, accept her decision. But remind her that research shows it takes most people many tries—seven to ten—to get used to new foods. In time, that gross new food may become one of her favorites.

The Breakfast Box
AND OTHER APPETIZING FOOD PRESENTATIONS FOR PRESCHOOLERS

Food is more appetizing to everyone when it is served in attractive ways. With preschoolers, you probably want to skip the parsley and fine china, but here are some ways to make their food look good to them. (These are most enjoyed if they are occasional treats.)

The Breakfast Box

Especially pleasing to children with older siblings who take lunches to school. Buy your child a bona fide lunch box of his choosing. Prepare a breakfast of small, packaged servings. (We use reusable containers.) Breakfast can actually resemble lunch (e.g., peanut butter sandwich, fruit, milk). Let your child pour her own milk from the thermos. Best of all, you can pack up this breakfast the night before (store in the refrigerator if it contains perishable items) and let your child serve herself in the morning. (I heartily recommend this if your child is an early riser on weekends.)

Bulldozer Breakfast

Use clean trucks or other toys as containers. Breakfast served in a new plastic dump truck from the dollar store is a meal your child will never forget. Use the opportunity to encourage him to try something new. Or, spread dry cereal around a clean placemat. Let your child use a toy bulldozer to push it around. She can use a loader to scoop it up and dump it into her bowl, ready to eat.

Doggie Diner or Dine-osaur Inn.

Buy a cheap pet bowl, and occasionally let your child eat face first. The dog menu can include "kibble" (breakfast cereal) or wet food (hot cereals, like oatmeal, or scrambled eggs). Be sure to offer a bone (pretzel or carrot stick) as a reward for performing his post-meal trick (carrying his bowl to the dishwasher).

Offer your dinosaur a primeval forest on a plate. The menu for carnivores, like Tyrannosaurus Rex, should include eggs or lunchmeats, while herbivores, like Stegosaurus, prefer an assortment of fruits, veggies, and cereals. Omnivores like a little bit of everything. Ask your child which sort he is.

Beverage Containers

Serve milk or water in interesting containers to make it more appealing. Try letting your child finish her milk from a kitty saucer on the floor or slurp it from a shallow container with a straw. Or serve healthy drinks in squeeze sports bottles. She can pour her own milk at the table from a little cow pitcher, rinsed pop can, or other cool container.

Stealth Veggies
AND OTHER SNEAKY GREEN STUFF STRATEGIES

My kid's pediatrician urged me to relax when I worried that my son refused to eat any remotely green foods (he even picked the tiny flakes of oregano out of the spaghetti sauce). "Preschoolers have hated vegetables for centuries," he said. "Offer lots of fruit, give him a multivitamin if you're very concerned—and then be patient. Eventually, most kids learn to like them, as long as they haven't been turned into an issue." And he was right, so I'll pass his advice on to you.

But you still want to make your kid eat spinach, don't you? In this day and age when we're bombarded with information about the importance of diets high in fiber and vitamins and phytochemicals, it's hard not to worry when your kid turns up his nose at every vegetable. So, if you don't want to just wait it out—but you don't want to turn it into a lifelong issue—try some of these tried-and-true ways to trick, I mean *persuade*, your kid into at least trying veggies.

Hide Them

Parents are always trying to hide vegetables by chopping them very fine and throwing them into the spaghetti sauce or sticking little chunks under the cheese on the pizza. Sometimes these strategies do work. I was successful in adding *shredded* onion to lots of sauces (which were rejected if they contained *chopped* onion), in sticking a variety of finely shredded veggies in meatloaf (for the kid who liked meatloaf), and in pureeing vegetable-based soups. My kids were totally onto the hide-green-stuff-under-the-cheese tactic, though, and my daughter is suspicious of pizza to this day. Ditto for the stick-little-bits-in-rice-or-macaroni-and-cheese approach. Keep in mind that the smaller the bits, the greater the likelihood of success. Pureeing is often best.

Overpower Them

Salad dressing, catsup, soy sauce, melted butter, cream cheese, melted cheddar—dips or toppings can completely hide the real taste of certain vegetables. And if your kid likes the disguising taste enough, he may be willing to eat the veggies to get his fix. Heck, he might eat cardboard if it was dipped in Cool Ranch dressing. See the next activity, "Little Dippers," for ideas for making this technique work.

Rename Them

Sometimes works—sometimes doesn't. As my middle kid once said, "You can call them broccoli trees or a whole forest—but they still taste nasty." Still, asparagus *swords* sound kind of interesting and might get you a test bite. Other popular veggie names include cauliflower bouquets, zucchini boats, and carrot coins.

Play with Them

This never worked at my house. Oh, they'd attach olive eyes to the sweet potatoes or make veggie landscapes on their pizzas, but they'd no sooner eat them than they'd consume their finger paintings. Still, this approach works with some kids.

TALES FROM THE TRENCHES

Once I was complaining to another mom that my daughter was anti-vegetables. She proudly announced that her son *loved* vegetables—he would eat carrots, corn, potatoes, red pepper slices, and salsa dips. Hey, I thought, my daughter eats all of those, *plus* artichokes, avocado, and the occasional lettuce leaf, cucumber slice, or fresh pea! Sometimes your kids like more vegetables than you realize—it never hurts to make an inventory and post it in the kitchen.

Get Cute Ones

Grape or cherry tomatoes are appealing—and often sweeter or milder tasting, as are baby eggplants and carrots, new potatoes, or lettuce leaves. And maybe your child will eat them if she's not taking care of them. My kids love the baby carrots and snack on them almost like potato chips. Well, like apple slices. And that's pretty good.

Sweeten the Pot

Do this by introducing veggies first as ingredients in tasty sweets. My kids thought zucchini was an occasional treat, since their first experiences were with zucchini bread and muffins. They felt a bit friendlier toward it by the time they encountered it as a dinner side dish. (But now they're a bit leery of zucchini bread.) Toss marshmallows or fruit in the salad to give your child a sweet incentive. Or get truly shameless and pay your child (money or another reward) to give a vegetable a fair shake. But, be careful, because this strategy can backfire big time.

Little Dippers:
FOODS TO DIP AND DRIP—AND EAT!

Preschoolers with purist palates may shun this eating style, but many young children will eat almost anything if they can dip it in something. Don't be surprised if your child prefers some *interesting* combinations, such as broccoli dipped in jam.

Serving Styles

Ice cube trays or muffin tins (one per diner for double dipping) will enable you to serve a variety of dips. Divided plates or trays are also useful for separating different items to be dipped. My children especially love the little Asian dishes we've collected (and fight over who gets the favorites, of course). Poking utensils—to use in place of fingers—also entice young appetites. Try various fancy toothpicks and cocktail skewers, fondue forks, and fancy forks like those for seafood.

Dips to Try

Catsup, salad dressings (ranch is a common favorite but you can find a bewildering array of choices at any supermarket or specialty store—or make your own), pizza sauce, cheese products (like Cheez Whiz), fancy vinegars (my kids love balsamic vinegar), salsa, plain yogurt flavored with your choice of seasonings, fruit-flavored yogurts, honey, cottage cheese mixed with salsa or crushed fruit, milk (for cookies or cake chunks), barbecue sauce, peanut butter thinned with a little peanut or sesame oil, hummus, baba ganoush, olive oil (try some flavored ones), jam or apple butter, syrup, thick soups or stews (cooled), pasta sauces (try pesto, meat sauces, and low-fat white sauces), bean dip, low-fat sour cream (plain or mixed with something like onion soup mix or salsa), other commercial dips, guacamole, orange juice concentrate (slightly thawed and stirred), Asian sauces like plum sauce or soy sauce, melted chocolate (or chocolate sauce), ice cream toppings, applesauce or other fruit sauces, lemon curd, and gravy.

Foods to Dip

Bread cubes, crudités (bite-sized veggies—try different colored peppers, summer squashes, sugar-pod or snow peas, cauliflower and broccoli, carrot matchsticks, celery, torn lettuce or cabbage leaves and other greens, cucumber slices, avocado chunks, cherry or grape tomatoes cut in fourths for safety, artichoke leaves or hearts, crisply cooked asparagus spears), stick pretzels, tortilla wedges or chips, pita bread wedges, quartered chunks of hot dogs, cocktail-size meatballs, chunks of other cooked meats, cooked shrimp or seafood chunks, fruits (strawberries, apple slices, orange segments, mango, papaya, starfruit, pineapple chunks), cookies or cake chunks, pastas (mini-tortellinis or raviolis, penne, rotini, and so on), cheese cubes, larger cereal pieces (like mini-wheats or other squares), and strips of French toast.

Fondue Fun-Do

Real fondue pots are risky around impulsive preschoolers. Pseudo fondue is fun and safe, though. Heat the cheese mixture or other dip-in food and serve it in a bowl in the middle of the table while it's still warm and melty.

My kids' favorite fake-fondue is pizza fondue. In a large bowl, combine your favorite pizza or spaghetti sauce with shredded cheeses (we use mozzarella or cheddar). You can also add "toppings" like crumbled sausage or chopped veggies. Microwave on High, stirring after each minute, until the mixture is warm and the cheese is melted. Serve with bread chunks, twists of baked frozen pizza dough, or veggie chunks.

Read It and Eat:
SNEAKY LITERARY FEASTS

Pairing an appropriate meal with a book will make the story come alive for your child—and, even better, may tempt him to try some new foods. I still remember asking my mom to serve spinach because I loved Popeye (okay, so that's not exactly literary)—and choking it down even though I wondered how he could eat that disgusting slime.

Three Bears Breakfast

Want your child to try hot cereal? Read a version of the classic "The Three Bears." My favorite is the version illustrated by James Marshall. (A silly four-year-old will also like *The Dumb Bunnies,* a spoof of this tale written by Sue Denim and illustrated by Dav Pilkey—but, of course, discourage your child from pouring the "just right" porridge down his pants as Baby Bunny did.) Serve oatmeal, cream of wheat, or other hot cereal in three different-sized bowls. (If your child has not been a hot cereal fan, try some of the flavored oatmeals, or offer toppings like cream or brown sugar.) Go for a short walk, and then taste-test to find the one that feels just right. Is it the baby bear–size bowl?

Vegetable Soup Suppers

There are some great choices to encourage kids to eat this nutritious meal. Serve it with fresh bread after reading the colorful *Growing Vegetable Soup* by Lois Ehlert. Or add some alphabet noodles to the soup, and sip it while you chuckle over the antics of the dog who ate alphabet soup and had the letters go up to her brain, instead of down to her stomach in *Martha Speaks* by Susan Meddaugh.

But my favorite vegetable soup tale is the classic *Stone Soup* by Marcia Brown. I started making this with kids back in my teaching days and was amazed at how it got my picky students to eat a wide variety of vegetables. We always used a real stone (run through the dishwasher and added just before serving), but if that grosses you out, substitute a bouillon cube for the rock. Simply have your child plop the stone in some canned soup along with a few canned or frozen vegetables—or better yet, let your child help prepare a homemade recipe.

Peter Rabbit Salad Bar

Set out little dishes of different dressings to use as dip. In Beatrix Potter's story, Peter ate lettuces, French beans, and radishes, followed by a bit of parsley to settle his stomach. We often add some other vegetables as well. Your good little bunny will undoubtedly enjoy some milk and blackberries for dessert, as Peter's well-behaved siblings did. A little chamomile tea, sweetened with honey, is an interesting sleepy-time drink.

LITERATURE LINKS

Picture books with edible themes are very common. Try *How Pizza Came to Queens* by Dayal Kaur Khalsa; *Cloudy with a Chance of Meatballs* by Judi Barrett; and *Miss Spider's Tea Party* by David Kirk. You can also dish up a teddy bear picnic, serving berries, honey treats, and other bear goodies, while reading the Winnie-the-Pooh stories by A. A. Milne, the Blackboard Bear series by Martha Alexander, and *The Legend of the Teddy Bear* by Frank Murphy.

Bread and Jam-boree

The finicky badger in *Bread and Jam for Frances* by Russell Hoban was beloved in my family, as was her diet. Serve bread and jam for breakfast followed by bread and jam for snack. If your picky eater is still feeling jam-ish, go ahead and serve her bread and jam again for lunch and afternoon snack. (It won't hurt her to eat a restricted diet for one or two days—but offer milk and fruit on the side.) By dinner, your child will probably be hungry for a boxed meal spread like Frances's—arranged on a doily and eaten with careful bites to make everything "come out even."

Little Red Hen Bread and Butter

Read the classic version illustrated by Paul Galdone or the boldly illustrated one by Byron Barton. Then make some bread and butter to go with it. Feel free to use a bread maker or frozen bread dough instead of your favorite bread recipe (but you won't have nearly as many opportunities to ask "Who will help me_____?") We have substituted muffins or biscuits for bread, too, because they're easier. Have your child help you stir honey or cinnamon and sugar into some softened butter. This makes a great alternative to a sugary dessert—it definitely feels like a treat.

Minimum Security Manners:
EATING WITH KIDS WITHOUT FEELING LIKE BARFING

Face it. Preschoolers do not generally have good table manners. They'll consider mashed potatoes a delightful finger food, impress the crowd with their burping prowess, and abruptly disappear without a word before they've even tasted their turnips. Unless you stop them. Which you will, gently and consistently—while still overlooking much that wouldn't pass muster at a palace, because the most important thing is that they learn to enjoy sharing meals with other people. Here, then, is a list of minimal manners that most preschoolers can *start* to master.

Use Utensils

Preschoolers have generally grasped the general concept that many foods are better eaten with forks or spoons. But they'll forget, since playing with mashed potatoes feels nice, and they like taking out their vegetable frustrations on the peas, squishing the very life out of them. So you will gently remind them, "We eat that with a *fork*," or whatever. Smile proudly and nod when they follow through.

Take Turns

Wait until someone passes the basket of rolls, instead of reaching across the table and grabbing one from your brother. Introduce the phrase, "Will you please pass the _____ ?" at three or four, and expect it to be remembered by five. Even more importantly, expect kids to take turns in the conversation. Vary who gets to tell about his day first, and take care that everyone gets at least a little turn in the spotlight.

No Grossing People Out at the Table

This is a good rule, since it covers many possible scenarios, from a child who wants to discuss his classmate's habit of eating boogers to another who insists on showing the family what cole slaw looks like after it's been chewed seventy-two times. It also gets at the heart of table manners—making other people feel comfortable and hungry.

Remember—and Teach—the Difference between Manners and Etiquette

Knowing etiquette—the rules for "proper" behavior—will be useful for your child, and you will want to teach her gradually which fork to use for salad and to ask to be excused before leaving the table. But the more important concept to learn as a young child, and to remember forever, is good manners—behaving in a way that is considerate of others. Some evening, tell this story (supposedly about Queen Elizabeth) to help your child understand the difference between the two—and watch her fall all over herself trying to be magnanimous to her baby brother who thinks that applesauce is a finger food.

The president of a small country was invited to a fancy banquet at the palace. The poor president, who had never attended such a party, was completely bewildered by the many forks and spoons and knives at his place. Several guests frowned in disapproval as he ate course after course with the wrong utensil. But the worst moment came at the end of the meal, when servants brought each guest a bowl of warm water with a lemon floating in it. These were fingerbowls, for the guests to wash their hands. But the confused president mistook them for soup. He picked up a dessert spoon and began to sip the lemony water. The other guests gasped! What poor etiquette! But the kind queen picked up her dessert spoon and sipped all her lemon water, too. What absolutely perfect manners!

LITERATURE LINKS

Manners books for children tend to be—how can I say this politely?—very *serious*. Here are a few that are fun: *Goops and How to Be Them*, a classic by Gelett Burgess, *Manners* by Aliki, which has a pleasant cartoon format, and my personal favorites, *What Do You Say, Dear?* and *What Do You Do, Dear?* by Seslye Joslin and illustrated by Maurice Sendak (these are very funny and useful—I still refer to them when I'm not sure what to say).

Conversation Starters:
THINGS TO DISCUSS AT THE TABLE
BESIDES HOW FAT YOUR STOMACH IS

Ask a preschooler what he did during the day, and you'll probably get an answer like, "Played" or "I don't remember." Questions like those tax not only a young child's memory but also his organizational skills. He feels overwhelmed and simply decides to avoid the difficult task. (The same thing happens when you tell him to pick up his messy room.) Instead he'll try to shift the conversation to concrete subjects like how french fries look after they get chewed up or how fat your stomach is. To avoid these charming topics, take control and try some manageable conversation starters like these.

The Day in Review

Here are some questions to get the ball rolling:
- "What did you have for morning snack at school?" (This question nearly always works, and often leads to a flood of other memories.)
- "What was the *best* thing you did this afternoon?"
- "Let me guess. Spider Man came over to play today. Right?" (Humor is very good at jogging young memories and engaging minds.)

What If?

Classic dinner conversation with children is concrete—but there is no law that it has to be. Some of the favorite dinner (and car) talks with my kids revolve around "what if . . ." questions.

- What if we invited an elephant to dinner?
- What if we lived in a cave in the woods?
- What if a fairy would grant a wish for you?

Rememberies

One of the best ways to get children to tell a story is to tell one to them. Use this structure to tell your children about their family and personal history. Try simple tales like these:

- "I remember when you were a little baby, and one time you put your spaghetti on your head!"
- "I remember when I was little, I had to eat all the food on my plate or no dessert. And one night there were lima beans for dinner and I hated them. But there was chocolate cake for dessert, and I loved that! I didn't know what to do. . . ." (Stories about when you were bad are favorites.)
- "Do you remember the book where the Man in the Yellow Hat took Curious George to his house far away? I wonder how George felt the first time he ate dinner at the man's house."

LITERATURE LINKS

Highlights for Children magazine includes a monthly feature called "Headwork." The column consists of a series of questions that challenge children to use knowledge, their imaginations, thinking skills, and sometimes even their bodies. These questions often make excellent conversation starters. (I clip them to keep in the car for traffic jams.)

Define "One Bite"
AND OTHER COMMON FOOD FIGHTS

A reluctant eater is a lawyer in the making. Tell him he just has to try one bite, and be prepared for an hour of argument and briefs on what exactly constitutes a "bite." To help you with your case, here are the latest citations and findings by the food courts (not always what you want to hear).

Define One Bite

In the case of *Eric v. Mom & Dad*, the official ruling was that a bite could be microscopic—a matter of molecules even—and still count. Despite numerous appeals, the ruling stands and is now an accepted part of common law. Even if the kid held his nose while the bite went into his mouth and then spit all the molecules into his napkin. (Oddly, adopting this definition was associated with later willingness to eat two or three bites of the offending substance.)

How Much Is Half?

This is not the simple mathematical problem it first appears, since food is magically much less as soon as it is spread out over the plate. If you are going to require a child to consume a certain portion of his meal (say, before he gets dessert), physically isolate the required quantity and require the child to place *all* of it into his mouth and thence to his stomach. (But avoid getting caught in this web if you can—this seemingly clear-cut guideline has more loopholes than the IRS code on capital gains.)

When is "Too Close to Dinner"?

This is a difficult call. I finally gave up on this issue—mostly. I have healthy snacks available (often those hated vegetables) in smallish portions, and allow them to be noshed freely, even if it's almost dinnertime. I just consider the intake to be part of the meal. And kids still have to sit with us at family meals, so it doesn't really buy them free time. I offer fruit or even dessert to those who are full when the rest of us are eating. But when they were younger, I cut off sweets and junk food at least two hours before dinner, because my kids filled up quickly. Now they *mostly* do a good job of monitoring their own snack-meal timing and variety.

"I'm Not Hungry Now"

I say respect this claim, even though you may suspect it's a ruse to be excused to go finish his Tinker Toy construction—or a way to avoid the broccoli in favor of the pumpkin pie set aside for dessert. But, require everyone to stay at the table for the bulk of the meal, eating or not. (It's amazing how appetites can sprout up suddenly when kids are bored.) And substitute dinner for the pie at snack time when your kid is finally hungry again.

Yuck! Gross! Disgusting!

When the kid is talking about the dinner you spent hours planning, shopping for, and preparing, it's not surprising that your feelings are hurt, and you feel cranky. Been there, done that, as they say. So make a rule banning these expressions. As my oldest son would say, "But that's illegal! What about freedom of speech?" Sorry, there's none at the dinner table. In our house, if you don't care for the meal, you can decline it (saying something like, "No thank you") *and* thank the chef for his efforts ("Thanks for working so hard on the dinner, Dad."). Kids who have to say "Yuck!" can go mutter it in the bathroom, by themselves. The preschool years are not too soon to learn this lesson.

Gimme Sugar, Buster!
NAVIGATING THE SHOALS OF BIRTHDAY PARTIES, JUNK FOOD JUNKETS, AND HALLOWEEN CANDY

Spend much time with parents of preschoolers, and sugar, junk food, and other troubling eating habits are sure to be discussed—and argued fiercely. You'll encounter parents who never permit sugar to touch their children's lips and others who have no problem with serving Coke with Pop Tarts for breakfast. In the face of this extremism (and your child's craving for sugar or simply to be part of the crowd), it can be hard to sort out reasonable positions on these issues. Here is some food for thought.

Birthday Parties

Over and over, I've read about research studies that find that sugar is not the culprit in kids' wild behavior at these functions—it's just excitement say the experts. The studies sound reasonable and well-conducted, but I must admit I'm somewhat skeptical about their results. I know that my kids seem jazzed in proportion to the amount of sugar they consume. Still, I think you have to let kids go to parties and eat what others are eating, and simply cope with their hyper behavior afterwards. But don't hesitate to turn down parties that fall during inconvenient times for you (just before bedtime, for example, or a couple of hours before your in-laws come for a visit). With each successive kid, I also declined more of the invitations issued by acquaintances, as opposed to close friends, especially if they took place at party centers with flashing lights, tokens, costumed characters, and candy.

Junk Food Shopping Junkets

To buy or not to buy? That is the question. The answer seems to be to buy some, but not too much. Learning to enjoy "treat" foods in moderation leads to the healthiest attitudes and habits over time. Research confirms what to me is common sense: When parents severely limit access to junk food, their kids crave it and will sneak it given the opportunity. And for obvious reasons, you don't want to completely indulge your child's desire for it, because most kids will want more than would be good for them. So go ahead and have an occasional chip break while you watch a family video, go out to lunch now and then at McDonald's, and dispense cookies and milk after preschool. We also let our kids pick their favorite disgustingly sugary cereal to eat on their birthdays and our vacations.

Halloween Candy and Other Sugar Mother Lodes

Most preschoolers have regular opportunities for acquiring candy windfalls—holidays, especially Halloween, parties, even visits with indulgent grandparents or neighbors. My position has always been that, after a reasonable period of inspection and a little heavy-handed taste-testing, preschoolers must fork over their candy bags to be stored out of reach (and sight). At chosen times, I return the bags so the kids can select what they'd like. And somehow, after a week or so, the candy bags just seemed to "disappear." (Too often into my stomach, especially when they contained chocolate.) I tried getting the kids to donate some of their candy to local charities, but for preschoolers the greed vs. good conflict tended to become overwhelming, so I stopped asking (but sometimes I just did it for them).

Have You Had Your Sugar Today? Teaching Moderation

Ultimately, your goal is to help your child set and adhere to reasonable limits *without your intervention*. It helps young kids (and older folk, too) to have guidelines, even if they are occasionally violated. For example, you might set a limit of one (or in my family, which has a mom with a sweet tooth, two) treat foods per day. Sometimes kids might choose to eat them before breakfast, *but that's their choice*. You can just remind them that that's it for the day.

CHAPTER EIGHT

Sleep-Ease: From Twilight to Nightlight

My friend Mark Sullivan-Hanson has a theory that there are two kinds of people in the world: those people who must actively power down to go to sleep at night and those for whom every moment of the day is a struggle to stay awake. Unfortunately, preschoolers nearly all fall into the first category, or insist that they do, while most of their tired parents fall into the latter category. This fact can make bedtime a battlefield, often strewn in our house with the bodies of snoring adults and frolicking tykes.

And it's why you really have to heed the advice of all those earnest childcare experts (I guess that includes me) who insist that you develop a consistent bedtime routine. A routine may give you the structure you need to stay awake until your children are safely in their beds. And it will also help your child shut down properly so that you don't get that sanctimonious message the next morning about how, since he wasn't powered down the right way, you'll have to stand by while he runs scans on every drive. Oh wait, that's the computer. But your child will complain just as much if you omit any expected procedures. In the long run, those omissions will cost you time and aggravation, so you might as well try to do the thing correctly in the first place.

And what is the correct way to put a kid to bed? That depends on your family—on your child's needs and the structure of his day, on the work schedules of parents, and a multitude of other factors. *You* are the expert on your family, the grownup in your household, so *you* get to pick and choose what components and rituals you include.

Ideally, your whole evening spirals down to sleep, like bath water swirling lazily toward the drain—not like the *whoosh* of a toilet flush. The evening routine may include chores and getting set for next day, family play time, a snack, a bath, and the usual tuck-in stuff. But it doesn't have to include everything every single night. Just make sure you and your child are clear on what components are essential. The bare bones minimum for kids in our family was brushing teeth and going potty, reading a story in bed, tucking in with their special blankies or animals, putting a story tape on, and exchanging smooches. Not one of these things could ever be left out unless the kid fell asleep in his spaghetti, but we could and did skip other things, like baths, pajamas, and cups of water. Still, bedtime takes a *loooong* time to accomplish, and you might as well just accept that fact.

Speed bumps and even major derailments are common in the bedtime routine. Most preschoolers are masters of delay tactics aimed at easing their separation anxiety, warding off fears, or simply prolonging their fun. And many preschoolers are troubled by intermittent night waking due to illness, bedwetting, nightmares, and other disturbances. Your child may suddenly insist that only one parent can tuck him in, or that there are major monsters lurking throughout his room. You may feel too exhausted to accommodate his demands that you pull his shade to the perfect point or give his teddy seventeen kisses. All this stuff is normal and distressingly common, if that makes you feel any better.

Having said that, bedtime really can be a pleasant, even favorite time of day. There is something so greeting-card poignant about reading a story about little bunnies to a soapy-scented youngster in his Batman pajamas. This chapter contains ideas for increasing the pleasure of the satisfying parts of nighttime routines, as well as suggestions for combating many common problems. It is divided into ideas for getting ready for bed, tucking in, and dealing with difficulties.

So get to work tinkering with that routine. Before you know it, you'll be staying awake until your child isn't.

Ready, Set ...
PREPARING FOR TOMORROW

After dinner, your child can help with preparations to ease the morning rush, practice skills or help with family work, and get ready for upcoming events. I admit that this approach may simply transfer some of the morning fuss to the evening, but the level of whining tends to be less near bedtime (after all, your kid will think it's a good delay tactic). Also, most parents find the squabbles easier to manage at 7:00 P.M. than 7:00 A.M. Finally, these habits will serve your child well as he enters school age, and it's easier to establish them before you need them desperately.

Lay Out Clothes and Supplies

Even if your child will simply be staying home, your morning will go more smoothly if you have your child lay out his clothes the night before. Check the weather forecast and the calendar together (in case he'll need something special). By four-and-a-half, he can probably handle this task with direction from you. (See chapter 1 for ideas on helping your child manage clothes selection.) He can also get his backpack ready if he's going to school or daycare in the morning and can pack nonperishable lunch items. A picture checklist can make these tasks easier for him to do all by himself.

The Homework Habit

If you have school-age children, your preschooler may be dying to have homework of his own, in which case he'll probably want to spend a few minutes each night doing things like practicing his letters and numbers (though they may look like lines or squiggles). Otherwise, give him a sit-down task or two he can do by himself, like drawing, threading a sewing card, matching socks, or sorting small toys while you finish work from the office, pay bills, or make phone calls.

Let him work near you, and keep this session brief. You can expect your child to "work" for five to ten minutes at age three, and you can add another five to ten minutes of work time each year after that.

Make Like an Ant

And prepare for the future. Show your child how you plan for upcoming events and break down big jobs into a series of small steps. Your child can help you make a card for grandma's birthday next week, wrap the present another day, and call or attend a celebration on the special night.

You can also use this time to do a few minutes' work on an ongoing or intermittent project, like putting photographs in an album, attending to small repairs, or working on a craft. Your child can help with sorting, fetching and carrying, or simply by watching over your shoulder and providing company.

Bathtub Carwashes and Laundromats
(AND YOU THOUGHT BATHS WERE FOR BODIES)

Something to wash (other than himself) can encourage a dirt fan to use the soap. As a bonus, you end up with clean toys and a child who has learned a new skill. Here are some of our favorite accessory scrub jobs.

The Carwash

Float small vehicles on a foam tray or a logjam of commercial foam bathtub blocks. Offer your child an old toothbrush and cut a small square of sponge to scrub the cars with (and let the child use the remainder of the clean sponge on himself). You can fashion miniature buckets from plastic caps and fill them with soapy water. To hose off the cleaned vehicle, show the child how to suck clean water (from a cup) through a straw or length of narrow plastic tubing, squeeze a finger over the end, and release the water over the car. He can polish chrome with a little toothpaste dabbed on a washcloth. Your child will enjoy polishing his teeth the same way—which makes an interesting comparison with the toothbrush method.

The Laundromat

Let your child wash doll clothes, washcloths, or hand towels. He can either wash them in the tub with him (add bubble bath or a small squirt of dishwashing soap for bubbles) or use a floating half-filled basin. This activity can spark some interesting discussions and investigations. For example, have your child observe the ways that cloth changes when it gets wet—weight, color, feel, how well it sticks to the side of the tub, etc. An old-fashioned toy washboard (if you can find one—try a flea market) will spark some good history discussions along with vigorous rubbing.

SAFETY ZONE
Supervise clothesline play carefully to prevent strangulation. It's best to suspend the line just above your child's head and not permit him to stand up.

Finally, you can fashion a clothesline by attaching a short length of string between two suction cup hooks (against the wall, not across the tub). Show him how to use clothespins to hang his laundry to dry. Check back to see how long it takes. Try comparing drying times of wrung-out cloths versus dripping ones, and of different kinds of fabrics.

More to Wash

- *The Tub* Use a little shaving cream or baking soda on a washcloth to scrub the sides of the tub and the surrounding tile. Rinse with a watering can.
- *Baby Dolls and Stuffed Animals* Provide real or toy accessories for wannabe parents. Encourage your child to model bathing

techniques and face-wetting courage for their unskilled or fearful tots. Fashion dolls with long tresses are good for practicing shampooing.

- *A Buddy* A sibling or friend is company and the kids can help each other with the hard-to-reach parts like backs and toes.

Fun Floats and So Does a Pumpkin:
THE TUB AS A SINK-AND-FLOAT SCIENCE LAB

This activity won't actually get your kid clean. It will lure him into the tub, though, and maybe you can soap him up while he's distracted. Besides, preschoolers love these experiments. One of my kids went through a phase of wondering about nearly every object he found, "Is this a sinker or a

LITERATURE LINKS

King Rollo's Bath by David McKee tells how a wizard solved the problem of a reluctant royal bather. On second thought, it may give away your secret tactic....

floater?" A few dramatic items to test, like a pumpkin, will make the activity especially exciting and interesting.

Before he gets in the tub, have your child sort all the items into two containers, labeled sink and float. Call this "predicting" or making a thinking guess. (You can also introduce the word "hypothesis"—your child will like the way it feels on his tongue.) When he gets in the tub, hand him the objects one at a time and have him check the accuracy of his guesses. He can use soap crayons to tally his hits and misses. Older preschoolers can use four categories to compare the two predictions with the two possible outcomes (sink-sink, sink-float, float-float, float-sink).

Items to Test

- A pumpkin—and then the jack-o'-lantern made from it
- Rocks, including pumice (which floats!)

- Various toys
- Aluminum foil—flat, shaped into a boat, crumpled in a ball
- More produce—apples, celery, carrots, lettuce leaves and head, cucumber, pepper, watermelon
- Cups, cartons, bowls, trays—fill to varying capacities
- Wood, including a log
- Soap bars, including Ivory (which floats because it's whipped and has air in it)
- A piece of bubblegum, a bubble blown with bubblegum
- Balls—superballs, ping-pong balls, playground balls, etc.
- Sponges, corks
- Balloons—before and after inflation, a water balloon, an ice balloon
- Ice, including a large block (try this on a hot day)
- Pinecones, acorns, other found objects
- Floaters with "passengers"—like pennies in a cup. Predict how many will make it sink

Displacement

A related fun activity is to have your child notice displacement. Have her use a soap crayon to mark the water level before she gets in. Then have her notice the change in level. Think about why it might have happened. Add more items to the tub (floaters and sinkers). What happens to the water level again?

TRY THIS!

Preschoolers are also impressed with the trick of trapping a bubble of air beneath a floating washcloth. Have him take a dry or wrung-out washcloth, hold his palm under the middle, and slowly lower it to the surface of the water. With luck, it will float for several minutes with a "bubble" just above the water, before it absorbs too much moisture and sinks.

LITERATURE LINKS

Who Sank the Boat? by Pamela Allen is a fun look at a sink-and-float problem.

Home Spa Soaks:
SENSORY PLEASURES FOR THE BATH

Many of the same sensory luxuries that you enjoy will bring pleasure to your child. Here are some ideas to try.

Scent

Wrap herbs (fresh or dried) in a square of fabric (cheesecloth works well). Tie the "bag" up and hang it beneath the spigot as the water runs in. Squeeze it out afterwards for maximum scent. (Or just float a handful in the tub and make your kid fish them out with a sieve before you pull the plug.) Good herbs to try include lavender, lemon balm, chamomile, mints, and scented geraniums. Many of these herbs may soothe or help skin.

Powdered spices or liquid flavor extracts will also add pleasing scents. My children liked vanilla and cinnamon particularly. These will make your child smell good, too.

Or, float slices of fruits or veggies for scent, visual beauty, and interesting "toys" (they make good rafts). Try citrus fruit slices, cucumber slices, or apple slices with a little cinnamon (stick or a dash of ground) for a bath—and a child—that smells like apple pie. In the fall, brightly colored leaves or a branch from a pine tree add an invigorating outdoorsy smell.

Sight

Cut spirals from paper plates or construction paper circles. Suspend them with thread from the center strip and hang above the tub. The rising warm air will make the "snakes" spin in slow circles. Or hang stars or any other shapes. (Attach them with sticky putty or tape.) These will give your child something to look up at when you rinse her hair and help keep water from running into her eyes.

You can also add objects to the water for their visual appeal. Flowers (or simply petals) will float. Try glow-in-the-dark items and briefly dim the lights. Or light the bathroom with a nightlight or other soft light, like pink bulbs in the fixtures. We have also bathed the kids by candlelight (keeping the candles well away from the tub and blowing them out before the kids got out).

Sound

Music can shape the mood in the bath. Play something upbeat while your child scrubs, and quiet music for a soothing playtime.

Touch

Bubble bath is the classic bath additive, but it can cause vaginal irritation in girls. Grind oatmeal in the blender to make a soothing soak for itchy skin (or purchase commercial oatmeal preparations like Aveeno). It, like bath salts, makes the water feel soft and smooth, so be extra careful to guard against slipping.

Also, try various scrubbers and cloths to stimulate your child's skin. A bath brush or rough washcloth feels especially nice rubbed gently on your child's soapy back. Your child can scrub her nails with a soft brush. (Remember that a child's skin is more delicate than yours.) Experiment, too, with different soaps formulated for children's sensitive skin. Try liquid as well as bar soap. Glycerin soaps are pretty as well as smooth.

SAFETY ZONE

Be careful that your child can see adequately and that there are no cords or electrical fixtures near the tub to pose an electrocution risk.

SOUND BITES

Some favorite bath tunes: *Rubber Ducky* as sung by Ernie and others and *Baby Beluga* by Raffi.

SAFETY ZONE

The American Academy of Pediatricians recommends against *ever* using bubble bath for young girls (or even letting girls sit in a soapy or shampooey tub!). My personal experience has been that an occasional bubble bath doesn't hurt for girls who aren't overly sensitive. If you're concerned, talk to your child's doctor.

"Hare Do's" and Sham-pooches:
HAPPIER HAIR WASHING

Try these ideas for clean tresses with fewer tears:

"Hare Do's"

Offer a mirror so your child can fashion interesting 'dos with her shampoo-covered hair. Rabbit ears are easy to sculpt, as are Mohawks, alien antennae, antlers, Cinderella buns, triceratops horns, Batman "ears," and dragon spikes.

Sham-pooches

Suds up your human puppy's fur while you narrate a nice doggy bath, preferably in a French accent. Shape her poodle curls or comb out her retriever "feathers" with your fingers. Close the shower curtains after you rinse, and have her shake like a dog. Ham it up good and let her finish up with a drink from her water bowl in the kitchen.

Wash That Spinach Right out of Her Hair

Put some shampoo on her head and start washing. Then say, "Oh, no! I must have grabbed the bottle of spinach instead!" Or fleas, or peanut butter, or dinosaurs, or something else silly. Then sing, "I'm Gonna Wash That Man Right out of My Hair" from the musical *South Pacific*, substituting spinach or whatever for "man" while your child (or you) scrubs her head vigorously. You can use this joke over and over—just ask your child what she'd like to scrub out of her hair tonight.

Dry-Eyed

Water or shampoo in the eyes is a major problem for many pre-schoolers. Some possible solutions:

- Let your child wear swim goggles, a scuba mask, or a shampoo visor. (I always found it hard to scrub my daughter's hair with the strap, but other parents seem to cope.)
- Wet hair with a mister and rinse with a hand-held sprayer, a squeeze bottle (like a water bottle) that lets you direct the water precisely, a watering can, or a cup.
- Get your child to point her face toward the ceiling. (Have her pretend to look for fairies fluttering overhead, or hang something from the ceiling for her to look at.)
- Have her hold a tightly rolled washcloth or hand towel to her eyes.
- Add cold water to the tub before rinsing—water feels warmer on faces.
- Practice getting eyes and face wet at the pool.
- Wash her hair in the kitchen sink. Have her lie down on her back on the counter and hang her head over the sink. Use the hand-held sprayer to wet and rinse. Pretend it's a beauty parlor visit.
- Put just a couple of inches of water in the tub so that your child can lie down and wet her head without getting anything in her eyes. Show her how to swish her head from side to side to help rinse the shampoo out. Hold a hand mirror above her so she can watch her hair swirl like a mermaid's.

Control Tactics

Giving your child more control may reduce her fear. Offer her a choice of shampoo or body washing first (but save play for after), of having you pour the water over her head or doing it herself, of washing it in the shower or bathtub, or of using this bottle of shampoo or that one.

The Dry Through:
OUT OF THE TUB AND INTO THE TOWEL

Ironically, it can be as difficult to get your child *out* of the tub as it was to get him in. These ideas may help remove your child from the bath—and maybe the ring from the tub, while you're at it.

Send in the Cleanup Crew

Announce that it's shift change—bathers out, custodial staff in. Have your child swim around "sweeping up" the bath toy litter (this is especially fun with a colander or large strainer). Then he can "wash the walls" or windows (use a sponge with baking soda for cleanser, or offer a mister of water and a squeegee to try). Finally, he can mop the floor (use a child-sized mop or an oversized sponge). Be sure to praise the cleaning crew and write him an imaginary paycheck.

Whirlpool Watchers

If your child is not afraid of going down the drain, simply pull the plug when it's almost time to get out. A bath is not much fun when the water's gone, though you may let your child slide around a bit in the last slick. Hand him an old towel to dry the tub and remove the ring. Many children enjoy watching the whirlpool created as the water runs out and will let you pull the plug so they can do so. Give him a floating toy to get caught in the whirlpool or let him put his hand flat over the hole to feel the suction. This is a good demonstration to watch repeatedly (from safely outside the tub) if your child does fear going down the drain. Just make sure the toy *is* too big to go down!

Dry and Wax Your Car

Use your magic wand to turn your child into a car. Make him something cool, like a 1922 Silver Ghost Rolls Royce, the Batmobile, Cinderella's pumpkin coach, or a Formula One race car. Hustle him out of the car wash, so you can towel him dry, polish his chrome, and rub hot wax (moisturizing lotion warmed by floating it in the bathwater) all over him.

Warm! Snuggly!

Cold is what often deters kids from exiting the tub. Heat towels on the radiator, have someone else deliver towels warmed in the dryer, or use an overhead bathroom heater. My daughter always demanded "Wrap me round!" as she got out of the bath. Oversized bath "sheets" or beach towels are perfect for that operation. Snuggle your child up, fully wrapped in her towel cocoon as you rub everything dry and let the terry absorb any lingering moisture. This is a good time for a rhyme, fingerplay, or song.

The Big Blow Dry

Many preschoolers hate having their hair blown dry. Some are frightened by the noise, but the most common problem is that their sensitive skin is bothered by the heat of the dryer. Try making a "tent" for your child's skin by wrapping a towel around the base of his hairline and clipping it closed. Or, use a brush to lift strands of hair above his head and direct the blower upwards. Towel drying works well for children with short hair. Another option is simply to cover the child's pillow with a towel, removing it once he's asleep and his hair is no longer damp.

Down at the Comb-and-Clip:
DETANGLING AND UN-NAILING

The Tangle Attack

- Apply cream rinse liberally—and spray detangler—on hair prone to major knots (forget those two-in-one shampoos—they're not adequate for fine kid hair).
- In the case of a major rat's nest, apply several rounds of conditioner in the tub, working out more of the knots each round.
- Use your fingers first to work out big tangles. (Try doing it underwater.)

- Let your child comb her own hair before you do. Show her how to work the tangles out from the bottom up, bit by bit.
- Use one hand to lift the hair closest to the scalp, so you're not pulling on the roots while you comb out knots.
- Count, sing, tell jokes, or distract your child some other way while you comb.
- Let your child work on a doll's hair or the dog's fur while you work on his.

Nail Notions

- Play manicurist. Put out a dish of warm soapy water to soak their fingertips, and use a small brush to paint their nails with water or lotion when you're done (or finish up with some kids' polish).
- My most successful approach was to have my kids' nails talk (in a high squeaky voice)—all of them clamoring to be cut first. "My turn, my turn. You got to go first last time!" and so on. The nail-cuttee got to pick whose turn it was and generally act as the grownup voice of reason to the high-spirited nail kids.

LITERATURE LINKS

See the Klutz book *Nail Art* by Sherri Haab for some really inspired ways to paint a kid's nails—and it comes with six bottles of kid polish!

- Use finger plays and toe-tickler rhymes to move from nail to nail. You can adapt the rhymes to suit the task, which may tickle your child's fancy, too. For example, sing "Where Is Thumbkin?" as a call and response song. Your child produces each finger, singing, "Here I am!" and you continue with, "Let me trim your hair, sir." Your child can sing back instructions for his guy, like, "I would like a Mohawk," or "A trim and perm is perfect" while you quickly do the snipping. Wrap up with, "That looks great!" or something similar.

- If your child has tickly toes, have him curl them just over the edge of the tub while he sits in a chair. Hold them steady by pushing down from the top, instead of grasping them individually.
- Experiment with different tools. You can try rounded nail scissors, small clippers, or even a nail file (which may work better for kids who fear being cut).
- Trim dinosaur or lion claws instead of fingernails. Much more appealing. Pretend to shape them into sharper points and make believe that the actual rounded results are very scary.

Goodnight, Molars:
OFF TO BED, BRUSHED, AND FLOSSED

For ideas on encouraging and timing toothbrushing, see "To Tell the Tooth" in chapter 1.

At night, an adult should help your child brush her teeth. Before the age of six or seven, children cannot clean their teeth adequately without assistance. You can let your child have a first go, and then you can "finish up." Some children may be content to let you take over the chore altogether when they are tired. Tips for getting the job done right:

- Use only a small amount of toothpaste. Children who swallow toothpaste may consume too much fluoride, which can stain developing adult teeth. Make sure your child spits and rinses his mouth when you're done.
- Play dinosaur dentist. Have your tyrannosaurus open wide—very wide—and carefully brush his fangs one-by-one, hamming it up as you work.
- Pretend to be an artist creating a masterpiece. Or a restorer, removing grime from a famous monument. Or a custodian scrubbing a very dirty room. Your child can choose the evening's brushing theme.

- Name your child's teeth. Clean Walter and Joe and Henrietta and all the others.
- Say goodnight to each tooth you brush. Goodnight molar, goodnight incisor, etc.

ON THE WEB

Games, explanations, and tooth-brushing tips can be found at www.ada.org, the homesite of the American Dental Association. You can also find information on tooth care and other health issues on www.healthykids.com.

- Make a game of spitting by having her try to hit the drain. Use silly words like "Ptooie!" and "Sploot!" Spitting is fun because it is normally forbidden.
- If your child resists having you brush his teeth, try an experiment. Have him brush one-half of his teeth; then you do the other half. Afterwards, he can chew a disclosing tablet (available at most pharmacies or from your dentist) to see which half is cleaner. If he can clean his teeth as well as you do, maybe he really doesn't need help!

Flossed and Fancy

The American Dental Association recommends that you floss your child's teeth nightly as soon as he has two teeth that touch. I never managed nightly, but I did try to do it occasionally. For easier flossing:

- Use bubblegum- or grape-flavored floss.
- If your child's teeth are tight, the newer "glide" style flosses work better.
- Experiment with different floss holders.
- Wiggle the floss between the teeth rather than pushing down hard. Slide it along the inside surfaces, taking care not to jab tender gums.
- Floss your child's teeth while she lies on the bed or sofa with her head in your lap.

- Pretend to be a miniature spelunker (cave explorer) descending into the depths of the crevices between your child's teeth to excavate food "ore."

The Pajama Game:
NO-SWEAR EVENING WEAR

Put pajamas on immediately after the bath or before the fun parts of the evening (like snack or story). Avoid many battles simply by choosing comfortable pajamas. What's comfortable varies from child to child, but here are some common concerns:

- *Feel* Avoid itchy lace or lumpy trimmings like bows and other decorations.
- *Long nightgowns* Some find they tangle; others like the warmth and curling up in them.
- *Elastic* Some complain if it is too tight; others, too loose.
- *Fabrics* If stiffness is a problem, try hand-me-downs or a different pair.
- *Smell* Flame retardant bothers some kids; try pre-washing them several times before wearing. Use unscented detergents. Or choose different fabrics.
- *Footed jammies* Some kids love them; some hate them. Mine despised them.
- *Temperature* If your house is warm or your child uses heavy bedding, he may prefer short pajamas even in the winter. Similarly, your child may choose long, heavy pajamas in the summer if the air conditioning or night air feels cold to him.
- *Style* Many kids like pajamas that make them feel a particular way (powerful is popular, as is beautiful). My favorite was a flannel "fairy gown" that my mother made for me (and that I wore for Halloween); my kids all preferred a pair of threadbare Superman pajamas that they wore well past the point of outgrowing them.

Invite children to put on their pajamas with appealing instructions. Tell them, "Pajama Party Time!" "Time to jump into your jammies!" or "Where's my Pajama-Mama (and/or Llama)?!" Sing dressing instructions or play one of the games recommended in chapter 1 for getting changed. And, don't forget to have your child take care of dirty clothes.

Avoiding the Pajama Police

There is actually no law that says children must wear pajamas to bed. Over the years, mine have slept in parents' and siblings' T-shirts, bathing suits, undies, sweatsuits, their clothes for the next day, their shoes, baseball caps, and other assorted odd garments. I was never arrested.

That said, there *are* good reasons to try to wrestle your kids into conventional sleepwear most nights. First is safety. Children's sleepwear must be flame retardant and free from strangulation hazards. If you do choose to let your child sleep in something other than pajamas, make sure the clothes fit tightly and are not particularly flammable. (Snug long cotton underwear, though not flame-retardant, has been approved as sleepwear because it meets these criteria.) Avoid any clothes with cords or loose pieces that could entangle or choke a sleeper who fell out of bed.

MORE TO KNOW

Spirited children who have trouble with transitions may be overwhelmed by one more change, especially when their energy is used up. You may want to let these kids sleep in some of their clothes at times (or maybe the next day's, to prevent morning battles). Strip them down to shirt and undies, wait to undress them after they're asleep, or aim for a daily bath (they'll have to get dressed in something afterwards, so it's a less noticeable transition). Go along with their insistence on sameness or particular features in sleepwear (buy at least two pairs of the same acceptable set).

The other reason is practical. Changing clothes is like suiting up for the big game or putting on a favorite costume—the ritual and the clothing shift mind (and body) into the right mode. For some children, the effect is powerful, for others negligible. If your child doesn't wear jammies and is having trouble settling down, try adding this component to the evening wind-down ritual. It just might help.

Wind Me Down, Scottie:
THE FINAL POWER-DOWN ROUTINE

Wouldn't it be great if you could just stop at this point and the whole bedtime thing would be done? Sorry, you can't unless you don't mind having everyone awake and jumping on your bed all night. This last step is really the most important one anyhow. These tips should help your wide-eyed guys snuggle in and relax their lids—and maybe help you discover some pleasure and peace in the process, too.

Step One: *Get the Kid Physically in the Bed*

Naturally, this is easier said than done. Unless you're my husband. He just threw the kids in bed. Literally. They loved it—and they stayed put. That's because the penalty for getting up again was that the next night Dad *wouldn't* throw them in bed. This method breaks all the rules about no wild play just before bed, but it can work, as long as the rest of the routine is quiet and calming.

The throwing technique, though, was not effective for me. Apparently I lacked Dad's power and flair. Instead, my kids liked me to carry them "like a baby." Being held or carried is still popular among preschoolers at bedtime (try piggyback if they're getting heavy or just giving them a "jump" into bed). The psychologist in me believes that a final display of your physical prowess gives children a sense of security before they surrender to sleep. Probably, though, they just want one last dose of fun.

If you have your kid say his prayers, you can do it just before this step in the classic kneeling-by-the-bed way. Personally, I prefer to save those intimate interactions (whether it's a prayer or something else) for last—in bed with the lights out.

Step Two: *A Story. Or Two*

Very, very important. Reading at bedtime is probably the most influential thing you will do to teach your child how *and why* to read. Snuggling up and sharing books with your child is a powerful opportunity to show him that reading is a pathway to excitement, knowledge, beauty, humor, and even emotional support. Trust me, many kids never make this discovery in the best school reading classes. Read something very short if you must, but skip this step only in dire emergencies. This is also the time to share memories or plans, guide your child through relaxing imagery, or write a fairy note together.

Step Three: *Arrange the Scenery*

Turn on the nightlight. If your child has trouble with the quiet, try a tape or white noise (e.g., a fan, a radio tuned softly to static, a tabletop fountain, or a nature-sound maker). Tuck in the teddy bear or smooth the security blanket. Check or spray for monsters. Offer one last sip of water, and then turn off the light. Just take care not to add too many essential elements. And be sure to let the sitter know these routines when you go out.

Step Four: *A Smooch and a Charm*

Give your child a final hug and kiss. A prayer or charm-like saying repeated every night just before you go out the door can be very powerful for your child.

Adjust these elements to suit your child and your family. I think it's a good idea to give each child at least five minutes of undivided attention at bedtime, but that may not work in your household. You may even be one of those lucky people who commands "To bed!" and the kids hop in and leave you alone until morning. But if not, and you're not following a routine like this, give it a try.

Goodnight, Moon:
A CELESTIAL INTO-BED STRATEGY

The moon is magical to young children (and to some of us old ones). Saying goodnight to it has great appeal. With your toddler (and possibly a three-year-old) you might have been able to get away with a generic "Night, night Moon!" à la *Goodnight Moon,* the classic book by Margaret Wise Brown—but your preschooler is likely to find that gig babyish. He wants to go outside and *really* say goodnight to the moon.

LITERATURE LINKS

Moon stories abound, of course, but we always loved *Owl Moon* by Jane Yolen, about a child's adventure with a protecting parent to see the moonlit sky and an owl.

Every night, once your child is washed, brushed, flossed, jammied, and ready for bed, take him out on the porch (or wherever you can see the moon) and simply say good night to it. You could sing a moon song, like Cat Stevens's "Moonshadow" or examine the moon through binoculars. Then pop the kid into bed. Wait! you say. Every night—really? What if it's cold? Cloudy? Raining, even?

Okay, you don't have to do it every night. If there are thunderstorms or torrential rain, skip it. But otherwise, you might want to give it a try. It only needs to take two minutes. You and your child will learn so much about the moon and the night sky—including the fact that the moon disappears when it's cloudy. More importantly, you'll share a few moments in the dark and experience the awesome hugeness of the sky. The sky is more amazing in the dark countryside, but still pretty wowser beneath city lights. If it's cold, wrap your kid in a blanket and hold him in your arms. If it's raining, share an umbrella. Even if he can't see the moon, reassure him that it's still out there, just as you are there for him when he can't see you. Pretty powerful stuff.

More Moon Magic

Put a moon—and some stars while you're at it—up in your child's room. You can find glow-in-the-dark heavenly bodies at nature stores, Spencer's Gift chains, toy and discount stores, even dollar stores. We like the "anatomically correct" ones sold at museum shops best. Or just hang a paper moon from a thread over your kid's bed.

SOUND BITES

Raffi sings the daytime version of Mr. Moon ("Mr. Sun") on his *The Singable Songs Collection.*

Moon and star songs are ever popular. In addition to "Twinkle, Twinkle Little Star" and Van Morrison's "Moondance," try singing one of these traditional songs to the night sky:

I see the moon, the moon sees me.
The moon sees somebody I'd like to see.
God bless the moon and God bless me.
And God bless somebody I'd like to see.

Mr. Moon, Moon, Mr. Silver Moon,
Please shine down on me.
Mr. Moon, Moon, Mr. Silver Moon,
Hiding behind a tree.
These little children are asking you,
To please come out so they can dream with you.
So, Mr. Moon, Moon, Mr. Silver Moon,
Please shine down on, please shine down on,
Please shine down on me!

Stories and Stretchers:
GOOD READS FOR GOOD NIGHTS

If you have a preschooler, you need a library card. Unlike toddlers, who want to hear the same book ten bazillion times, preschoolers want to hear ten bazillion books one time. Plus maybe their favorite again when you're done with the others.

The books listed here are ones that preschoolers I have known have loved. Some of the choices may seem "young" but everyone regresses a bit at night. I have also included ideas here and there for "stretching" the story and bringing it into your child's life. These simple extensions are powerful for building listening and comprehension skills.

Sweet Lovey Bedtime Books

- *Owl Babies* by Martin Waddell. Have your child chime in with Percy's repeating line, "I want my mama." And don't forget to kiss your little Percy goodnight.

- *Guess How Much I Love You* by Sam McBratney. The distance to the moon is 238,900 miles from Earth. How far would it be there—and back?

- *Good Night, Gorilla* by Peggy Rathmann. After you turn out the lights, sneak some stuffed zoo friends in bed with your child, giggling with him as you do so.

- *Throw a Kiss, Harry* and other Harry cat stories by Mary Chalmers. These are old, but they come back in print periodically. Naturally, your child will wait to throw your goodnight kiss *after* you leave the room. Catch it anyhow and send one back.

- *Good Zap, Little Grog* by Sarah Wilson. Playful take on language. Take turns saying things with made-up words and see if the other person can understand what you mean.

- *When Mama Comes Home Tonight* by Eileen Spinelli. Nice for families where Mom is gone all day. What does your child like to do when Mama comes home?

- *Tell Me Something Happy Before I Go to Sleep* by Joyce Dunbar. About a game played by siblings at bedtime. Tell each other happy things before you go to sleep.

TRY THIS!

Read in a lively, expressive voice, using different "voices" for different characters (unless that totally bugs your kids like it does mine). Occasionally run your finger along under the text. Your child will naturally pick up the left-right, up-down progression without any direct instruction. From time to time, point out words and show how you can tell what they say. Take time to really look at the illustrations and admire them. What can your child predict about what will happen on a given page from the picture? Look at wordless books like David Wiesner's *Tuesday* or *Sector 7*. Let your child try to "read" them with you.

**Funny Stories You Can Still Read at Bedtime
without Getting Everyone So Stirred Up They Can't Fall Asleep**

- *Olivia* by Ian Falconer. Have your child list all the things she is good at.
- *George and Martha* and other books in the series by James Marshall.
- *Frog and Toad* and other books in the series by Arnold Lobel.
- *The Three Little Wolves and the Big Bad Pig* by Eugene Trivizas. Has good repeating lines for your child to recite.
- *You Be Good & I'll Be Night: Jump-on-the-Bed Poems* by Eve Merriam. Try to memorize one poem with your child. Test your recall the next night.

Books for Advanced Listeners

These are chapter books, longer picture books, or books with fewer or plainer illustrations.

- *Lotta on Troublemaker Street* by Astrid Lindgren. A perfect book for spirited, persistent children. It has short chapters, colored illustrations, strong emotions, warm resolution.
- *The Mouse and the Motorcycle* and other books in the series by Beverly Cleary. Short, lively chapters, some illustrations. A toy mouse and motorcycle are good props for your child to play with while you read.
- Collections of comic strips. *Calvin and Hobbes* by Bill Watterson, *The Far Side* by Gary Larson, and *Peanuts* by Charles M. Schulz are favorites of younger children, but be prepared for advanced vocabulary at times and some jokes that will need explaining.
- *Winnie-the-Pooh* and other books by A. A. Milne.

ON THE WEB

Want more ideas? Go to the website www.chinaberry.com, an independent catalog and online children's bookstore. It has the best catalog you'll find—completely annotated and indexed. I would absolutely trust its recommendations. The catalog also includes books on tape, project kits, and some books for adults.

Pillow Talk:
BOOSTING YOUR CHILD'S MEMORY AND HAPPINESS

Research has shown that things we think about just before bed are more likely to be transferred from short-term memory to long-term memory while we sleep. (That's why a bedtime review was a good idea before a school test.) Use this knowledge to help build your child's recall of positive emotional episodes and information. And to get her set for happy dreams.

Family Tree

Bedtime is a good time to look at family pictures and tell family stories. Your child will like pictures of when she was a baby, but she will really love all the tales about your childhood (especially when you were bad—and how it all worked out). Examine photos of faraway relatives, too, so your child will recognize them next time she sees them—and so she has the knowledge of their love, too, to keep her safe and snug all night. Hang a collage of friends and family by her bed as a focal point for her to gaze at while she falls asleep.

The Good Times

Talk to your child about "the best thing" from her day. You might want to get in the habit of recording her assessments nightly. Keep a pencil and a journal or a calendar with large squares next to your child's bed. Each night, have your child dictate her best or favorite thing. Next month or year, re-read the corresponding entry for that date. This will help your child build a repository of good memories and a sense of optimism.

Souvenir Sleep Buddies

Let your child bring one thing from her day to bed each night. If it's appropriate, she can sleep with it; if not, she can place it somewhere she can see it while she falls asleep. Suggested items include found natural objects, a new toy or book, an art project she made, or a photograph of a friend she played with.

Great Expectations

Once your child is in the expecting-good frame of mind, make predictions for the future. What might happen tomorrow? Next week? A year from now? When she is a grown-up? Discuss planning and what she can do to make good things and wishes come about. Children this age have a hard time with imagining the future, but your child will enjoy the pictures you paint for her. The near future will be easier to grasp, especially by the time she is four.

Worry Stones

Nighttime is when many children's (and adults') worries come to the forefront. This is a good time to have a quiet discussion about problems your child raises—in part because she may not bring them up during the day. The extra minutes you spend will be well worth it to you and your child. (If she has worries every night, schedule talking time during the day or evaluate whether she has more significant problems.) If she has trouble telling you her worries, let her whisper them to a set of worry dolls.

Let's Sleep at the Beach Tonight:
"YOU ARE GETTING SLEEPY" STORIES

Guided imagery is powerful for relaxing a child who has a hard time unwinding. I'm including a script you can read, but it's better to tell the relaxing stories in the dark, tailoring details to match your child's passions and needs. Pitch your voice deep and quiet, let your own breathing slow down, and feel your tension dissolve too.

"Let's Sleep at the Beach Tonight"

"Take a moment to snuggle in and get comfy…. Now notice your breathing. Take a slow breath in…and let it out. Another slow breath in…and let it out. Continue breathing slowly and comfortably in… and out.

"Now imagine that you see a door in front of you that is just your size. You walk over to the door and turn the handle, and it opens easily. When you look through, you see white sand, blue-green water, and a deep blue sky with little wispy white clouds. You are at the beach! Go ahead and step onto the sand in your bare feet. Doesn't it feel nice and warm beneath your toes? Walk closer to the water, hearing the sound of the waves, the cries of seagulls, and the whisper of the breeze. For a moment stop and watch the waves crashing onto the sand, one after the other, and then sliding back into the sea. Feel the spray mist your face. Lick your lips and notice how salty they taste.

"The sky is beginning to turn pink, and you see a little sliver moon hanging low in the sky. You watch a beautiful little boat wash up on the sand in front of you. A mermaid with long silver hair invites you to climb in the boat. She and her dolphin friends will take you on a safe nighttime ride. You step in and see that the whole boat is a soft bed, with fluffy cushions almost like clouds and a fuzzy golden blanket. You rest your head on a satiny pillow that smells like roses. In a moment, you feel the mermaid and the dolphins push the boat into the water. See the stars twinkling overhead? They look like jewels. Suddenly one slides off the sky and right into your hand. It feels cool and smooth when you rub it. The boat is rocking up and down and up and down, and you are feeling sleepy. You can hear the soft voice of the mermaid singing to you. You drift off to sleep, feeling completely happy and safe, as the night snuggles close around you. (Pause.)

"In a moment, I will count from one to five. When I get to five, you will go to sleep still rocking in your mermaid boat. In the morning, you will wake up feeling refreshed and ready to tell me about your trip on the ocean. One...two...three...four...five. Goodnight."

Give your child a kiss and leave the room. You can try other themes, like sledding down a long hill, swinging from a tree swing, riding on a winged horse, playing in a fairy garden, going in a submarine, or flying on a magic carpet.

SOUND BITES

Jim Weiss, who is a wonderful storyteller, has a whole tape (or CD) of longer, more elaborate sleepy stories like these, called *Good Night: Enchanting Stories and Visualizations with Music.* His stories will take your child to visit a cabin in the woods, meet a unicorn, or enjoy a snowy day before drifting off to sleep.

Monster Repellent
AND OTHER WAYS TO DISCOURAGE THINGS THAT GO BUMP IN THE NIGHT

Monsters

Preschoolers often believe fervently in these regardless of the firm proof you offer that they don't exist. Leaving a nightlight on may help—monsters are as afraid of the light as your child is of the dark. If that doesn't do it, try filling a perfume atomizer with distilled water and some scent, like a couple of drops of cologne. Label it carefully as Monster Off or something similar and include directions for use. Monster-scaring wind chimes hung by the child's bed can help, too.

Bad Guys

Older preschoolers may fear robbers and other "bad guys" breaking into their homes while they are asleep. During the day, take your child around the house, and show him all the ways you have to protect it—and him. I let the kids practice locking the doors and reassured them that their dad and I locked up every night. We pointed out posted numbers for the police, and the neighborhood watch decal on the front window. These reassurances helped some, but the best approach to the problem came from a nature special on mother animals. After we watched a demonstration of the fiercely protective actions of a mother bear, I told my brood that I was just like those mama bears—and would attack any threat to my cubs with as much vigor. And the kids believed me! Try it!

Nightmare Proofing

The best nightmare-proofing tactic is, of course, to monitor your child's media consumption, especially near bedtime. Sometimes, though, despite your best efforts your child will be exposed to something that leads to "bad thoughts" (as one of my kids called them) at bedtime. For example, one of my kids once overheard part of a very tame ghost story that his aunt was reading to an older child. He had trouble falling asleep for the next six months!

When something like that happens, you may ultimately have to let time resolve the problem. But meanwhile, try hanging a Native American dreamcatcher above his head (look for them at nature stores) or make one yourself from string and an embroidery hoop. (It should look like a web that bad dreams can get tangled in.) Hang a picture of a superhero by your child's pillow for him to look at while he falls asleep. Distract him during the falling-asleep phase with a story or music tape, and give him a bell or buzzer so he can ring for you if he needs you.

TALES FROM THE TRENCHES

Despite his yearning, I would not allow my oldest son to have toy guns. But one day our next-door neighbors moved away, leaving a perfectly good neon orange toy gun behind the daylilies. My son swooped over and grabbed it as soon as the moving van was out of sight. That night after lights out, my husband and I heard a strange clicking sound from our son's room. When my husband went in, he found Kyle busy shooting all the monsters lurking in the shadows. And that night for the first time in months, he did not come in our room seeking refuge from monsters and bad guys. We decided to let him keep his anti-monster gun, and for months we heard its click, click, click as he drifted off to sleep.

Happy Dream Seeds

Help your preschooler sow happy-dream or good-mood seeds before she goes to sleep. Have your child assemble a collection of small objects that represent things or events that she likes. Items could include a tiny pretend present, plastic friendly animals like kittens and puppies, toy crowns or other fancy doll clothing, a beautiful key, a sea shell, tickets or tokens, coins or play money, a plastic flower, miniature play food, vacation souvenirs, and so on.

Place the items in a fancy-looking cloth bag or special box. Each night before bed, let her choose one or two items from the bags. Discuss the type of dream she might have based on these objects.

LITERATURE LINKS

There are many good books about kids dealing with monsters or nightmares and such. Some kids are actually more frightened by these, but many find them reassuring. My favorites: Mercer Mayer's *There's a Nightmare in My Closet* and Judith Viorst's *My Mama Says*.

Then let her plant her happy-dream seeds under her pillow. When she wakes up, talk about the dream that grew from her seeds.

How to Smooch Your Sweetie:
THE VERY BEST WAYS TO HUG AND KISS AND SAY GOODNIGHT

A ritual goodnight game is great. Its predictability soothes your child, and the touching makes you both feel connected before you separate (with luck, for the whole night). Here are some hug-and-kiss routines we like:

Full Face Coverage

We start with a tickly "massage" from the forehead to the temples to the cheeks. Lightly stroke over both closed eyes and zip a finger down the nose. Draw circles around the lips and stroke the jaw line from ears to tip of chin. Finish up with kisses—one for each eye, one for the tip of the nose, each cheek, the chin, and the last one on the lips. Ahhh!

Om-a-lom-a

This was a tradition from my mother-in-law's grandparents, and I've never met anyone else who does it—but my kids love it. Hold your child in your lap, facing you. Both of you tilt your heads back, saying, "Om-a-lom-a-tootsie . . ." Draw out the last syllable, then suddenly say "Buck!" and touch foreheads gently. Finish up with some nice smooches.

Kisses à la Carte

Let your child choose five to ten different kinds of hugs and kisses. For example, he might request a bear hug, two eye kisses, a butterfly kiss (flutter eyelashes on his cheek), an Eskimo kiss (rub noses), a snaky lick, a belly zlerbert, an air kiss (kiss near but not touching each other's lips or cheeks), a European hello kiss (each cheek), and one big squeeze. The question is, can you remember his whole order without writing it down?

Goodnight Sayings

The traditional favorite:

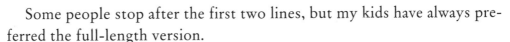

Goodnight, sleep tight,
Don't let the bedbugs bite.
But if they do,
Squish a few,
And they won't be back
tomorrow night.

Some people stop after the first two lines, but my kids have always preferred the full-length version.

You can also try this classic good-bye exchange, taking turns saying the lines:

See you later, alligator!
In a while, crocodile!
Not so soon, you silly baboon!

Some people say something even less kind for the last line, but we, of course, are too polite to repeat it in public.

Prayers

Try reciting a final short prayer together. The traditional one with "If I should die before I wake" has always given me the willies, and I can't imagine it would promote a restful night for a fanciful child. Instead, choose a favorite one from books like *In Every Tiny Grain of Sand: A Children's Book of Prayers and Praise* collected by Reeve Lindbergh or *A Child's Book of Blessings* by Sabrina Dearborn. Or make up one of your own.

Charms

Basically just a saying, too, but one that promises safety and/or comfort. Here's one my daughter and I made up and like:

Turn out the light
And hug you tight.
So love will keep you
Safe all night.

Some kids also like to hold a small "charm" to remind them of you and give them a secure feeling. (There's a good chance they'll lose it during the night, so make it something easy to replace. We use pieces of seashell worn smooth by the ocean—and collect tons of them every vacation so we have a full year's supply.) Traditional comforters, like teddies and security blankets, can also be "blessed" with the right words to make them extra effective.

You Got a License to Do That?
DEALING WITH DELAY-OF-GAME PENALTIES

Nearly every preschooler likes to drag out bedtime, squeezing as many "Just one mores" out of you as she can. Don't overreact—but go ahead and set firm limits. You're entitled to some alone time at the end of the day, and your child needs to go to sleep. Try some of these strategies to keep your child in bed—without you.

LITERATURE LINKS

A little humor helps everyone tolerate this situation. Read *Bedtime for Frances* by Russell Hoban, which will give parents a chuckle, and help suggest ways for kids to work out the problem themselves.

License Your Child

Sometimes. For birthdays or other special occasions, give your child a "stay-up-late" license that entitles the bearer to an extra fifteen minutes of awake time. Be sure to specify how many times it can be used. When your child begs for one more drink, another story, extra kisses, etc.—just ask if she wants to use her license. Often she'll decide to save the opportunity. You can also give out extra-drink-of-water or one-more-story tickets as rewards for good behavior. Reserve veto power—there may be nights when the tickets aren't good.

Send Them to the Penalty Box

Kids who keep getting out of bed may find themselves in the penalty box. Not then, but the next day when they'd rather be out playing. This is really just the "No TV tomorrow if you don't get back in bed this minute!" threat in disguise, but it is more fun. We sometimes used an actual cardboard box (a refreshing change from the time-out chair, don't you think?) where the child had to serve five minutes of playtime.

Ooze Away

Kids who are scared at bedtime may beg you to stay with them. An occasional night like this is not a problem—but this need tends to be very persistent. Some parents claim not to mind hanging out, reading a book or doing needlework. I couldn't stand it on a regular basis. I suggest a program of gradual withdrawal instead. Tell your child you will sit with her tonight. Tomorrow you will sit on a chair next to her bed. The next night, by the door. Keep increasing your physical distance. Use a firm, matter-of-fact tone when you tell your child the arrangements. Kids sense hesitation as keenly as mosquitoes smell blood.

The Great Check Back

Also for the child who can't bear to have you leave. Stay with him for five minutes. Then leave—returning to check back after five minutes. If he's asleep, let him be. Otherwise, stay a few minutes (but not more than five) if he needs you. Next, though, stay away for ten minutes before checking back. Return as often as your child needs, but never stay more than five minutes, and keep increasing the time that you are gone. This way you are not abandoning your child, but you are communicating your confidence in his ability to be by himself.

After Midnight:
KEEPING THOSE LITTLE BED BUGS OUT OF YOURS

How could Amahl have stood those night visitors? Try these ideas for dealing with common middle-of-the-night interruptions.

Unwanted Visitors

How you handle these depends on your family's values, your tolerance for elbows in your face (or urine on your pillow), and even the size of your mattress. Maybe even on your mood and level of sleep deprivation. Some approaches:

- Welcome the little buggers and make room. Clean up puddles in the morning. Warning: They'll be *ba-a-a-a-ck!*
- Allow sick children to stay. All others get a five-minute cuddle and a return ticket to their own beds.
- Put a sleeping bag on the floor next to your bed. Night visitors are welcome to bed down there. (Or put the sleeping bag just outside your door.)

- Hand a scared child *your* special Nightmare Teddy that she can borrow just for this night. As soon as she goes back to her own bed.
- Take them back to their own beds immediately. Do a mini-practically-no-talking re-tuck-in. Put on a nightlight and a soothing tape. Return to your own room with your fingers crossed.
- Trade beds. Yours is less appealing when you aren't in it. Maybe. Depends whether the kid already peed his.
- Use a sticker chart. Five straight nights of "all night in my own bed" stickers earns a reward.
- Lock your door. Really. I couldn't do it, but some desperate people do until they break their child of night wandering. Or, gate your child into her room—but use a monitor so you can hear if there's a problem that requires your presence.

Blood Curdling Screams

Sometimes caused by nightmares or ear infections. More often, they're the result of night terrors. During a night terror, your child may appear awake (eyes open) but he doesn't seem to "see" you and won't respond to your attempts to comfort him. He is actually asleep, and there's not much you can do except stay with him and keep him safe. Murmuring soft reassurances helped me feel better, but never seemed to shorten the time of terror. In the morning, most kids have no recollection of waking or of being scared.

Another possibility is "growing pains." Some kids seem to be prone to these, often around age four and again around six. Rub their legs (which are the usual site of pain), apply warm compresses or an ice bag (like frozen peas), whichever feels better, and try to limit pounding or jumping activities during the day.

Dry Trying:
DEALING WITH NIGHT WETTING

Bedwetting is extremely common during the preschool years, and you should never punish your child for it. It doesn't make your child any happier than it makes you. Try these strategies to minimize the problem in the first place or to cope with it once it occurs.

A *Half* Ounce of Prevention

- Make sure your child goes potty just before bed. Make him try even if he doesn't think he needs to go. Run the faucet to encourage his flow.
- Limit fluid intake near bedtime. Be reasonable—you don't want to risk dehydrating your child, but you also don't need to offer six cups of water just before you turn out the light. I recommend *tiny* cups for bedtime drinks of water (like a doll's tea-party cup).
- Place a potty in his room. He may not be able to wake soon enough to make it to the bathroom, but he might manage to get out of bed.
- Take your child potty when *you* go to bed. She may seem three-fourths asleep, but often she'll pee (though with no recollection in the morning). Experts don't recommend this method—it doesn't train the child to recognize his full bladder—but I know many parents who swore by it until their children matured and gained control on their own.
- Put your kid in disposable undies, like Pull-Ups. Also not recommended by many experts because they don't make kids uncomfortable enough to want to learn control. But those experts aren't waking up with your kid every morning at 2:30 or washing five loads of sheets a week. Also make sure you have a rubber sheet on the mattress.

Daddy, I Peed the Bed

Man, I wish my kids had said that. Instead they always substituted "Mommy" for "Daddy" who slept like a corpse anyhow.

- Get up and strip the bed. Older preschoolers (fives and sixes) can learn to do it themselves, especially if it's a common problem. Keep a plastic laundry basket in their room to hold the wet sheets.
- Place towels and a clean blanket down on the bed or spread out a sleeping bag for the rest of the night.
- Take the kid potty, just in case he has anything left.
- Give him a clean shirt to sleep in. Deal with the wet laundry in the morning.
- Keep talking to a minimum so you don't wake him completely.
- Run through a quick version of the bedtime routine if necessary. Put on a tape or music box to soothe.
- If a five- or six-year-old is still wetting the bed most nights, talk to your pediatrician about trying a bedwetting alarm or other behavioral program.

CHAPTER NINE

The
Mush
Pot

As the middle child in my family, I learned to be competitive at an early age. I struggled mightily to keep up with my big sister and her friends, and I lived in terror of the possibility that my younger sister might best me at something. But a week or two into kindergarten, I discovered that winning was not necessarily The Best Thing.

This discovery had nothing to do with any high and mighty principles of fairness or cooperation. It was because most days my class played a rousing game of "Duck, Duck, Goose"—and I soon realized it was better to lose quickly and get stuck in the Mush Pot, where one could laugh, talk, and goof around with one's fellow mush-ees than to sit tensely on the edge of the circle, every fiber straining so you'd be ready to run like the wind when you got goosed. Plus, those Mush Pot kids were a fascinating group with lots to teach me, like how to tie my shoelaces in knots more tangled than the famous Gordian one.

Since then, I've had a warm spot in my heart for the Mush Pot concept. That's why I'm including this last chapter, with a mixture of activities and ideas that I hope will be as interesting and informative as my kindergarten Mush Pot gang was.

All right. That's a lie. Really, I just had lots of activities and ideas left over that didn't fit into the earlier chapters and didn't go together either. So I'm throwing them together and pretending there is a rationale for putting them in the same chapter. But I'm still hoping that you'll find them intriguing or at least useful.

This chapter is where you can find suggestions for getting your child to take his medicine without having to call in the National Guard to restrain him. And, of course, the ideas you've been waiting for on preventing or coping with down-on-the-floor-kicking-and-screaming-tantrums (your kid's, not yours). Finally, there are tips to help you understand and manage your kid's own style of fussing.

And if none of the activities in this chapter proves helpful to you, at least take away my lesson about the Mush Pot. Because even if I lied about why I was putting the chapter together this way, I was being completely truthful about my kindergarten discovery. Life *is* better in the Mush Pot. Invite your kids and their friends to join you there for a little camaraderie and maybe some cookies and lemonade, too—and leave the goose chase to others.

Creature Comforts for Sick Puppies:
SOOTHING AND BOOSTING

I think another good term for "preschoolers" would be "germ factories." Or maybe Typhoid Mary. Preschoolers tend to be sick quite frequently in my experience, and they share germs far more willingly than their favorite green trucks. This means you, too, should expect to be sick constantly. (Naturally, no one will coddle you when you're puking your guts out—they'll call through the bathroom door to find out when you'll have dinner on the table—but you should still be noble and give them lots of comfort when they're sick.) Consult your doctor or children's medical guides for giving proper physical care, but here are some ways to provide TLC:

Special Snugglies

In the book *When Vera Was Sick* by Vera Rosenberry, the miserable little girl is comforted by cuddling with the special silky pillow that's reserved for illness. You might want to set aside a nice pillow, blanket, or stuffed animal to comfort little guys who are under the weather. (Just make sure it's washable.) The ultimate special snuggly is getting to hang out in your big bed. I still remember my mom cuddling me up in her bed when I was about three and miserably sick.

Ache and Pain Relievers

In addition to acetaminophen, trot out the old-fashioned comforts, like cool washcloths for feverish or achey heads, and hot water bottles (or those pillows you can heat in the microwave) for stomachaches. (These kinds of pain relievers probably work largely because attention feels good, but who cares why.) Heat feels good, too, on growing pains or strained muscles. It often eases the intense pain of an earache, but ask your doctor first because heat may cause eardrums to rupture. Earache pain may also be soothed by cupping your hand over the affected ear or applying pressure to the side of the head. I spent many nights with an earachey child's head propped on my chest as I tried to sleep sitting up—it really helps.

Cold Comforts

For kids with stuffy noses, coughs, or sore throats, run a vaporizer. Tabletop fountains add soothing moisture to the air, too. You can make a steam tent for a child with a bowl of very warm water and a big towel to drape over kid and bowl. Vaseline applied under the nose and on the lips at the first sign of a cold may prevent or limit chapping and soreness. The old-fashioned remedy, Vap-O-Rub, is surprisingly effective for congestion, too—just be sure to follow the directions carefully. A bad cough—

especially a croupy barking one—may improve with a quick trip outside or to a steamy bathroom.

Food and Drink

Sick kids are at risk of getting dehydrated. Pedialyte or similar electrolyte solutions are recommended by doctors as the best fluids for kids with severe vomiting or diarrhea. Otherwise you may be able to get enough fluids in with crushed ice, Popsicles, flat soda (add one-quarter teaspoon of sugar to flatten it—watch out, though—it foams like mad!), Jello water (mix Jello powder with twice the recommended water and serve warm), or watery foods like watermelon. Naturally, whatever liquid you serve will be much more appealing and soothing if it's doled out in a special cup with a straw or a paper umbrella. When I even look at the little Danish cups my mom served Jello water in when we were sick, I get an urge to snuggle on the sofa with my fuzzy pink blankie.

My kids have sworn for years that chewing gum or sucking on ordinary lollipops soothes scratchy sore throats. I myself was skeptical, but a doctor friend told me that increased saliva production does help—and gum and lollipops are good for that.

TALES FROM THE TRENCHES

One year on my birthday, my son woke me at 5:00 A.M. with a sweet-voiced, "Mommy?" "Yes, honey," I answered, half-opening my eyes and expecting birthday kisses. "I feel . . ." he said, and threw up *right on my face*. Parenthood. There's nothing like it.

Special Activities

I have one word for you: television. We allowed *way* more TV when folks were ill, especially if Mommy was too. Other comforting activities include being read to over and over, and playing with toys set aside for use only on special occasions. You will also grant permission to be whinier and clingier than normal. For kids who are sick for more than a day or two, wrap up a little something (it doesn't really have to be new, just forgotten). A gift of something novel will give your child something to do and remind her that she hasn't been forgotten. Loneliness and boredom can make kids feel even sicker than they are.

Working Parent Comforts

Guilt is never stronger than when your kid is sick and you can't be there. If at all possible, have a caregiver come to your home—if just feels better to be home when you're sick. Try to call home periodically during the day. In the short run, talking to your child may prompt fussing and begging for you to come home, which feels lousy for everyone. In the long run, though I think it's more important for your child to know you're the kind of person who will be there for her in some way when she's ailing. Leave behind some special comforts, like something of yours to snuggle, and try to bring home a little treat. You won't spoil your child by coddling her when she's sick.

Just a Spoonful of Sugar:
GETTING THE MEDICINE DOWN WITHOUT MARY POPPINS

The combination of yucky medicine, a sick, crabby kid, and an overtired parent is not a good one. Try these ideas to reduce the number of Bad Mother moments when you find yourself, medicine cup in hand, chasing your sick kid around the kitchen table.

Yucky Taste Busting

The main reason kids resist medicine is that it tastes bad. The pink stuff (amoxicillin) isn't too bad, and some over-the-counter medications are also palatable, but most taste, well, *yucky*. Ideas to try:
- Have the kid suck on a Popsicle before and after the medicine. The cold will slightly numb the taste buds, and the strong flavor will overpower the medicine-y taste. At a minimum, have a strong-tasting drink ready as a chaser.

- Use a syringe or dropper to shoot the medicine toward the back of the mouth (aim for the back molars), along the side of the tongue. This will reduce the medicine's contact with taste buds.
- Ask your pharmacist about mixing the medicine with other foods. We've found that mixing some medicines with a tablespoon of chocolate or strawberry syrup makes them completely palatable without affecting the efficacy of the drug. Some pills can be crushed and mixed with applesauce, ice cream, or chocolate syrup (just be sure your child finishes all the food).
- Have your child hold her nose—smell is an important part of taste. Some kids also like to close their eyes.
- Help your child learn to swallow pills, which are less likely to taste terrible.

How to Teach Pill Swallowing

Older preschoolers will generally learn this more easily, but if your younger child has to take yucky medicine regularly, you can talk to your doctor about teaching him how to take pills.

- Practice swallowing chunky drinks, like shakes with bits of frozen fruit, or eating chunky foods like applesauce with bits of apple.
- Learn by swallowing small, coated pills. Our pediatrician recommends practicing with a Tic-Tac candy. We've had good success starting kids with Junior Advil tablets, which have an appealing (and slippery) sweet coating.
- Have your kid take a drink *before* putting the pill in his mouth—that way it won't get stuck in a dry throat.
- Place the pill far back in the mouth, taking care not to activate the gag reflex. Have the child use a flexible straw to take a drink, tip his head back, and swallow quickly. The straw may provide a little extra oomph to power the pill down.

Cooperation and Remembering Tactics

- Give a small reward each time your child takes his medicine. Sticker charts may work fine, but candy is especially effective since it also chases the bad taste, and may motivate your kid to remind you that it's time for his medicine.

- Give your child some control, like where he takes his medicine, whether he uses a syringe or a medicine cup, or what he has to drink afterwards.

- Make a paper chain (or better yet, a candy chain) with links for each time your child must take his medicine. Use different colors to separate each day's worth of doses. That way you and your child can tell at a glance whether he has taken each dose. You can also set aside coins to equal a day's doses, and let your child make a piggybank deposit after each dose.

- Set an alarm clock or timer to go off when it's time for the next dose. Post visual reminders in the bathroom, on the kitchen table, the steering wheel of the car, and other places you see frequently.

- On the go with medicine that has to be refrigerated? Keep it in a cooler or put your keys in the borrowed fridge along with the medicine. That way you won't leave the medicine behind.

The Poop Scoop:
DEALING WITH ASSORTED POTTY PROBLEMS

Parenting books usually address toilet training and associated issues as toddler concerns. But in truth, they're often preschooler issues. According to one study I saw recently, half of all boys are not trained on their third birthdays, and one-third of girls aren't either. And even though most parents are more relaxed about training today, problems are extremely common—and distressing for everyone concerned. Here are some ideas for the problems I get asked about most frequently.

The Kid Won't Poop in the Potty

Most kids learn to urinate in the potty first. Some, however, persist for an impressively long time in refusing to poop in the pot. Many kids will even ask to have a diaper *put on* so they can poop. Time will usually solve the problem, but you can try these strategies to encourage your child to make his deposits where they belong.

- Tell your child, "The rule is that poop goes in the potty." Each time she goes, dump the poop immediately from the diaper into the potty while she watches. Encourage her to sit on the potty while she poops, so she gets used to the position.
- Make sure your child's feet are supported, either in a sturdy potty seat or on a step stool. Some kids prefer to sit backwards on the toilet so they can hold onto the back.
- Put the diaper *in* the potty cup as a transition. After a while, switch to a paper towel or plastic liner (but be careful not to flush them).
- Find another child willing to model how to poop in the potty, or let your child watch you.
- If your child is slow to give up the potty chair for the big toilet, try using a seat cover—many kids rightly fear falling in.
- If your child is afraid of flushing, let her practice flushing toilet paper or other safe objects. Or flush the toilet after she leaves the room.
- Offer rewards. Keep them small, so your child doesn't get the idea it's a big deal.

Constipation

I get more calls about this issue than any other potty problem. Most parents complain that their pediatricians were unsympathetic and unhelpful. Having been through this with one of mine, I know what they mean. It takes only one painful poop to set off a long bout of withholding—and this can lead to serious problems. Here are some things that often help:

- *Diet* Increase fruits and veggies *and* decrease milk products and anything you suspect your child might be allergic to. You can mix prune juice with Coke or orange juice to hide the taste. Drinking lots and lots of fluids (water or juice) works, too.
Chocolate is a good reward for pooping, and has the added benefit of being a mild laxative.
- *Warmth* Constipated tummies hurt. A hot water bottle on the tummy feels good—and may get things moving. A warm bath after a meal will also stimulate the urge and may relax your child's muscles enough to reduce or eliminate the pain. Use warmed wet wipes on his sore bum.
- *Exercise* It helps kids as well as adults. But when a kid's tummy hurts, he may be reluctant to run around, so you may need to increase outings to fun playgrounds.
- *Medical Help* Your child may need a stool softener or laxative if she is seriously constipated. You may have to really push your pediatrician to okay these, but if your child is having pain when she poops, they're necessary.
- *Talk* Get out one of the many potty books and talk openly with your child about the whole process. I recommend *Everyone Poops* by Taro Gomi. Be comforting and reassuring—I promise you, your child feels lousy.

Poor Aim

This is usually a boy problem. It may not bother him at all but encourage him to fire more accurately by:

- Letting him play "crossfire" with another male or practice "writing" his name in the snow or dirt to improve control.
- Putting a drop of red or blue food coloring in the toilet bowl as an incentive (his pee will turn it orange or green).
- Floating a square of toilet paper for him to sink. Tissue paper confetti and cereal "O's" work, too.

Lousy Wiping

Preschoolers' arms are often too short for them to wipe adequately. They also may lack the coordination and strength. Most kids will need help until sometime between ages four and five—and some even longer. Try using wet wipes (available in flushable varieties) to improve the quality of their handiwork.

Accidents

These are common during the preschool years.

- If the child has never been fully trained, you should revisit materials on training your child. But, never put a preschooler who has been trained *back* in diapers—it is too humiliating.
- Many kids wait too long because it's inconvenient. Make sure their clothes are easy to operate, and schedule potty times when everyone must stop and try, even if they don't feel like it. Set a timer if necessary.
- Watch your child for signs she needs to go. The pee dance is a sure sign, but so are general restlessness and irritability, clamping legs together, standing with weight to one side, and holding genitals.
- Go before you go. Anywhere. Take a portable potty seat cover if the big potty feels uncomfortable. Or, tote a potty chair in the car. And take a set of clean clothes.

Remote Control:
CAGING THE TELEVISION MONSTER

Like most parents, I have a love-hate relationship with television. I love it when I'm sick and need an hour of peace. But I hate it when I see my kids parked in front of it, slack-jawed and glassy-eyed, instead of running around and playing. By now we all know that television viewing can make kids more aggressive, frightened, fat, and material-istic. The American Academy of Pediatrics recommends that you not let your kids watch more than one to two hours of TV daily, and that you closely supervise your children while they watch. Try these ideas to get your family closer to meeting these guidelines.

Put the TV in the Dark, Scary, Lonely Basement

At a minimum, that will ensure the kid won't want to watch alone. The only problem is that when you *want* the kids to go watch the telly and leave you alone, they won't. A portable set (or even better, one of those little TV/VCR combos)

SAFETY ZONE

Television sets are heavy and unstable. Children have been killed by acciden-tally pulling them over on themselves. Make sure you locate the set too high for kids to reach, place it on the ground, or anchor it securely. Use a barrier or marker to keep kids from sitting and playing too close to the set as well.

stashed in a closet can give you the best of both worlds. At a minimum, hide the TV in a cabinet, so it's mostly out-of-sight and maybe sometimes out-of-mind.

The Anti–Couch Potato Approach

Locate the set away from comfy chairs but near equipment that encour-ages physical exercise while viewing, like a mini-trampoline, rocking horse, or Sit 'N Spin. Exercising also seems to prevent kids (or adults) from getting into that zombie-stare mode. In turn, the kids seem to be less glued to the set. Ban eating (and drinking) while watching—that rule will keep the kids from mindlessly pigging out, and may make them turn off the set sooner if they get hungry.

Rely on Tapes

Tape shows to watch when *you* choose, instead of when the schedule dictates. Dab bright nail polish on the fast forward button and teach your kids to zip through commercials to get to the "good stuff." Most public libraries are now well stocked with quality kids' videos, and you can buy inexpensive used ones from most video stores. And remember, you don't have to watch longer videos in a single sitting. Treat them like chapter books and break off at exciting points until another viewing slot.

Schedule It

Having designated times (and shows) for TV viewing is one of the best things you can do. Some families select shows weekly from the *TV Guide,* and others have standard time slots, like while parents shower or on Saturday morning so the adults can sleep in. Other families rely on tokens or timers to limit viewing.

Have a Regular Family TV Night

I know it's weird to recommend watching more, but this routine ensures that you will at least occasionally watch with your kids. Doing so gives you a chance to discuss how advertisers manipulate viewers or to explain scary or confusing content. You'll also plant the idea that TV is an occasional treat, the entertainment equivalent of dessert.

Don't Get Cable or Satellite—or TV

Sticking to the main broadcast channels means your kids will miss out on some of the quality shows on the Discovery Channel, but offering fewer choices leads pretty automatically to less TV time. Plus, it means that you are less tempted to be a poor model for your kids. The extreme:

Give up TV altogether. My family did for a while when I was young—but I have to tell you it did make me feel different from my peers and led me to spend lots of time watching TV at friends' homes.

Offer Better Alternatives

Most kids will pass up the telly for the chance to do messy science experiments at the kitchen table or visit the science museum. This is more work for you—but in the long run, it's also more pleasure for everyone.

Take an Occasional Vacation from the TV

Going without for a week or even a day can change everyone's patterns.

Your Kid Sucks!
AND YOU THINK IT'S TIME FOR HIM TO STOP

As it does for babies, sucking provides comfort for many preschoolers when they're stressed. Sucking (often accompanied by twirling or stroking hair or an object) is also frequently part of the routine that soothes them to sleep. Nonetheless, most parents become uncomfortable with their preschooler's sucking, especially in public. And, although most pediatricians and dentists no longer insist that you force a child to give up his sucking habits by a certain age, there are good reasons for encouraging your preschooler to reduce or eliminate the habit, including these:

- It makes the child seem babyish and may make him a target for teasing by his peers.
- Frequent sucking can interfere with language development. A child with something in his mouth speaks indistinctly and may sound unintelligible, particularly to people outside the family. And it encourages the kid to use grunts and gestures to communicate since his mouth is busy.
- Relying on a pacifier or thumb may delay his learning of other, more mature ways to soothe himself or solve his problems.

- It often accompanies watching TV, and the two tend to become circularly related—when he sucks, he wants to watch TV, and when he watches TV, he wants to suck.

If he's at all willing, enlist your child's cooperation in reducing his habit. I wouldn't worry about nighttime sucking in this age group, but you can help him stop walking around with his plug or popping in his thumb all the time. Here are some approaches to try.

Limit Where and When Your Child May Suck

Ideally, you will only allow sucking in the bedroom. This is easier with a pacifier, of course, but even thumb suckers can be told, "If you want to suck your thumb, you need to go to your room until you're done." Being separated from the action is enough to encourage many kids to stop, or at least spend much less time doing it. Another option is to remind your kid that sucking is only for special circumstances, like bedtime or when he's hurt. You can also reduce sucking gradually by allowing it only during certain hours, like an hour in the morning and an hour in the evening. (This approach also works well for other bad habits, and for masturbating or running around naked.)

Make Him Aware

I've never been a big fan of the put-something-yucky-tasting on the thumb or pacifier method, unless the kid wants you to. But try using jingle bells on the plug or around his wrist to make him notice when he sticks his thumb in. Some kids like to wear finger puppets on their sucking fingers— if they want to suck, they must first remove the puppets. You can also require your child to ask you for his pacifier or to get a "sucking permit" from you before putting his thumb in his mouth.

Refuse to Talk While He's Stoppered

"When you take out your pacifier (or thumb) I can understand you. I'll listen to you then."

Help Him Find an Alternative Behavior

Give him other things to do with his hands. Some kids like to wear loose rubber bands or stretchy bracelets around their wrists to pop or play with when they have the urge to suck. Chewing gum can help during the quitting phase, much as it does for smokers. Let your child sip through a straw (especially thick liquids like shakes or smoothies) to satisfy his sucking urges. Offer lots of extra snuggles and sensory pleasures like swinging during the quitting phase.

Avoid Mean or Deceptive Approaches

In the short run, tricking your kid by "losing" his pacifier or cutting a hole in it may "work," but it just doesn't feel right to me. And certainly don't tease him or call him a baby—he'll get enough of that from his peers.

MORE TO KNOW

If your child is still sucking on a bottle, the preschool years are definitely time to give it up. Even more than pacifiers or thumbs, bottles will get your kid teased. And probably his bottle contains milk or juice, which are not good for his teeth. Wean gradually by watering down the contents more and more until he's just drinking water. Tell him that's all that big kids can have in their bottles. Of course, most preschoolers occasionally like to pretend to be a baby. A bottle of water then is harmless—and most will have forgotten how to suck effectively on one anyhow.

Thar She Blows!
ADVICE FROM THE FEDERAL TANTRUM MANAGEMENT AGENCY

Every child has occasional tantrums. Mostly, preschoolers have fewer than toddlers because their verbal skills give them other ways to solve problems and understand their feelings. Some kids, though, will continue to have Mt. Vesuvius–caliber eruptions throughout the preschool years. This tendency is temperament driven. But whatever the frequency and quality, try these approaches to dealing with tantrums.

Remain Calm!

Easier said than done, of course. I find it helps me (a spirited tantrum-prone type myself) to visualize myself as having a reservoir of calm, cool water that I can pour on my child when he's melting down. I think of my kid as "a poor bunny" or some other sweet term to keep me focused on the fact that I love him and that he's really pretty powerless and in need of my protection. Because, otherwise, I totally get sucked into his whirlpool of emotions and want to clobber him or at least squeeze him a good one.

Remain Near

Some kids need physical distance when they're worked up, but most are frightened by their powerful emotions and need the comfort of your presence and protection. If possible, move your child to someplace quiet and relatively dark. Remind her that you are there for her and that you will keep her safe. Don't bother trying to reason or bargain with a tantruming child, but you can label her feelings (e.g., "You're frustrated because you wanted to do it yourself") and let her know you'll talk things over when she is calm again. If you're losing it, too, leave the room, but reassure your child that you will stay nearby and help her when she's ready.

Restrain If Necessary

If your kid is trying to hurt someone or break things, say something like, "I know you're upset, but I can't let you hurt anyone." For many kids this will be enough for them to stop. If not, you may have to restrain your child. Cross your arms around him from behind, holding his wrists if needed, and ease him to the ground. Then wrap your legs around his and hold him firmly. Breathe deeply. Most kids will "melt" into you after a minute or two of this holding.

Douse the Fire

You know how in the movies someone always dashes cold water on the hysterical person and stops him cold? It would probably work in real life, too, but I'm too chicken to try it. But I do know that a cool washcloth on the kid's face helps him catch his breath, and a drink of cold water is calming, too.

Don't Give In

Most tantrums, in my experience, are "overflow" tantrums—the kid has had too much stimulation, frustration, embarrassment, whatever, and the dam bursts. Some tantrums are manipulative, though—the kid wants you to get him something or do something and is bringing out the big guns to force you to comply. But whatever the motivation, *don't give in to terrorist demands*, or you're sunk. It's fine, though, to be sympathetic and understanding.

The Aftermath

No need to punish a child after a tantrum—he has already punished himself plenty. Praise him, in fact, for regaining control, forgive

LITERATURE LINKS

If your child is prone to tantrums, I strongly, strongly recommend that you get a copy of *Raising Your Spirited Child* by Mary Sheedy Kurcinka. Put it on your bedside table and read a little every night and morning, the way some people read Bible passages. Keep reminding yourself that the same temperamental characteristics that make your child likely to have tantrums can make her a pretty nice adult. (Just ask my mother about me.)

him, and move on. A hug and a kiss will clear the air and let him know you still love him.

Preventive Maintenance

It is definitely better to avoid tantrums in the first place. Pay attention to conditions that make your kid more likely to lose it—hungry, tired, hot/cold, over-stimulated, and frustrated. Certain situations, like a birthday, a new baby, starting school, and other important life changes make kids walk around for weeks or months as if their emotional reservoirs were already three-quarters full. During these times, it takes much less stress to cause their dams to burst.

When you notice warning signs (muscle tension, voice shifts, upset expressions) move quickly to stick a finger in the dike—try to satisfy your child's needs, support her, or even remove her from troubling situations. At a minimum, talk her through the problem (e.g., "It's hot in here and that feels bothersome. Let's try fanning you and blowing on your skin," and so on). Helping kids *breathe* deeply is usually calming. Try humor, surprise, or a big hug to provoke a full breath.

Wild Things and Whiners:
GETTING TO KNOW YOUR CHILD'S FUSSING STYLE

Everyone has a preferred style of fussing. You might as well get acquainted with your kid's (and yours), because then it will be easier to target interventions that will work to prevent or stop his fussing. Here is a crash course on some of the more common styles of making a fuss, as well as tips on working effectively with your child's preferred approach.

Wild Things

If you have one of these, you already know it. These are the kids who pitch fits, who have strong and dramatic reactions and do not hide them. Many of these kids grow up to be perfectly nice, civilized adults, so don't worry. But during the preschool years, Wild Things need careful management so they'll learn how to live with their powerful emotional responses, and so they don't get labeled as "bad kids."

With Wild Things, anticipate likely trouble spots and work to reduce their exposure to conditions that trigger their meltdowns. Choose your battles (for example, don't fight about clothes—you'll lose), schedule one-on-one playdates with carefully matched buddies instead of joining big play groups, and limit the demands you make on them, especially when they're tired or hungry. Provide regular opportunities for soothing activities like water play. Finally, and this is really important, avoid people who criticize them—or you—excessively.

Whiners

This style is almost the most annoying to me. These kids rarely have full-blown tantrums, but *that voice!* They tend to be a bit clingy and dependent, and like to follow you around all day. Some whiners are remarkably powerful—even other kids will give in to them to stop that awful noise.

Help Whiners get ready for new situations. They like warnings about what will happen and how it might make them feel. They prefer to have you stay near them when they start something new. Schedule a daily cuddle and offer frequent physical reassurance in the form of hugs, supportive pats, and boosts. Remind them to use "a big kid voice" (if they're baby-talkers). Tell them, "I will listen when you talk in a pleasant (or calm) voice."

Dawdlers and Mules

These are the passive and active resisters, respectively. Dawdlers take *forever* to complete expected tasks or follow through with requests. They often seem dreamy—or deaf. Mules say, "No!" as often as two-year-olds, challenge your authority, or dispute the reasonableness of your requests. Both may ask endless delaying questions, go limp or rigid when you try to force them to do something, and just take a lot of *your* energy to move them along.

Dawdlers need structure and frequent calm reminders. Give them one-step directions and check back frequently. Gently guide them where they need to go. Use nonverbal cues as much as possible—clap your hands to get their attention, flick the lights, touch them. Say, "Look at me" before you give directions and get them to repeat what they are to do. Make sure you schedule some time for them to be off in their own worlds without external demands.

Dangle carrots in front of mules. Say, "Let's go get some ice cream!" and then casually mention that you're going to stop at the dry cleaners and the bank on the way. Offer choices instead of making demands, like "Do you want to *hop* or *run* to the bus stop?" instead of "Time to go to the bus stop." Walk away from fights and refuse to argue. Give them lots of physical activity and vigorous touching like bear hugs and swinging around. Tell them, "It takes you a while to get used to changes. Wait and see before you decide you don't like it."

"I'm Counting to Three!"
AND OTHER TRANSITION-TAMING STRATEGIES

Preschoolers are most likely to fuss when they are required to make a change. They're playing and it's time for dinner. They're in their pajamas and they need to put on their clothes. They're at home and you want them to go to grandma's. Try these strategies to reduce fussing and increase cooperation with changes throughout the day.

Five-Minute Warning

Get in the habit of alerting your child to upcoming transitions. "In five minutes, it will be time to put away your toys and take your bath." "In five minutes, Joe's mom will be here to pick him up." My computer-obsessed middle child has taught me another phrase, "Time to find a stopping point." This is helpful for kids who need closure to their activities before they can move on.

Make It a Game

Or a contest. Few preschoolers can resist these, and in the process they may not even notice that you've shifted them to something new. "Let's see who can get dressed first." "I'll be a horse and you be the driver. Make me go to the dinner table." Imagination is one of the most effective tools with balky kids.

Be Very, Very Silly

Humor is a super motivator, too, especially the warm and silly kind. Telling your child, "I command you to go wash your hands until they are so clean that your fingers fall off," will generally provoke giggles and a dash to the bathroom (followed by showing you their fingerless hands, which you should absolutely admire).

Sing It, Baby

It's hard to argue with you when you're singing instructions. I also make my kids sing their arguments back when I'm in the singing mode. This approach falls into the silly category, too, so it makes us all feel a bit cheerier.

Pick 'Em Up

One of the great things about preschoolers is that most of them are still small enough to be shifted bodily. Sling the kid over your shoulder like a sack of potatoes, cradle him like a baby, or even just gently push him along. Keep your tone cheery, silly, or sympathetic, and you might just circumvent the fuss.

Count to Three

This is the classic for parents who are crossing over into the Fussing Zone themselves. I generally prefer the unspecified threat (because I know I tend to overreact when I've reached the end of my rope), saying something like, "If you don't do it by the time I count to three, you'll be sorry." Specifying a reasonable consequence is better, though, if you're a calmer sort than I am. Naturally, you will count with numbers like "two and a half" for kids who are starting to comply but have to move slowly to save face.

Time-Out Teddies:
WHEN FUSSING WON'T BUST

No matter what you do, periodically your child will fuss. That's the way kids are. When you have to respond to fussing that's escalating or simply not ending, you need to give everyone a break. The classic time out is often not as effective as the experts say—mostly because most parents are totally crabby themselves by the time they implement it. I like this approach a little better, because it lets you step in earlier and, with luck, gradually transfers responsibility for monitoring and regulating her emotions to your kid.

Time Outs versus Benching

A *time out* is just that, a break from the action. Players request time out when they're exhausted or not performing up to snuff. It is not a punishment (though it may be strongly encouraged by the coach). *Benching*, on the other hand, is a forced removal and exclusion from play, imposed by the coach or umpire. You want your child to learn to give herself a time out when she needs it, so take care to distinguish it from benching.

When you see your child start to lose it, ask her gently (and privately) if she's ready for a time out. If she resists, tell her what you notice that indicates she needs one. Signs you might see in your child include these:

- *Physical* Clenched fists, upset or angry facial expression, jerky or clumsy movements, wild or flailing movements, tensed shoulders, clenched teeth, unfocused eyes, droopy or dragging posture, slack jaw, and other physical indications of fatigue, anxiety, or anger.
- *Voice* Overly loud or quiet tone, high pitch, whining, slurring, stammering or stuttering, baby talk, growling, staccato pattern, and other atypical speech patterns.

- *Behavior* Using threatening words or actions, balking or refusing, clinging or acting dependent, being unusually easily upset or frightened, being careless with possessions, tattling or teasing, losing normal prosocial skills (unable to share or take turns as well as usual, not offering compliments, being less cooperative than normal with peers), and so on.

Teddy Bear Time Outs

Make time outs inviting. You can give the time out more appealing names, like "a break in the action," "a snuggle moment," "putting your brakes on," or "a breather." Most children will prefer to remain near you during a time out.

Use traditional comforts during time outs. Designate a special teddy bear as Time Out Teddy. Try handing your child the teddy wordlessly when you see that she needs a break. If your child likes being snuggled or touched when she is upset, gather her into your arms or lap. If she prefers to be alone, settle her in a comfortable chair. Silky-edged blankets, twiddlers (things to play with using fingers), a cool drink, a warm wash cloth, a little hand lotion and other child-friendly luxuries will make the time out relaxing. Use your own slow, deep breathing to transfer calm to your child. As she calms down, you can talk quietly about the positive changes you notice in her body. When she has been calm for several minutes, ask her if she is ready to rejoin the play or if she would like a change of activity.

Benching

Explain, in a calm moment, that coaches bench their players when they are too upset, angry, or hurt to play properly. Players do not get to choose whether to stay in the game; the coach makes the decision. Once benched, a player cannot return to the game until the coach says so.

Preschoolers should be benched for use of physical aggression, willful property destruction or endangerment, and any behavior that is crossing over into a tantrum or meltdown. A benched child should be physically separated from his friends and family. You may need to remain nearby, but avoid giving him attention, except to narrate how to calm his body. You can take a child off the bench once he has regained his cool *and* made amends for his behavior. This should include saying he is sorry and repairing, as best he can, any damage he has caused.